SOCIAL POLICY REFORM IN CHINA

Social Policy Reform in China

Views from Home and Abroad

Edited by
CATHERINE JONES FINER

Routledge
Taylor & Francis Group
LONDON AND NEW YORK

First published 2003 Ashgate Publishing

Reissued 2018 by Routledge
2 Park Square, Milton Park, Abingdon, Oxon OX14 4RN
711 Third Avenue, New York, NY 10017, USA

Routledge is an imprint of the Taylor and Francis Group, an informa business

Copyright © Catherine Jones Finer 2003

The author has asserted her moral right under the Copyright, Designs and Patents Act, 1988, to be identified as the author of this work.

All rights reserved. No part of this book may be reprinted or reproduced or utilised in any form or by any electronic, mechanical, or other means, now known or hereafter invented, including photocopying and recording, or in any information storage or retrieval system, without permission in writing from the publishers.

Notice:
Product or corporate names may be trademarks or registered trademarks, and are used only for identification and explanation without intent to infringe.

Publisher's Note
The publisher has gone to great lengths to ensure the quality of this reprint but points out that some imperfections in the original copies may be apparent.

Disclaimer
The publisher has made every effort to trace copyright holders and welcomes correspondence from those they have been unable to contact.

A Library of Congress record exists under LC control number: 2002074724

Typeset by Martingraphix, Cape Town, South Africa.

ISBN 13: 978-1-138-71845-6 (hbk)
ISBN 13: 978-1-138-71842-5 (pbk)
ISBN 13: 978-1-315-19456-1 (ebk)

Contents

List of Tables	vii
List of Figures	ix
List of Contributors	xi
Acknowledgements	xiii

1   Foreword   1
Catherine Jones Finer

PART 1: ON DRAWING LESSONS, IN THE CONTEXT OF CHINA

2   When all other Conditions are not Equal: The Context for Drawing Lessons   5
Richard Rose

3   The Context of Social Policy Reform in China: Theoretical, Comparative and Historical Perspectives   23
Sheying Chen

4   The Policy Process in Contemporary China: Mechanisms of Politics and Government   37
Bo Peng

5   Paradigm Shifts in Social Welfare Policy Making in China: Struggling between Economic Efficiency and Social Equity   51
Hsiao-hung Nancy Chen

PART 2: POLICY SECTORS UNDER SCRUTINY

6   Policies Geared to Tackling Social Inequality and Poverty in China   69
Xinping Guan

7   Reflections on Inequality and Poverty in China   89
David Piachaud

8   Labour Market Construction and Labour Mobility in Urban China   97
Fenyu Wang and Yandong Zhao

9   The British Labour Market and Labour Market Policy in Comparative Perspective   117
Jochen Clasen

10	Pension Reform in China *Nelson Chow and Yuebin Xu*	129
11	Reforming Pensions *Alan Walker*	143
12	Financing Health Care in China's Cities: Balancing Needs and Entitlements *Gerald Bloom, Yuelai Lu and Jiaying Chen*	155
13	China's Health Policy: A Comparative Footnote *Rudolf Klein*	169
14	Progress and Problems of Urban Housing Reform *Ya Ping Wang*	177
15	Housing in China: A View from the West *John Doling*	191
16	Women's Rights and Protection Policy in China: Achievements and Problems *Peiqun He*	203
17	Women's Rights and Gender Issues *Jane Lewis*	215
18	Social Care and Voluntary Action in China: The Policy of 'Societalizing Social Welfare' and its Effects *Tao Chen*	225
19	Voluntary Action, Social Care and Social Work: A UK Response *Nicholas Deakin and Ann Davis*	233
20	Afterword *Catherine Jones Finer*	245
	Index	*247*

List of Tables

2.1	Desirability and feasibility of applying a lesson	14
5.1	Chronological account of key events of the social welfare system reform in China, by different economic planning phases	53-56
5.2	Expenditures on civil affairs establishments 1950–1996	57
5.3	Labour insurance and welfare expenditure 1952–1995	60
5.4	Changes in the situation of urban employees by type of ownership, 1978–1998 (million persons)	62
5.5	Social insurance coverage 1986, 1989, 1992	64
6.1	Urban inequality 1990 and 1998	72
6.2	Annual average foreign capital into China (billion US$)	73
6.3	Annual average foreign trade (billion *yuan*)	74
8.1	Annual employment growth by ownership in China 1990–1997 (%)	98
8.2	Average years between job changes in different eras	100
8.3	Means of job changes in labourers' careers for different age groups	100
8.4	Impact of an individual's unit characteristics on the signing of labour contracts and the social security obtained: logistic regression	109
8.5	Mean annual household income (in *yuan*: total, per capita and per adult equivalent), poverty incidence and poverty gap	111
8.6	Correlation matrix between social welfares and securities that an individual obtains	112
12.1	Number of employed persons by type of enterprises (million)	160
14.1	Housing entitlement in different periods	181
14.2	Housing problems and policy responses	187
17.1	Economic activity of women aged 16–59 with dependent children, Great Britain 1973–1996 (%)	221
17.2	Divorce rate per 000 married population	221
17.3	Marital and extramarital births per 000 women aged 15–44, 1940–1998	222
17.4	Percentage of women aged 18–49 cohabiting by legal marital status (Great Britain)	222
17.5	Distribution of the different types of lone-mother families with dependent children 1971–1999	223

List of Figures

5.1	Industrial structural change in China 1991–2000	51
5.2	Economic growth rate vs. urban registered unemployment rate in China over different planning phases	63
8.1	Changes in methods of getting the first job 1949–1998	99
8.2	The structure of urban poverty population	110
12.1	Health needs and entitlement groups in urban areas	162
12.2	Agenda for urban health development and reform	164
15.1	The housing provision chain	199
15.2	Housing regimes	200

List of Contributors

BLOOM Gerald is a Fellow of the Institute of Development Studies (IDS) and Deputy Chair of the China Health Development Forum, University of Sussex, Brighton, UK.

CHEN Hsiao-Hung Nancy is Professor and Dean of the Department of Sociology and College of Social Sciences, National Chengchi University, Taipei, Taiwan. At the time of writing, Professor Chen was spending six months as an academic visitor at the Department of Social Policy and Social Work, University of Oxford, UK.

CHEN Jiaying is Associate Professor in the School of Public Health, Fudan University, Shanghai, China.

CHEN Sheying is Associate Professor in Public Policy and Development Strategy, City University of New York, USA.

CHEN Tao, Dr, teaches in the Department of Social Work and Administration, China Youth College for Political Science, Beijing, China.

CHOW Nelson Wing-sun is Professor of Social Work and Social Administration at the University of Hong Kong, China.

CLASEN Jochen is Professor at the Centre for Comparative Research in Social Welfare, University of Stirling, Scotland, UK.

DAVIS Ann is Professor of Social Work at the University of Birmingham, UK.

DEAKIN Nicholas is Emeritus Professor of Social Policy, University of Birmingham, UK; and Visiting Professor at the London School of Economics, UK.

DOLING John is Professor of Housing Studies at the University of Birmingham, UK.

GUAN Xinping is Professor in the Department of Sociology and Deputy Director of the Centre for European Studies, Nankai University, Tianjin, China.

HE Peiqun is Associate Professor in the School of International Politics and Public Affairs, Fudan University, Shanghai, China.

KLEIN Rudolf is Emeritus Professor of Social Policy, University of Bath, UK; and Visiting Professor at the London School of Economics, UK, and the London School of Hygiene and Tropical Medicine, UK.

LEWIS Jane is Professor of Social Policy at the University of Oxford, UK.

LU Yuelai is Senior Research Associate in the Overseas Development Group at the University of East Anglia, Norwich, UK; and Executive Secretary of the China Health Development Forum (Sussex, UK).

PENG Bo, Dr, was a Senior Associate Member of St Antony's College, Oxford, UK (2000-2001); and is Lecturer in the Department of Public Administration, Fudan University, Shanghai, China.

PIACHAUD David is Professor of Social Policy at the London School of Economics, UK.

ROSE Richard is Professor and Director of the Centre for the Study of Public Policy, and Editor of the *Journal of Public Policy*, at the University of Strathclyde, Glasgow, Scotland, UK.

WALKER Alan is Professor of Social Policy and Director of the ESRC Growing Older Research Programme on Extending Quality Life, Department of Sociological Studies, University of Sheffield, UK.

WANG Fenyu is Professor and Director of the Sociology Section, National Research Centre for Science and Technology for Development (NRCSTD), Beijing, China.

WANG Ya Ping is Reader in the School of Planning and Housing, Edinburgh College of Art/Heriot-Watt University, Edinburgh, Scotland, UK.

XU Yuebin is Associate Professor in the Department of Social Work, Administrative College of Civil Affairs, The Ministry of Civil Affairs, Yanjiao, East Beijing, China.

ZHAO Yandong, Dr, is on the staff of the National Research Center for Science and Technology for Development. In particular, he was a member of the team led by Wang Fenyu to conduct The Survey of Occupational Mobility and Migration (SOMM), a joint research undertaking by the National Research Center for Science and Technology for Development (NRCSTD), China, and Fafo Institute for Applied Studies, Norway, in three cities of China in 1998.

Acknowledgements

As might be expected, this has been a 'rolling collective' undertaking from start to finish. So there are not merely many contributions to acknowledge, but many different orders of contribution.

Thanks are due, first of all, to our sponsors: The British Academy (Sino-British Fellowship Trust) and the Economic and Social Research Council's (ESRC's) Future Governance Programme under the direction of Professor Edward C. Page. It was this combined generosity of funding which permitted the original, innovative China-UK/Europe comparative social policy workshop ever to take place and which then ensured the present book's completion.

Next and no less conspicuously, thanks are due to the Asian Studies Centre of St Antony's College, Oxford, and indeed to the College in general, for hosting the workshop and assisting in its preparation and operation in every way. In particular, the contribution of Dr Steve Tsang, Director of the Asian Studies Centre, to the co-chairmanship of workshop proceedings, was decisive and much appreciated. Much valued, also, was the contribution of the secretary of the Asian Studies Centre, Jennifer Griffiths, to the otherwise 'thankless' detailed burden of workshop preparation and support.

Next again – most conspicuously – thanks are due to those of our contributors who braved flying to attend the workshop, from New York as well as from China, in the month after September 11. Only one participant from China (Professor Wang Fenyu) was unable to get official clearance in sufficient time, but he was able at least to send material for another Chinese colleague (Professor Guan Xinping) to present on his behalf. Meanwhile, the response from leading, UK-based comparativists – most of them professedly ignorant about China hitherto – to the challenge of the workshop, was as impressive as it turned out rewarding. All of the contributors, Chinese and western, have since confirmed their commitment to this project by their willingness to rewrite and revise for this book, in response to editorial – and each others' – suggestions.

Not least, although last in this order of proceedings, thanks are due to Pandora Kerr Frost, who is quite possibly the best UK-based copy-editor in the business – certainly one most sensitive to unconventional, potentially block-busting, publication demands. In the preparation of MSS for CRC, *par excellence*, it is her order of expertise that in this case has triggered the difference between finished and unfinished copy.

Chapter 1

Foreword

Catherine Jones Finer

This collection is the product of a workshop on 'Social Policy Reform in Socialist Market China: the Scope for Lessons for and from Abroad', organized through the Asian Studies Centre, St Antony's College, Oxford, funded by the British Academy in conjunction with the ESRC[1], for October 19–20, 2001. The purpose of this chapter is to outline something of the background to the workshop, before commenting on the event itself and thence on the contents of this book.

The promotion of East-West comparative social policy – in the global rather than merely European sense of this expression – has long been a priority for this editor. An ESRC-funded year-off in the mid-1980s, researching social policy development in Hong Kong (Jones 1990a), first prompted her to question how far 'the Hong Kong way of social policy' might reflect *regional* traits over and above the idiosyncracies of this then famously unique British colony. Since when, without prejudging the issue of how far it made sense to talk of 'an Asian Pacific welfare model' (cf Goodman et al. 1998), she has been urging the case for incorporating Asian Pacific perspectives (not merely western perspectives on Asia Pacific) into the mainstream of international comparative social policy (e.g. Jones 1990b, 1993; Jones Finer 2001).

The ambition remains to encourage ever more comparativists, and others active in the fields of social policy-making and delivery, to look on comparative social policy (CSP) as being about more than the comparison of western style welfare states (even with occasional reference to Japan), from western points of view. However, just as the development of the subject so far has largely been a product – and indicator – of the quantity and quality of academic networking to date, so its prospects for further expansion will depend on broadening the club membership. But on what terms and on whose say-so? Thanks to the 'luck of the draw' and the impact of the Internet, the extent of the CSP network is bound to depend, at least for the time being,[2] on the willingness and capacity of relevant academics to address one another in English.

Yet further constraints arise from an underlying disagreement within CSP, as to how far it is to be regarded as a form of moral crusade (e.g. Beck et al. 1997) as against a 'purely academic' specialism – as against (as in the present case) something pragmatically in between. Witness the inconsistencies evident in western universities' treatment of non-western graduate social policy students and visiting academics. Are the students there merely to be taught or also to inform? Are non-westerners attending western-organized social policy conferences expected primarily to conform or to offer alternative points of view?

Finally and most decidedly, CSP is constrained by the fact that much of the world remains as yet unpossessed of what might be termed 'social policy', for comparative purposes. Social policy implies some sort of top-down role for government in society i.e. some intention and capacity, on the part of a government, if not actively to manage key aspects of its society, then at least to count 'society oversight' as being part of its brief. CSP is thus neither to be confused with international aid nor – at the opposite end of the spectrum – with traditions of local custom-and-practice. By the same token, therefore, it is bound to have more to do with the developed and fast-developing parts of the world, than with those swathes of it still locked in a sheer struggle for existence. In short, social policy is what better-placed national governments – or, conceivably, even regional federations of governments such as the European Union – have the time, will, political authority and material resources to decide on for themselves.

It is against this background that China offers such a striking challenge – as much to its own experts as to CSP specialists viewing the country from outside. As will become increasingly clear in the following pages, China boasts everything from first world metropolitan city trading centres to vast tracts of rural primitiveness whose inhabitants must be amongst the poorest people in the world; all ostensibly under the single governance of the Chinese Communist Party (CCP). In practice, much – though by no means all – of the social policy emphasis in this book will be on urban and semi-urban, socialist market China. But even within this 'sector', the practical limits to the reach of central government – across a country so vast and varied – swiftly become apparent. Policies may be centrally decided, but key decisions as to their implementation are liable to depend more on local officials' susceptibilities to the interests of local enterprises, than to the distant dictates of Beijing.

Nevertheless, the idea of launching a high-profile China/UK CSP workshop (already discussed with a number of colleagues in China) turned out to be a timely proposition – for two main reasons.

First, the experience of uneven, unfettered economic liberalization had alerted Chinese authorities to the importance of responding to some of the consequences of this upheaval, not least in the interests of maintaining vital social stability. Hence, for instance, 'Social Policy' was finally accorded its own sectional status within the Academy of Social Sciences in Beijing (December 1999), atop a network of social policy-interested university academics apparently stretching right around the country.[3] The subject was still, by definition, 'non-political' – in the sense that academic experts were expected to act in a consultative rather than in an openly critical capacity *vis à vis* government. Nevertheless there was obvious interest in the idea of learning from the experience of other countries; not of course about their processes of policy-making *per se*, but about the operation of the policies that these processes had given rise to.[4]

Meanwhile, the second factor has been the intervening build-up of western social science interest in contemporary China, not merely as a consequence of its much awaited entry into the World Trade Organization but, more fundamentally, as a result of China's unprecedented drive to catch up with the developed world, via its very own crash course in economic liberalization *without* political liberalization. In this context, a CSP project committed to linking Chinese expertise with useful outsider comparative perspectives, turned out to have convincing appeal both ways. Hence the willingness of both the British Academy (Sino-British Trust) and the Economic and Social Science Research Council (*Future Governance Programme*) to fund an international workshop, and the willingness of the government of China (despite

September 11) to allow a selection of its key social scientists to travel to Britain for the purpose.

Ideally, this was intended to be a two-way exchange of views, between Chinese experts in search of ideas and advice from elsewhere and experienced UK-based comparativists intrigued to discover more about the situation in China. In other words, the object was to ensure a balance between, on the one hand, Chinese expertise on China (such as had typically not been exposed to mainstream CSP audiences hitherto) and, on the other, authoritative CSP expertise on the part of distinguished academics not hitherto professionally familiar with the Chinese case. Furthermore it was made clear from the outset that the workshop was to serve as preparation for this book.

Thus the design of workshop proceedings was contrived very much with the eventual book in mind. Part One of both workshop and book was designed to serve as a composite introduction to the point and substance of this coming-together. Crucially, it proved possible to secure the services of no less than Richard Rose to open with another famously incisive piece on the scope for drawing lessons ('when all other conditions are *not* equal') between countries. In response to which Sheying Chen then offers his own measured analysis of the state of GPP (general public policy) in China and thence of the country's openness to differing types of lesson-learning from abroad. Bo Peng follows with a frank and illuminating introduction to the current 'Policy Process in China'. Hsiao-hung Nancy Chen then concludes this section with a masterly overview of key trends, to date, in Chinese social policy reform, in the context of the country's striking economic transformation.

Thereafter the layout of Part Two is in a sense more predictable, in that successive areas of social policy concern are respectively to be 'dealt with' by pairs of China experts and senior UK-based comparativists. The actual choice of themes and policy sectors for discussion was determined by a mixture of Chinese specialist availability, the extent of relevant coverage in the CSP literature – and the willingness of leading UK-based policy specialists to involve themselves in this project Nevertheless it proved possible to account for most major social policy sectors (at least from a UK-based perspective on what counts as 'social policy'), as befits an introductory venture such as this.

Every paper represents a version of its workshop original, revised in the light of workshop feedback, in addition to editorial advice. Just three of the final Chinese papers presented (Chapters 6, 10, 12) include co-authors additional to those actually present at the workshop (but present in the list of contributors here included). We were delighted, in this connection, to be able to include Professor Nelson W.S. Chow of the University of Hong Kong (unable for personal reasons to attend the workshop) as a co-author, with Yuebin Xu, of the revised presentation on pensions reform.

The sequence of substantive papers on China – Guan on Poverty/Inequality; Wang/Zhao on Labour Market Construction; Chow/Xu on Pensions Reform; Bloom/Lu/Chen on Health Care; Wang on Housing; He on Women's Rights; Tao on Social Care and Voluntary Action – is unparalleled for its range, thoroughness and originality. No less impressive – and proof in itself of the generosity of famously senior colleagues – is the roll-call of respective UK-based respondents: Professors Piachaud, Clasen, Walker, Klein, Doling, Lewis, Deakin and Davis: great names in their respective fields of comparative social policy. In short, this has been a memorable coming-together.

Notes

1 See Acknowledgements page for details.
2 There could be an eventual 'Chinese takeover' – if China ever becomes rich enough to replace the US in the international linguistic stakes.
3 Personal interviews, Beijing, April 2000.
4 Almost as if the authorities in China were content to allow the deliberations of other peoples, elsewhere, to serve as a short-cut substitute for throwing key questions open to their own people.

References

Beck, W., van der Maesen, L., Walker, A. (1997), *The Social Quality of Europe*, Kluwer Law International, The Hague.
Goodman, R., Kwon, H-J., White, G. (1998), (eds), *The East Asian Welfare Model: Welfare Orientalism and the State*, Routledge, London.
Jones, C., (1990a) *Promoting Prosperity: The Hong Kong Way of Social Policy*, Chinese University Press, Hong Kong.
Jones, C., (1990b) 'Hong Kong, Singapore, South Korea and Taiwan: Oikonomic Welfare States', *Government and Opposition*, XXV, 4. 445–62.
Jones, C., (1993) 'The Pacific Challenge: Confucianist Welfare States', in C. Jones (ed) *New Perspectives on the Welfare State in Europe*, Routledge, London, pp. 198–217.
Jones Finer, C. (2001), (ed), *Comparing the Social Policy Experience of Britain and Taiwan*, Ashgate, Aldershot.

PART 1

ON DRAWING LESSONS, IN THE CONTEXT OF CHINA

Chapter 2

When all other Conditions are not Equal: The Context for Drawing Lessons[1]

Richard Rose

'A society can move forward as it is, in spite of what it is, and because of what it is.' (Albert Hirschman, *Journeys toward Progress* 1963)

'To attempt to do something which is inherently impossible is always a corrupting enterprise.' (Michael Oakeshott, *Political Education* 1951)

Neo-classical economics and Marxist theories share a common assumption: universalist explanations are best for understanding behaviour in a given society. Capitalists and consumers and workers and bureaucrats are expected to behave in similar self-interested ways, whether they are in America or Africa, or in Britain or Burma. The development of increasingly abstract economic theories omits references to social institutions that other intellectual disciplines treat as central in making social science 'social'. It also leaves out information specific to the context of time and place. The host of excluded concerns are covered by the *ceteris paribus* assumption that 'all other conditions remain equal'.

Advisors on public policy similarly assume universality, treating their favoured policies as completely fungible. What works in one country is expected to work everywhere; contextual information is deemed irrelevant. Economists are particularly prone to this assumption. Lawrence Summers, chief economist at the World Bank when the market was introduced in post-communist countries, has asserted: *'Respect the universal laws of economics'*. Steve Hanke, a consultant on monetarist programmes, relies on fungibility in travelling from continent to continent: 'I tell everyone the same thing' (quoted in Rose 1993: 35f). Monetary policies are treated as if they would work the same in Sweden and Russia, just as the parts for a Ford automobile are expected to work the same in Scotland or Spain.

However, public policies are concerned with actions of government, and every government is embedded in a specific context of territory, institutions and national history – for better and for worse, as Albert Hirschman emphasizes. No government can ignore the constraints and opportunities of its national context. To attempt a great leap forward without regard for context is a policy of impossibilism. It is not only intellectually corrupting, as Oakeshott emphasizes, but also likely to be politically disastrous. Timing and sequencing are also crucial considerations in determining whether or not a policy recommendation is adopted. Policy analysts caught up in the everyday concerns of a government ministry have no time to consider what happens in the abstract; they are concerned with the here and now, disposing of good ideas that are inopportune in order to focus on what is possible today. Single-country studies of public policy are rich in information about specific events, individuals and institutions specific to the context of the problem at hand.

The analysis of public policy is more akin to epidemiology than to rocket science. An epidemiologist not only interprets biomedical symptoms of individuals in terms of universal principles, but also examines contextual variations in the incidence of these symptoms in order to find the most effective response. Similarly, individual governments around the world face many of the same problems – health care, social security, transportation, education and collecting the taxes to pay for these services. In the Organization for Economic Cooperation and Development (OECD), member states meet in committees to share their experiences. The European Union adopts policies affecting economic and social problems of its 15 member states, and its authority is backed with the resources of law and money. The World Bank and the International Monetary Fund offer policy advice to countries unable to deal with problems with their own national resources, and Britain and Korea, as well as low-income countries, have turned to the IMF for help. When prescribing policies to deal with foreign exchange problems, IMF officials invariably invoke lessons based on their experience in other countries and other continents.

Many scholars of China stress the importance of the Chinese context for understanding its public policies. However, although the People's Republic of China (PRC) governs a society with a history far older than any OECD country, the PRC government is not trying to preserve old traditions. It is trying to abandon 'backward' ways in order to advance towards its vision of China as a modern society. The Great Cultural Revolution was an attempt to create a new society by ignoring constraints of context and without learning from the failure of Soviet experiments. It was abandoned. Today, the PRC government is seeking to integrate China in the international economy. Entry into the World Trade Organization is practical evidence of this strategy, and international trade exposes countries to influences from abroad. Given a relatively low level of economic development, the Chinese government has incentives to give less priority to what is distinctively 'national' in national policy and to look to other countries for policies that appear more successful.

From the perspective of policy makers, differences between countries can be a source of threat, envy or learning. Comparisons of military strength are invariably based on appreciations of threat. Comparisons of wealth between rich and poor countries can induce envy or anger or cries of injustice. However, differences between countries can also be a means of learning about the causes and consequences of variations in the way that governments in different countries respond to the same problem. Academic students of comparative public policy seek explanations for observed differences, and the answers given invariably emphasize contextual details. Policy makers are more interested in learning about the consequences of policies. The results of comparing how different countries respond to a common problem can provide ideas about which measures are more effective and which are less successful.

Lesson drawing creates a comparative advantage from the empirical observation that countries deal with common problems differently and differ in the degree to which their policies are deemed successful. The object of lesson drawing is to adapt and adopt in one's own country a programme already successful in another, and thus reduce future differences in achievement. In developing countries, where all other conditions are palpably not equal to those in OECD countries today, the attractions of learning how to improve national conditions are great. The potential sources for learning are heterogeneous and scattered from universities offering ideas without money to development agencies dispensing cash grants on behalf of their governments. The intergovernmental and international agencies moving ideas across national boundaries are also heterogeneous and numerous. Rich countries offer attractive achievements, but the resources required for success for the moment are beyond the scope of many developing countries. Poor countries offer both positive and negative lessons, but their poor status makes them unattractive for emulation.

The following pages examine the tension between universalistic assumptions about the transferability of policies and contextual obstacles to lesson-drawing. Emphasis is given to the role of political values as well as resource constraints as criteria for deciding under what circumstances and to what extent lessons can (or should) be drawn. Where a country looks for lessons reflects psychological proximity more than geographical proximity. Developing countries are prone to make the mistake of focusing on the current policies of developed countries, rather than looking back in time to see what they did in order to move from being a developing to a developed country. The conclusion is that learning from abroad can contribute to making progress, but differences in starting points mean that national progress is not the same as international convergence or catching up.

Reality cannot be Exogenized

Economic models are both universalistic and abstract, and what is exogenous to a model tends to be treated as irrelevant. The rationale for doing so may be an aesthetic concern with keeping the model pure, or it may reflect a belief that the relationships specified in the model are just as valid universally as are the laws of physics. Even when a seasoning of stylized facts (*sic*) are added for illustration, the fundamental goal remains universalism. But abstraction has a price for, as Ian Little (1963: 81f) long ago remarked about pure welfare economics, it risks becoming 'an unmitigated stream of logical deductions which are not about anything at all'.

The free movement of ideas and of graduate students in search of education has given intellectual hegemony to the universalistic paradigms of economics. Able young people from throughout the world win grants to study economics in internationally renowned universities, and policy concerns shaped by national contexts are replaced by intellectual problems determined within the context of the neoclassical economic paradigm. Students are encouraged to become adept in analysing economic issues in terms of abstract mathematical formulae. This priority is complemented by marginalizing or eliminating contextual knowledge derived from economic history; by training in the collection and evaluation of statistical data that are inputs to mathematical formulae, and by awareness of institutions that are the means by which economic policies are in practice implemented. Able products of disciplined universalism are then recruited to jobs in national ministries, intergovernmental agencies and international financial institutions.

In imitation of economics, public management specialists promote best-practice policies on the universalistic assumption that 'one size fits all', that whatever policy is identified as best can be put into practice without regard to context and that there is an international political consensus about what is best. The assumption of normative agreement is the politics of the apolitical, a refusal to recognize that politics is about the expression of conflicting views about what government ought to do to achieve a given goal.

Limits of Universalism

The inspiration for economic model building is physics, which is both abstract and universal in its applications. However, the analogy is imperfect, for applied physics continues to flourish alongside theoretical physics and applications of physical principles endogenize the specifics of context in everything from civil engineering to space exploration. By contrast, the disjunction between economic theory and public policy means that economists are prepared to externalize the costs of applying their advice on to policy makers who carry the burden of figuring out how to endogenize the political realities left out of abstract prescriptions. The assumption that best practices can readily be transferred from one country to another overlooks the fact that governments in OECD countries have institutionalized commitments in almost every field of public policy.

The current policies of a national government are path-dependent; they are not chosen but inherited from predecessors (Rose and Davies 1994). The adoption of a best-practice policy involves not only adapting the measure to fit the context of another country but also disposing of prior commitments. However, path dependence makes it difficult to dispose of prior commitments. What was once contingent – for example, whether or not a pension fund should be pay-as-you-go or not – becomes a given in the present. However attractive another country's way of dealing with a common problem may appear, current policy makers tend to carry on as before, because of the political, economic and social costs of switching a policy they have inherited (see e.g. Pierson 2000; Mahoney 2000).

Resource constraints cause problems in developing countries, and thus encourage the search for better ways of doing things, and this search often focuses on sophisticated and costly policies of prosperous Western countries. Examining what is done in OECD countries is aided by funds that the latter provide for travel grants, followed up by technical assistance and foreign aid funding. However, the scope for developing countries to adopt best-practice programmes of OECD countries is immediately limited by constraints of resources. If a best-practice policy implies substantial expenditure, money is a constraint. For example, income-maintenance programmes regarded as best in the rich countries of Scandinavia may be impossibly expensive in middle-income or low-income countries. If programmes depend on large numbers of skilled persons, for example research and development policies, then personnel can be a constraint too.

Constraints of Context also Limited

Context has a double meaning for historians: it is about a point in time as well as about a specific place. A British historian examining the welfare state not only takes it for granted that it is a British institution, but also that it was created at a specific point in time. The Labour government's 1948 National Health Act, for example, is treated as the outcome of a configuration of influences in both time and place. When a historian documents individual policy-makers writing memoranda about legislation to colleagues in a specific political context, by definition such details are not generalizable to other countries.

When historians invoke the 'lessons' of history, there is the assumption that a country's past offers guidance for what can and cannot be done at present. However, every country has multiple histories: the United States has a history of promoting freedom and a history of slavery, and the lessons of British history in England are not the same as in Ireland. In countries with many centuries of history, such as China, there is a surplus of past events that can be drawn on – and no grounds for expecting agreement about *which* history is most relevant to the context at hand. When multiple histories are available, politicians can pick and choose from the past the historical example that gives them the answer they want, regardless of the stretching required to fit present circumstances (cf. Neustadt and May 1986; Rose 1993, chapter 4). For example, when inflation or depression threatens, Americans or Britons may point to Weimar Germany with the warning cry that inflation or depression threatens a turn to Nazism, for all that this did not happen in their own countries in the 1930s.

The principle of the classical Greek historian Heraclitus – you cannot step in the same river twice – implies, however, that national context varies from generation to generation, decade to decade or even year to year for, as a novelist has said, 'the past is another country'. While Heraclitus was correct in the literal sense, this did not stop Thucydides and Aristotle from seeking to draw lessons from what were then recent events. Nor does it stop contemporary policy makers from invoking experiences from the recent past as lessons to guide actions in the immediate future. However, in the due course of time policy makers repudiate their national past as irrelevant to the present. For example, while the Elizabethan Poor Law cannot be dismissed as 'un-English' because it was part of the nation's history from 1601 to 1834, it can be dismissed as out of date in the context of today.

When historians write books full of the specifics of national context, this is usually interpreted as meaning that events are due to causes specific to a single country. For example the most important feature of the welfare state in Britain is that it is British. Yet many of the causes invoked, for example, the influence of industrialization or urbanization or increasing national wealth, are generic. To bring out generic causes requires the examination of a multiplicity of countries. When compulsory education or national pension programmes are adopted in dozens of countries, then generic patterns and explanations are often offered to account for commonalities and variations around common themes, as in Esping-Andersen's (1990) study of *The Three Worlds of Welfare Capitalism*.

The uniqueness of place is usually assumed or asserted. Paradoxically, the only way to demonstrate the uniqueness of a national policy is through comparative analysis that endogenizes the experience of other countries. Systematic comparison can then measure the extent to which a country's policy differs from a larger OECD universe. The most likely outcome of comparison is that some differences, a few of kind and more of degree, will be identified with some countries. But it is a fallacy to treat partial differences as if they were total, or to argue that one particular difference in a complex set of educational or social security measures creates a total difference. Moreover, if one country is shown to deviate from a large number of OECD countries, in turn this implies that the great majority conform to a common linear model, for deviations can only exist within a framework that also recognizes regularities.

The interaction of universalistic and contextual influences is part of a dialectical process of policy development, with ample use and abuse of past history. Textbooks written by academics about national government, and national government manuals, are full of context-specific information about policies. By contrast, the world of commerce is full of examples of the universalistic adoption of many goods and services, such as Ford motor cars, Xerox machines or Sony Walkmans. Given that anthropologists treat food as culture- and context-dependent, the internationalization of food products is specially noteworthy. In Asia, McDonald's is a popular symbol of a product moving across national boundaries. A study of *Golden Arches East* (Watson 1997) not only documents the acceptance of McDonald's in many national contexts as families give greater attention to child-centred activities; it also shows that, just as policies imported from abroad can be changed in use by those receiving them, the way in which McDonald's is integrated into the lives of its customers varies from country to country.

Criteria for Lesson Drawing

Dissatisfaction is the starting point in searching for lessons. If a policy adopted in the past no longer delivers political satisfaction, this creates political pressure to search for something else to put in its place. The more intense the dissatisfaction, the less the concern with best practice, and the greater the desire to find something that will reduce pain, even if the new policy is admittedly a stop-gap measure that buys time until something can be found that will put an end to dissatisfaction. In search of something better, policy-makers can turn to speculation in hopes of finding an appealing policy. But even if this produces an attractive measure, because a speculative policy has never been put into effect, there is a difficulty in answering the practical question – will it work? Lesson drawing offers an alternative to speculation.

A *lesson* is a programme designed to deal with a problem in one country by drawing on the experience of other countries facing the same problem (Rose 1993). Thus, a lesson is not a prescriptive statement about what ought to be done, justified by a vague reference to 'experience shows' or 'what everyone knows'. Nor is a lesson just a description of what another country is doing, for that leaves out the point of the process, applying foreign experience in one's own national context. This is very evident when the lesson is negative, a conclusion not to follow what another country is doing. A lesson is about linking observations of what is currently being done in another country with what might be done here in future. If a lesson is positive, a lesser or greater amount of adaptation is required before it can be imported, to take into account differences between the exporting and importing country in administrative institutions and much else. Additional changes are also likely to be needed in order to satisfy the demands of the importing country's political constituencies.

Lesson drawing is about contingencies: *Under what circumstances and to what extent will a programme that works there also work here?* Foreign experience is examined in order to deal with a domestic problem better. Contingency emphasizes the need for policy makers to be sceptical about the ready adaptation of best practice policies. It also encourages scepticism about arguments that what is done there can never happen here. Japan's success in learning from the West is an example of national policy makers responding successfully when foreign force imposes the need to open up a country to international influences.

The *desirability* of a lesson is contingent, because it is determined by political values and ideology. When socialist and capitalist countries were in conflict, there was a big gulf between Western nations and the Soviet Union and China. Today, there are few countries so ideologically rigid, as the People's Democratic Republic of (North) Korea, that their policies are likely to be dismissed out of hand. Now that there are dozens of post-communist countries undergoing degrees of democratization and/or market liberalization, a national government can turn to countries further down the road in the process of 'de-communization' to examine responses to common problems, such as privatization. Within East Asia, there are negative lessons too, for example, the close and private financial interconnections of *chaebols* and the Korean government.

Since there are disagreements within every political system about desirable ends and means, a change in government, in the balance of power within a government, or in the appreciation of national policy by civil servants with critical roles in the policy process, can change what is deemed desirable. For example, in China the communist government has shifted from defining major urban enterprises as producing welfare for their workers to a new goal of producing goods and services that can compete profitably in national and international markets (S. Chen, chapter 3). In the previous political climate, cost was not an objection to adopting new social policies. In the current political climate, the insecurities of workers are not an objection to lessons promoting economic development.

Desirability does not ensure feasibility. Every programme involves a particular combination of laws, personnel and financial resources (Rose 1984). Programmes concerning freedom of speech are law-intensive; pension programmes cost a lot of money but require relatively few employees; while health and education programmes tend to be both labour-intensive and money-intensive. Within Western countries, the resource requirement of the average programme is usually much less than the average error in the ministry of finance's forecast of annual tax revenue, but the total of demands for new public expenditure is usually greater than discretionary income. The easiest way to finance the introduction of a lesson from abroad is if it takes over the budget allocation of a failing programme that is about due to lose its budget allocation.

In developing countries resource constraints are of fundamental importance. In a country where the average per capita income is estimated at less than $1,000 a year it is a luxury to worry about trade offs between equity and efficiency (Okun 1975) or about altering the fiscal basis of a nationwide social security system. Although the People's Republic of China is by world standards a low-income country, three characteristics augment its resources. First, the population of the People's Republic is so great that aggregate resources are large. For example, if 2 per cent of the population has special skills, their number is greater than the population of most European countries. Second, the concentration of resources in major cities creates growth points as well as divisions between cities and the countryside. Third, the economic potential of China – as exporter and importer – attracts overseas resources, some controlled by the Chinese and some in foreign hands.

Logically, there are four ways of combining concerns with practical feasibility and political desirability (see Table 2.1). Two are very straightforward. If a lesson is deemed desirable by politicians and practicable by experts, it is doubly attractive. Reciprocally, a programme is doubly undesirable if it is disliked by politicians and likely to fail if put into effect. Conflict arises when politicians are attracted to a policy successful elsewhere but likely to fail if imported. As in Greek mythology, such a programme is a siren call: it is alluring but if followed it leads to shipwreck. While the veto of a lesson that is technically practical but inconsistent with the government's political values and interests may frustrate its proponents, it does not cause failure since no action is taken.

Table 2.1 Desirability and feasibility of applying a lesson

Feasibility	Desirability	
	High	Low
High	Doubly attractive	Unwanted technical solution
Low	Siren call	Doubly rejected

The current PRC government policy for the Internet is an example of the tension between what is desirable and what is feasible. On the one hand, government policy wants to promote internet use for communication between producers and buyers in competitive international markets. On the other hand, the government wants to control the Internet in order to prevent its use to access and circulate political information that Chinese censors would not allow to be published in print. In addition to competing goals, there are also differences of opinion about whether or not it is practical for the state to censor internet communication abroad through control of internet service providers or to attempt to monitor billions of email messages and connections (cf. Dai 2000; Pei 2001; Rose 2001a; Wong 2001).

Where to Look – and When

The problems facing developing countries are long-term problems; thus, there is plenty of time for national policy-makers to look abroad for examples of what to do and what not to do. Many countries offer evidence to policy-makers looking for programmes that produce political satisfaction. Given time and opportunity to travel to different countries, where should policy-makers turn?

Sources of lessons tend to *vary with the problem* at hand. A country that is an exemplar in maintaining full employment may be only average in dealing with inflation, and vice versa. In the late nineteenth century, Japan consciously adopted a policy of looking for lessons from the leading country in each sector. Thus, officials were sent to Britain to study how to operate a postal service and to the United States to learn about establishing agricultural education. Initially, the Japanese looked to France for lessons about creating a modern army, but after its defeat in the Franco-Prussian war of 1870, they turned for lessons to Berlin (see Westney 1987). The stimulus to search also varies within a country. For example, within the People's Republic, there are big issues of urban development and there are big issues of rural development and, while they are related, they are not the same. The lessons appropriate for major Chinese cities such as Beijing or Shanghai are more likely to be found in countries with massive cities that are magnets internationally, while lessons relevant to the mass of the population in the countryside may well be found in very different countries.

For most of the post-1945 era, *ideological harmony* was an important influence on where countries looked for lessons. From Berlin to Beijing, countries with Communist governments and a non-market economic system tended to look to Moscow for lessons, while market-oriented countries looked to the United States or Western Europe, and developing countries with competing or unclear ideological commitments could shop around between them. Today, the Russian Federation offers both positive and negative lessons about how to make the transition from a non-market party-state. As a Chinese researcher in Beijing, Zhou Xincheng, told an American journalist:

'When you Americans argue about the fall of the Soviet Union, it is a matter of history or international affairs. But when we argue about it, it is a domestic issue and current affairs. People borrow Russia to express their opinions about China.' (Pan 2001)

There are now dozens of post-communist societies that have faced such common problems as introducing market institutions, shedding governmental commitments to finance 'value-subtracting' enterprises, and dealing with the consequences for civil society of totalitarian-inspired efforts to control the behaviour and thoughts of citizens. Post-communist countries offer positive examples of how to do it (e.g. East Central European countries now negotiating entry into the European Union) and how not to do it (e.g. Ukraine).

Geographical proximity is less important than *psychological proximity* in looking for lessons. While London is geographically closer to France and Ireland than to the United States or Australia, the latter are psychologically closer. Likewise, Australians prefer to look to America or Europe rather than to Indonesia for lessons. In post-communist countries, policy makers are more likely to look to European Union countries than to close neighbours with similar legacies. Scandinavian countries are exceptional in combining psychological and geographical proximity.

Given constraints of *resources*, it is logical to look for lessons to countries that have a similar amount of tax revenue and public officials with skills needed to deliver specialist services and a readiness to apply bureaucratic rule and follow the rule of law. There are few policies that do not require a significant commitment of money and personnel. The exceptions, such as laws on same-sex marriages or on the death penalty, may be opposed on normative rather than resource grounds. Costs are a valid argument against developing countries applying best practice policies currently in use in prosperous OECD countries. But for the same reason, policies in healthy and wealthy countries can be psychologically attractive because they promise so much more than governors of an indebted poor country can deliver.

The People's Republic of China is embedded in a complex of geographical, political, economic and cultural relationships involving different types of proximity. Institutionally, it is most closely linked with the Special Administrative Region of Hong Kong. Even though political relations with the Republic of China–Taiwan are strained, there is significant economic interaction. The dispersion of ethnic Chinese people throughout the region provides a 'bamboo network' that can be a conduit for the communication of ideas and resources (cf. Weidenbaum and Hughes 1996). In its current material resources, the PRC is at a similar level of economic development as Indonesia, the Philippines, Thailand or Vietnam, countries large and different enough to have the potential to offer positive or negative lessons. The size of the Chinese economy and the rapidity of recent developments makes it an attractive potential partner for the already-developed tiger economies of East Asia,

Within the region the Republic of Korea is a neighbour that is now much better off economically, but in the not too distant past was also a poor Asian country. When Chinese students are given the opportunity to study abroad, they prefer to study in a country that is 'most different' from China, such as the United States. In part this reflects the fungibility of knowledge, in fields such as medicine or electronics; in part it reflects the attractions of cosmopolitanism (learning to live and work in two very different cultures) and in part the aspiration to arrive at a remote goal. Entry to the World Trade Organization will increase Chinese contacts with countries that are remote geographically, economically and politically.

For activist policy-makers under pressure to reduce dissatisfaction by adopting a new policy, the answer to the question – *when to look?* – is: *Now*. But such is the speed with which information flows around the world that this response may be premature, for policy innovations attract attention, and their promoters are often ready to claim that their new initiative is a success before it has been implemented and before sufficient years have passed for the results to be evaluated. The United States is the prime example of success being claimed before implementation (cf. Pressman and Wildavsky 1973; Mossberger 2000: 202). Given the extent to which other countries follow developments in the United States from media accounts, there is the danger that foreign visitors arriving in America to study how a programme is working on the ground may find their visit premature by more than a year.

Where a programme is established, then examining how it is working on the ground is both possible and desirable; for people who administer an established programme, for example Value Added Tax, can explain how it works routinely. However, if the programme is long established, today's administrators may not know the problems faced by early initiators (for example, reliance on paper and pencil methods rather than computers) and what was done to overcome them. In so far as today's successful programme is added on to a programme that has developed over decades or generations, then the conditions for implementation and success will be radically different from those in a country where a programme is being introduced on a 'green field' site and administrative structures and public understanding must be built from scratch.

The question of *sequencing* is acute when developing countries look to OECD societies. The probability is high in OECD countries that current measures amend or augment pre-existing policies rather than starting from scratch, whereas in developing countries the opposite is often the case. For example, reforming social security raises very different issues from introducing a social security system in the first place.

The logic of a 'first-things-first' approach to lesson-drawing is that developing countries may be better advised to look to the more or less distant *past* of OECD countries rather than to current performance for lessons about how to introduce a programme. In addition to the logical argument for thinking in sequence, there are also practical advantages. The initial financial cost of introducing a programme is invariably less than that of a programme that has grown over the decades, and is thus likely to be more affordable for a country without the revenue resources of an OECD country. Examining how a programme has evolved over time reveals unintended consequences of an initial choice, and thus can provide negative lessons about avoiding immediately attractive measures that can have costly and unwanted consequences later.

Comparing welfare state policies in Europe and China can illustrate the importance of sequencing. In China today, a major problem is the substantial volume of welfare commitments that urban enterprises have as a legacy from their establishment as state enterprises in the time of a non-market economy, when enterprises were not evaluated on market-based criteria of making a profit but in terms of their contribution to the national plan. In such circumstances, enterprises could therefore undertake spending commitments that in a market economy would be separately funded through social policy ministries. By contrast, European welfare states have been established by enterprises and employees paying taxes to government, which takes responsibility for welfare policies. The European method guarantees the maintenance of employee pensions and other benefits, even if the enterprise goes bankrupt, while the Chinese system does not.

The model for Chinese enterprises was welfare provision in the Soviet Union rather than Sweden. However, detailed analysis has shown that the Soviet system created marked disparities between insiders covered by enterprises and outsiders left uncovered. Moreover, benefits were not distributed according to standard social policy criteria of need but according to place of employment, thus resulting in an inefficient, as well as inequitable, targeting of resources (Rose 1996). In so far as Chinese enterprises are now under pressure to concentrate on being market-oriented and shed the spending commitments of social security ministries, then it would be appropriate to look at what state enterprises have done since the introduction of the market in the Russian Federation a decade ago. The evidence shows that some enterprises have continued to maintain full social commitments, even though they cannot cover the cost of doing so from their revenue. In market terms, they are now 'value-subtracting' enterprises reducing the rate of economic growth (Gaddy and Ickes 2001).

Twenty-first-century European debates about how to reform mature welfare state policies are less relevant than the nineteenth-century measures which initiated the welfare state. When the welfare state was launched, it was selective in coverage rather than universalist. Some programmes were targeted at the very poor through means testing, while others benefited workers in steady employment who could contribute, along with their employers and the state, to a pool where payments were restricted to contributors. In countries such as France and Italy, where peasants were very numerous, there was also a marked differentiation between urban and rural coverage too. The move to universalism took generations to accomplish.

Political intentions differed greatly, for in some countries the expansion of the right to vote and welfare measures went together, whereas in Bismarck's Germany welfare policies were intended to be part of a strategy of 'authoritarian defence' by regimes that assumed economically secure workers would not want political rights. A similar assumption could be discerned in the 'welfare state authoritarianism' of the Soviet Union in Brezhnev's time (cf. Flora and Alber 1981: 46; Breslauer 1978; Cook 1993).

In addition to the fiscal dividend of a growing and increasingly rich economy, welfare states in OECD countries have also depended on social and political requisites (Rose 1991). Because a welfare state is a device for the collective provision of welfare, it presupposes a strong and also a broad sense of social solidarity. If this is absent, then individuals are likely to depend on their family, on close friends and neighbours, or on communal, religious, clan or other intermediate institutions rather than on the all-encompassing state. Francis Fukuyama refers to this phenomenon as the 'radius of trust', and emphasizes its importance for the scale of business enterprises. Where the radius is short, then enterprises will tend to be family-run for the welfare of the extended family of the owners, but where the radius is long then joint-stock companies can be created with a circle of trust that embraces impersonal shareholders and workers. He illustrates the point with a comparison of Chinese family enterprises as against Japanese enterprises with very large numbers of employees and shareholders.

Administrative honesty is required, if the state is to collect substantial tax revenues and disburse benefits to those who are entitled to them under the laws and regulations of the welfare programme. In developing countries, where resources are very limited, rationing can be according to legislation, for example, targeting or distinguishing between insiders eligible for benefit and outsiders not eligible. Rationing can also distinguish the distribution of resources between those who have connections and those who do not. The former can use what Russians call *blat* (Ledeneva 1998) and in China is referred to as *guanxi* (Walder 1986; Luo 2000; Wang 2000; Huang 2001; Lin 2001; cf. Transparency International 2001: 234ff).

Given multiple obstacles to introducing a European-style welfare system in an inhospitable context, inspiration may be gained by pushing analysis further back in time to look at what Europeans did for welfare before the state became important (Rose 1986). In the simplest circumstances, the family was the primary source of welfare provision in what was often a non-money or scarcely monetized system of household or village subsistence. It was sometimes supplemented by religious charities or by occupational guilds or other mutual benefit societies. In parts of the People's Republic of China the family is still often the primary source of welfare.

Industrialization brought with it urbanization and monetization. In mid-nineteenth-century England mutual aid societies were developed in which people known to each other pooled resources in order to make provision for those within their group who fell ill or lost their job, and for the funerals of those who died. The description of these organizations as 'friendly societies' emphasizes their origins as face-to-face groups of individuals known to each other, and deemed trustworthy and fair in financial matters. They thus resembled the *grameen* banks of contemporary India, where villagers pool the small amount of capital that they have because they trust those they know. In some cases face-to-face friendly societies slowly grew into large, nationwide agglomerations of capital, so-called mutual (that is, not-for-profit) insurance companies, while in other cases they were superseded by profit-making insurance companies and/or by the state. There are also examples of the shift from small-scale to large-scale funds generating abuse and even corruption, as in the case of some trade-union pension funds in the United States, which were not managed by workers known to each other, but exploited by national officials and their cronies. The hour-glass society of Russia also offers a caution against assuming that grassroots cooperation can be generalized to the national level. While 55 per cent of Russians trust most people whom they know, only 32 per cent trust most Russians. Similarly, while 66 per cent of Russians in work trust their employer to look after their interests and 66 per cent of the third of the labour force in trade unions trust their local union leaders, only 40 per cent trust their national union leaders and trust in businessmen in general and trade-union leaders in general is low (Rose 2001b).

In the medium term, developing countries want to look forward rather than backward to their own or to a European past. A low-income developing country such as China can, if it chooses, look to Asian countries that have recently used economic growth to create a society in which most people enjoy high standards of health, education and security in old age. The means of doing so differ from Esping-Andersen's (1990) three worlds of welfare, derived exclusively from European experience. Holliday (2000) describes the Asian model as 'productivist' welfare, in which economic growth is the overriding priority, and any increase in welfare provision depends on increases in production. High-income East Asian governments spend far less on welfare than do European counterparts. Among 28 OECD countries, Japan ranks 27th in public expenditure on education (3.6 per cent of GDP, almost a third below the OECD mean) and among the top countries in private expenditure on education. While Koreans spend relatively more on health than their GDP per capita would predict, less than half the spending on Korean health care is financed through the state, a big contrast with Europe where about three-quarters of health spending is state spending. While the United States is also a big spender on welfare, there too there is a much higher degree of market and not-for-profit provision of welfare services than in Europe, producing a pattern more congenial to Asians, who distrust the state, than to trustful Europeans.

Making Progress comes before Catching Up

Making progress is independent of a country's starting point. Given normative consensus on a goal – for example, increasing the proportion of young people completing secondary education – and accurate evidence of conditions here and now, measuring progress is relatively straightforward. Progress occurs if there is evidence of a fall in mortality or an increase in youths gaining qualifications on completion of secondary education. In the most favourable circumstances, the means to catch up involve a tested technology that is already working within a country. Progress therefore depends on providing more of the same, for example, medical clinics or secondary schools.

Catching up is more difficult, for not only is it a function of where a country is at a given moment in time but also of where other countries are and the lagging country maintaining a rate of progress higher than the country it is trying to catch (Rose 1995). When other countries are growing economically, absolute progress is insufficient to catch up with another country. Growth rates must be well above average. Japan has shown it is possible to catch up with Western countries through sustained high rates of growth. In the 1990s the PRC reported an annual average growth in Gross Domestic Product per capita of 9.5 per cent, a rate that is historically unprecedented. Yet after that decade it is still well behind the average of developing countries and further behind the minimum level of European Union countries.

A fixed target makes catching up much easier, for the target country cannot improve its current standing, for example, 100 per cent literacy or virtually all young people completing secondary education. A moving target is much harder to catch. If the PRC maintains its abnormally high economic growth rate indefinitely, then in about 16 years it could catch up with where Malaysia is as of the year 2000. But by that time, based on Malaysia's current rate of growth, its GDP per capita would have more than doubled (calculated from World Bank 2001: 44f).

Comparing public policies across countries or continents at a given point in time is bound to emphasize differences in context. Universalists ignore these differences at the risk of making generalizations that are irrelevant to the world as it actually is. But historians and area specialists risk insisting that differences at a given point in time are permanent, whereas the world is constantly changing. China is a prime historical example, for a millennium ago it could claim to be ahead of European countries in their dark ages.

The point of lesson drawing is to take advantage of cross-national differences in order to learn from the experience of countries where policies are different. The object is not to become so enamoured of a foreign example that one's own national context is ignored. Instead, it is to make the most of the positive achievements and failures of other countries to improve policy at home. Lesson drawing cannot overcome limitations of context, but it can offer a means of making progress from where a country is here and now.

Notes

1 This paper is a product of Grant L216252017 for a study of How to Draw Lessons, part of the British ESRC programme on Future Governance. It draws on ideas discussed at a Workshop convened by the editor of this volume at the Asian Studies Centre, St. Antony's College, Oxford, 19–20 October 2001. Useful comments have been received from Sheying Chen, Qihai Huang, Karen Mossberger, Edward C. Page and Raymond Saner.

References

Breslauer, George W., (1978). 'On the Adaptability of Soviet Welfare-State Authoritarianism,' In Karl W. Ryavec, ed. *Soviet Society and The Communist Party*. University of Massachusetts Press, Amherst, pp. 3–25.
Chen, Sheying, Chapter 3 in this volume.
Cook, Linda J., (1993). *The Soviet Social Contract and Why It Failed*, Harvard University Press, Cambridge, Massachusetts.

Dai, Xiudian, (2000). *The Digital Revolution and Governance*. Ashgate, Aldershot.
Esping-Andersen, Gosta, 1990. *The Three Worlds of Welfare Capitalism*, Blackwell and Polity Press, Oxford.
Flora, Peter and Alber, Jens, (1981). 'Modernization, Democratization and the Development of Welfare States in Western Europe', in P. Flora and A.J. Heidenheimer, eds., *The Development of Welfare States in Europe and America*. Transaction Publishers, 37–80, New Brunswick, NJ.
Fukuyama, Francis, (1995). *Trust: The Social Virtues and the Creation of Prosperity*. Free Press, New York.
Gaddy, Clifford G. and Ickes, Barry W., (2001). 'Stability and Disorder: an Evolutionary Analysis of Russia's Virtual Economy', in V.E. Bonnell and G.W. Breslauer, eds, *Russia in the New Century*, Westview Press, Boulder, 103–123.
Hirschman, Albert, (1963). *Journeys toward Progress*. Twentieth Century Fund, New York.
Holliday, Ian, (2000). 'Productivist Welfare Capitalism: Social Policy in East Asia', *Political Studies*, 48, 706–723.
Huang, Qihai, (2001). 'Chinese Social Capital: Guanxi'. University of Bristol Social Policy Department, New York, Bristol, duplicated.
Ledeneva, Alena V., (1998). *Russia's Economy of Favours*, Cambridge University Press, Cambridge.
Lin, Nan, (2001). *Social Capital: A Theory of Social Structure and Action*, Cambridge University Press, New York.
Little, I.M.D., (1963). *A Critique of Pure Welfare Economics*, Clarendon Press, Oxford, 2nd edition.
Luo, Y., (2000). *Guanxi and Business*, University of Hawaii Press, Honolulu.
Mahoney, Joseph, (2000). 'Path Dependence in Historical Sociology', *Theory and Society*, 29, 4, 507–548.
Mossberger, Karen, (2000). *The Politics of Ideas and the Spread of Enterprise Zones*, Georgetown University Press, Washington DC.
Neustadt, Richard E. and May, Ernest R., (1986). *Thinking in Time: the Uses of History for Decision-Makers*, Free Press, New York.
Oakeshott, Michael, (1951). *Political Education*, Bowes and Bowes, Cambridge.
OECD, (2000). *OECD In Figures: Statistics on the Member Countries*, OECD, Paris. Supplement to *OECD Observer*.
Okun, Arthur, (1975). *Equality and Efficiency: The Big Trade Off*, The Brookings Institution, Washington DC.
Pan, Philip P., (2001). 'Collapse of Soviet Union Still Troubling to Chinese', *International Herald-Tribune*, 21 August.
Pei, Minxin, (2001). 'Political Institutions, Democracy and Development', in Farrukh Iqbal and Jong-Il You, eds., *Democracy, Market Economics and Development: An Asian Perspective*, World Bank, Washington DC, 25–48.
Pierson, Paul, (2000). 'Increasing Returns, Path Dependence and the Study of Politics', *American Political Science Review*, 94, 2, 251–268.
Pressman, Jeffrey L. and Wildavsky, Aaron, (1973). *Implementation*, University of California Press, Berkeley.
Rose, Richard, (1984). *Understanding Big Government: the Programme Approach*, Sage Publications, London and Beverly Hills.
Rose, Richard, (1986). 'Common Goals but Different Roles: The State's Contribution to the Welfare Mix', in R. Rose and Rei Shiratori, eds, *The Welfare State East and West*, Oxford University Press, New York, 13–39.
Rose, Richard, (1991). 'Is American Public Policy Exceptional?', in Byron Shafer, ed., *Is America Different?* Oxford University Press, New York 187–229.
Rose, Richard, (1993). *Lesson-Drawing in Public Policy: A Guide to Learning Across Time and Space*, Chatham House, Chatham, NJ.

Rose, Richard, (1995), 'Making Progress or Catching Up', *International Social Science Journal* No. 143, March, 113–126.

Rose, Richard, (1996). 'Evaluating Benefits: the Views of Russian Employees', in Douglas Lippoldt, (ed.), *Social Benefits and the Russian Enterprise: A Time of Transition*, OECD, Paris.

Rose, Richard, (2001a). 'The Internet's Impact on East Asian Governance: Openness, Impersonal Rules and Accountability', *University of Strathclyde Studies in Public Policy No. 354*.

Rose, Richard, (2001b). 'Russians Under Putin: New Russia Barometer 10', Glasgow: University of Strathclyde Studies in Public Policy No. 350.

Rose, Richard and Davies, Phillip, (1994). *Inheritance in Public Policy: Change without Choice in Britain*, Yale University Press, New Haven and London.

Transparency International, (2001). *Global Corruption Report*, Transparency International, Berlin.

Walder, A., (1986). *Communist Neo-Traditionalism*, University of California Press, Berkeley.

Wang, H.Y., (2000). 'Informal Institutions and Foreign Investment in China', *The Pacific Review*, 13, 4, 525–556.

Watson, James L., ed., (1997). *Golden Arches East: McDonalds in East Asia*, Stanford University Press, Stanford.

Weidenbaum, Murray and Hughes, S., (1996). *Bamboo Network*, Martin Kessler/Basic Books, New York.

Westney, Eleanor, (1987). *Innovation and Imitation: The Transfer of Western Organizational Patterns to Meiji Japan*, Harvard University Press, Cambridge, MA.

Wong, Luong, (2001). 'The Internet and Social Change in Asia', *Peace Review*, 13, 3, 381–387.

World Bank, (2001). *World Bank Atlas*, World Bank, Washington DC.

Chapter 3

The Context of Social Policy Reform in China: Theoretical, Comparative and Historical Perspectives

Sheying Chen

Introduction

Western scholars, as well as academics in some westernized Chinese societies (e.g. former colonial Hong Kong), accustomed to think in terms of welfare state social policies, have tended to find that the socialist state of mainland China did not measure up to their expectations. For example, Chan (1993) observed China's official commitment to welfare provision to be relatively small. 'The budget allocation, the priority of service entitlements, the emphasis on family care and self-reliance, all reflect the state's reluctance to provide universal and comprehensive welfare protection for all' (1993: 137). In addition, she noticed that, in the wake of the economic reform, 'ability to pay' had become a new selection criterion for service utilization.

Such observations were strictly accurate. The behaviour of the Chinese state was often reported in the light of its 'reluctance' to invest in welfare provision. And this was not the whole story. The Chinese government was also frequently criticized for its lack of commitment to education, while the constant shortage of housing could be listed as a consequence of the unreasonable philosophy of 'production goes before living (well-being)'; and so on. After two decades of economic reform, social problems would seem to be overshadowing economic progress, thanks to widespread concerns over such new and old issues as inequality, unemployment, and inadequate social spending on services.

This discovery of problems over Chinese social policy could potentially involve all sorts of different perspectives and sentiments. For instance, one brand of popular opinion might stem from a negative attitude towards China's bureaucracy in particular; whereas an academic critique might rest on a holistic explanation of the interest conflicts within this socialist-communist society *per se*. Both such sets of insights are valuable and indeed indispensable for a discerning study. Nevertheless, neither, alone, can furnish a comprehensive analysis of the actual prescriptions of China's government. Indeed, this sort of incomplete or isolated understanding of Chinese social policy, if mingled with emotions as well as various preferences, prejudices and stereotypes, could conceivably be totally destructive.

No government can ignore the constraints and opportunities of its national context (cf. chapter 2, this volume), and this chapter will look into the context of social policy reform in China by offering relevant theoretical, comparative and historical perspectives. It will be argued that an adequate understanding of social policies and problems in any country requires attention to its general public policy (GPP), which cannot be achieved via the analysis of its various sectoral policies alone. Under the 'economic state in transition' framework, employed in apposition to the Western welfare state model (Chen 1996, 1998a, 1998b, 2002a, 2002b, 2002c forthcoming), factors affecting China's social policies are explored. Special attention will be drawn to the historical reasons for the Chinese state's often seeming to fail to address its social issues adequately. Its priorities, and preferred modes of policy making and policy operation, are indicated by reference to China's evolution from extreme politicization in the past to depoliticization and extreme economicization after 1978, and to potential de-economicization in the future.

Models of Policy Analysis and their Use in Chinese Settings

The Chinese adage is that a workman must first sharpen his tools (supposing him to be possessed of the appropriate tools) if he is to do his work well. The following will review some of the analytical tools frequently used in the West by examining their utility for studying public policy in China. Some new approaches will also be explored.

Policy Making as Rational Choice of One Governing Mind

The rational paradigm considers that a policy is rational if the ratio between the values it achieves and the values it sacrifices is positive and higher than any other policy alternative. Rational policy making entails several logical steps. First, goals have to be clearly defined and the levels of achievement to be regarded as satisfactory have to be set. Second, the alternatives for achieving such goals have to be canvassed, involving all the logical, scientific, and technical drawing-board work possible, on the basis of available information. These alternatives are then assessed and compared systematically, with their costs and benefits carefully calculated. Finally, the alternatives that would achieve the goals at the least cost are chosen.

Clearly, this rational perspective faces a number of challenges, it being evident that there are too many limits, in practice, to the achievement of comprehensiveness, unity, and rationality. For instance, it could be that some individual actors in the process are fairly rational but that, when many actors are involved and drift in and out of the process, the kind of rationality that might characterize a unitary decision-making structure becomes elusive.

This approach is important, however, for it sets an aim for an individual, a group, or the society as a whole for exploring barriers to rationality (DiNitto 1991). It also helps to develop methodologies for analysing public policies (Scioli and Cook 1975) and a framework for studying the 'policy paradox' in terms of the art of political decision making (Stone 1997). In sociology, rationalization is recognized as one of the historical processes that constitute the 'Great Social Transformation' (GST) (Curry et al. 1997; Schluchter 1981). The rational model seems to be especially suited for policy study in 'planned' societies, where the drawing-board work in guiding 'economic construction' and 'social engineering' carries special weight. In

China, economic planning has long been essential, and more recently such 'social' affairs as social security and community services have also been heeded (Chen 1988). In still other aspects such as international relations and defence, Chinese policy making has been characterized by a 'calculative strategy' (Swaine and Tellis 2000). Such a rational system of policy making is now considered a major legacy of Deng Xiaoping (Shambaugh 2000).

Nevertheless, in certain historical periods Chinese policy making could hardly be explained according to a rational model. Indeed, economic calculations were actually overlooked or deliberately defied for decades before the era of 'open door' and market reform (Chen 2002b).

The Role of Politics

A political perspective in policy analysis holds that policy development is a result of political disagreement over the nature of the problems confronting society and over what, if anything, should be done about them (DiNitto 1991). Focusing on political actors or players involved in the policy process, the political paradigm stresses those severe limits placed by a political context on rationality: political movements, pressure groups and special interests, civil servants and elected officials. Deep-seated conflicts of interest mean that any action taken is likely to be a compromise, such compromises seldom producing 'perfect solutions' for any troublesome social condition.

China is known for its major intra-national 'fierce fights', referred to as 'a game to win all,' over political power in its ancient and modern history (Womack 1991; Tsou 1995). Certainly, political processes in China have been different from those typical of latter-day Western democracy, involving open or free politics (Pye 1988). Since the founding of the People's Republic, political movements in the form of official 'class struggle' have had unique influence over governmental decisions. Although the manoeuvre for power may have been ubiquitous (Nathan 1973; Tsou 1994), politics has never been recognized as a legitimate field for open, personal career building. During the 'Great Proletarian Cultural Revolution' (1966–1976), any compromise in carrying out the presumed rational policies of the central power was deemed unacceptable, for all that the 'revolutionary' government was split into adverse parts in many localities and politics was – in practice – bursting free at all levels. For the most part, however, while not necessarily nonexistent or inconsequential, lobbyists and pressure groups were invisible in the creation of policies. There were semi-official organizations representing such groups as women and youth (i.e., the Women's Federation and the Communist Youth League), but these were organized as helping hands of the Chinese Communist Party (CCP) rather than as independent interest groups.

So, the typical image of the impact of Chinese politics is that of a form of elite politics (or, traditionally, palace politics), in conjunction with an element of bureaucratic politics (Fewsmith 1999). Western academics have typically divided the Party elite into three categories: the left wing (Maoist followers and associates of the 'Gang of Four'), the centrist or center-left groups – also referred to as the 'conservatives' after 1978 – and the right wing who were also called the 'liberal reformers' (Jackson 1992; White 1993). China watchers have produced numerous accounts of such elite politics, while some 'democrats' may have fallen into this category themselves (e.g. Jing 1999). It seems clear that such researchers could benefit by drawing on a broader context when studying the loci of political forces and defining the use of the political model. This suggested a broader contextual approach to politics would be more of a grassroots perspective than an elite one; such as could balance the traditional approach with an appreciation of the views and interests of common people (as opposed to those of elite politicians and scholars) in the particular sociopolitical settings of China. With older, revolutionary strongmen quitting the scene and a civil society or political pluralism conceivably in the ascendance, such a perspective could carry more and more weight for policy analysis in this context.

The Impact of Organizational Structure

In a sense, the political paradigm is also based on rationality, since it does not rule out logical reasoning for individuals and groups but rather emphasizes the calculative or speculative nature of their activities. However, the policy process may contain things that are truly irrational and/or impersonal, and organizational theorists foresee the potential impact of an organizational structure on policy formulation and implementation. It is possible that an organization may adhere to its own sets of rules and procedures, in preference to pursuing any (latest) rationally defined purpose; and that it may, in so doing, override the preferences of powerful political players. The policy-making machine is often a complex bureaucracy, and such organizational issues as funding, manpower/staffing, communication and leadership may significantly influence policy formulation and implementation.

The organizational paradigm demands knowledge and understanding of the structure and culture (e.g. rules and procedures) of the policy-making body in addition to information about the thoughts and behaviours of individual policy makers. The study of policy making in communist countries (China in particular) requires special attention to the impact of the party state structure (Teiwes 2000; Walder 1995). On the one hand, the CCP is renowned for its organizational prowess, which helped greatly to achieve its political objectives before and after the founding of the People's Republic. On the other, even the presumption of dictatorship would not rule out organizational restrictions on the dictator's seeming free will over policy making. Indeed, such restrictions could be so serious that even the private lives of very important members of the CCP, such as Mao's marriage and divorce, could be heavily affected.

Human Sources of Irrationality

The central argument of the organizational paradigm against the rational model is based on the impersonal or inhuman aspects of an organization, particularly of a highly differentiated modern bureaucracy. By further scrutinizing the role of irrationality in influencing policy making, more sources of complication can be identified; including insufficient information, inadequate knowledge, and/or inappropriate understanding. On the one hand, these psychological factors reflect the cognitive capacity and limitation of human individuals, groups, and societies, as well as policy making as a learning process (which naturally involves mistakes). On the other hand, the fluctuation of individual emotions as well as national sentiments may also divert policy making from rationality.

I have formulated an 'irrational model' of policy making based on my own and other authors' observations (e.g. Lindblom 1968). The hypothesized irrational paradigm considers that public policy is sometimes irrational in the sense that it may proceed largely or completely without rationality. Yet, unlike the organizational model, this approach emphasizes people, or the human side, rather than impersonal organizational structures and bureaucratic rules. Nor does it presume that people, including individual politicians, are always rational, calculative, or speculative, which is often the source of interest conflicts under the political model (now called 'rational choice theory'). The irrational model focuses on the role of ignorance, stereotypes, misunderstanding, and emotions of individuals, groups, and society as a whole. Such factors may divert a rational policy making process and also render political conflicts nonsense, since they may bear no relation to the actors' real interests. In the historical analysis of Chinese policy, the irrational model renders additional insights into a complicated process called politicization of the economic state (Chen 2002b, forthcoming). The irrational model highlights the inherent human limits at both individual and organizational levels. From this point of view, humans make mistakes, as do states (Cipolla 1980). Indeed, the Chinese party state has made (and admitted, if reluctantly) many major mistakes that went against its own interests (CCCCP 1981), of which the most fundamental, if implicit, one was straying from its main mandate as an 'economic state' (Chen 2002b, forthcoming). The progress of human society in (Weber's) terms of rationalization will not be completely illuminated without analysing the potential changes in the irrational aspects of public policy. Likewise, the improvement in the cognitive capacity of human society, including greater access to information and use of other technologies, will alter the whole scene of policy making. The information superhighway is, indeed, rapidly reducing ignorance and misunderstanding between and among human communities (despite the fact that some new problems are being created, such as information overload for individual players and security concerns for organizations and states). This may not eliminate political conflicts or emotional reactions but will profoundly help to rationalize Chinese policy making by supplying a better information base as well as more educational channels (Rose 2001).

The Structure of the Policy-Society System

On the whole, models like the above may do well to illuminate a policy-making system. However, as Lindblom (1968) indicates, policy is moulded by a variety of forces beyond those within the policy-making system itself. Policy analysis using these models may not always do justice to all the forces, causes and effects of the policy change process. A broader view is needed to integrate the policy-making system with the society within which it operates (Miller 2000).

In this regard, Morris's (1985) scheme for policy analysis supplies a more comprehensive framework for understanding policy making in the societal context. By taking social policies as guiding principles for public actions, Morris discerns several elements that affect their evolution and implementation. These include: (a) society's aspirations or goals; (b) societal policy (i.e. social norms); (c) general public policy (i.e. a guide to the priority aims and preferred means); (d) sectoral public policy (e.g. income security, housing, health, personal social services, the family domain, and the aged); (e) the leadership role of governmental units in moving beyond or in modifying social norms; (f) advocated vs. adopted policy; and (g) criteria for assessing policy guidelines (e.g. charity vs. rights or middle-class viewpoints, and distributive-regulative vs. redistributive).

Public policy as a subfield of political science and China as an area of international relations/politics have naturally made political perspectives the dominating paradigm on the subject. Under Morris's framework, however, it seems that the political model is but one of the essential perspectives needed for a discerning policy study. If political accounts were used as the sole basis for investigation, any effort in public policy making would only be interpreted as manipulation of interests and reallocation of political power. A society's goals and aspirations, its social norms or 'societal policy', and its general public policy in terms of a guide to priority aims and preferred means, would all be lost. The last, which I have referred to and elaborated further as the GPP (Chen 2002b), could be particularly useful in comparative and historical studies since, from a sociological point of view, such inquiries could be of fundamental significance in specifying structural functional patterns of the state.

Welfare State vs. Economic State: A Comparative Approach

A country's GPP is the result of an often complex and complicated interplay between various elements of its policy society system. And the priority aims and preferred means for the multi-level and multi-faceted system may be viewed in many different ways. Although this field has only recently been opened up for inquiry, there exist some long-standing, dominant stereotypes relating to different nations' public policies. In respect of Eastern socialist-communist states and Western industrialized nations, 'state socialism' and 'welfare state' are two of the most popular labels used by Western academics to symbolize what they see as two major worlds. Although not without challenge, such notions have survived as the dominant models for decades. The beginnings of systematic inquiry into GPP, however, have revealed serious theoretical flaws and practical drawbacks, with regard to these two conventional paradigms in their application to the socialist-communist states in general and to China in particular (Chen 1996, 1998a, 1998b, 2002a, forthcoming).

Socialist States and State Socialism

My previous research has scrutinized the roots of the notion of state socialism and its relations with socialism and anarchism and examined socialist-communist states as a Cold War and post-Cold War subject. My view is that in the greatly changed world environment, the notion of state socialism keeps with it a historical anti-state undertone and appears to be more and more handicapped in representing the experiences of the reforming socialist states (Chen 1996, 1998a, 1998b, 2002a). In sum, this notion, with its close ties to anarchist attacks on the state (Bakunin 1968, 1990), has its historical/political limits (it might be more destructive than constructive) and theoretical drawbacks (it confuses Marxism with state socialism). Therefore, it can hardly provide us with the necessary analytical power. In social policy study especially, welfare professionals have usually stressed state responsibility for service provision in both capitalist and socialist societies. If the state is simply to be dismissed, how come welfare states, and where should we look for state responsibility in socialist countries? It seems rather inadequate to use anarchism as the basis for dealing with socialist states (cf. capitalist states, for all that socialism emerged historically as a result of widespread frustration with capitalism), even if politically it has helped to keep a balance from the alleged excessive statism. In real terms, anarchism, albeit attractive, has practised and succeeded in no (major) part of the modern world. Naturally, the notion of state socialism, with a heavy anti-state undertone and historical contribution to the Cold War, is becoming obsolete, if not already an anachronism. A more relevant and constructive framework is required to meet the purposes of present-day research favouring international development and a win win strategy. In other words, the GPP of socialist states in general and China in particular needs to be represented and characterized more appropriately to guide research and lesson drawing.

Western Countries and the Welfare State

The idea of the welfare state, on the other side, seems also to be experiencing some rise and fall in its life course. 'In the 1950s and 1960s [British] political and academic commentators seemed to assume that the welfare state was a uniquely British institution' (Johnson 1987: 3). By the 1980s, as Johnson observes, 'In spite of variations in scope, scale, aims and organisational arrangements, Wedderburn's view that "the welfare state is a common phenomenon of all capitalist societies" is now generally accepted' (1987: 4). The universal acceptance, however, was not only conditioned by variations in actual welfare state structures and performance, but also accompanied by worries about the welfare state 'in crisis'. As Esping-Andersen (1987: 3) narrates, 'Initially, the key issue was how to explain the phenomenal growth of welfare policies; the emphasis subsequently shifted to the welfare state's crisis.' This has made the centrality of the welfare state idea in capitalist Western countries less obvious than before. In real terms, the conservative forces opposing the development of welfare-oriented collective arrangements had been extremely strong in Europe before the Second World War. If they lost much of their strength after the war, they received new worldwide impetus through the victories of Thatcher and Reagan for the 1980s. It is apparent that the welfare state is now in trouble, in characterizing the GPP of capitalist Western countries without an effective solution to their current problems and any clear suggestion as to their future direction.

Notwithstanding this awkward situation, the study of social policy remains equated, in Western terms, with the study of the welfare state (including its variations and deviants) (cf. C. Jones Finer 1999 and chapter 1 in this volume). Even for the current and former socialist-communist countries, such a label as 'socialist welfare states' would be adopted for the study of their social policies. The inclusion of other nations could be justified with a belief in industrialism or technological determinism. Particularly, sociological convergence theory derived from functionalism has informed the study of social welfare development, though challenged by a conflict perspective emphasizing the role of class structure and ideology. According to Esping-Andersen (1987), the many contending modes of analysing the welfare state typically share a linear or stage-based conception of its development. These theories clearly assert cross-national convergence over time: '...as nations industrialize, democratize, or modernize, welfare states will emerge and become essentially similar in their scope and commitments' (1987: 3–4). Yet, functionalism applied this way has its limitations. The convergence theory may show some possibilities for socialist states to approximate to certain aspects of social welfare in capitalist societies. But the theory does not tell us what the realities are in contemporary socialist states. It may also lead to ignorance of the differences that cannot be wiped out during the convergence. As Esping-Andersen points out, 'General linear ideas of welfare state development give us the impression that growth and stagnation follow some inexorable common logic. But they clearly do not' (1987: 4).

The question of relevance in conceptualizing the experiences of different nations is far from settled. On one hand, although the welfare state did represent a great historical advance, as opposed to the GPP of the warfare states commonly seen in the world wars, it must now look for a way out/forward in the face of mounting demands to 'end welfare as we know it' as echoed tirelessly by US presidential candidates in recent elections. On the other hand, while the socialist-communist states seem no longer to care about communist principles as much as they did before, there are still huge differences with Western states in socioeconomic realities, and thus in their GPPs. The point is that we need to treat the welfare state as representing a particular GPP pattern rather than a universal and eternal phenomenon, by making an effort to identify other important patterns that may have also existed. Such an effort, if successful, could make for real two-way lesson drawing and bring to fruition EastWest lesson learning in public/social policy.

China as a Socialist Economic State

In a sense, any nation state is at once a welfare state (the socialist is a special kind for sure), an economic state, a political state, a military (warfare) state, and so on (e.g. Szelenyi and Manchin 1987). However, the conception of the welfare state as a definitive feature signals its priority aim and primary responsibility as a function of government. This conception has to do with the relative importance of various functions of the state. It does not mean that the state does not care about the country's economy, politics, defence, and other kinds of public affairs. But it does indicate an outstanding position for welfare provision by historical or cross-national comparison. For Western developed countries, such a feature of their GPPs is readily demonstrable by their welfare expenditures and the importance of social administration in government activities, although there are certain resistance and failure cases.

For the socialist-communist states and some other developing countries, however, it seems neither ratios of social spending nor the foci of the attention of governments would prove such an idea to be very relevant to their practice. Focusing on the period 1978–1984, when China was considered finally back on track before overall reform, my previous work has suggested that the country's GPP could be characterized as a socialist 'economic state' (Chen 1996, 1998a, 1998b). An economic state can be defined as a state in which the economy is promoted largely by the organized efforts of the government rather than by private institutions. In other words, it is the state that assumes primary responsibility for the development of the economy. The label of an economic state indicates that economic administration carries a big weight in state affairs. Like the welfare state, this characteristic has to do with the relative importance of various functions of the government. It does not mean that the state does not care about the country's welfare, politics, defence, and other kinds of public affairs. But it does indicate an outstanding preference for economic administration, by historical or cross-national comparison. Here, compared with our familiar welfare state, the economy has switched position with welfare in the state hierarchy of priorities, representing a rather distinctive pattern of GPP.

Theoretical grounds for this were provided in terms of the guiding principles of Marxism, the theoretical foundation of the People's Republic of China (PRC) (Chen 2002a). Legal and political provisions for the Chinese GPP were reviewed by analysing the 1982 Constitution and the official doctrine codified in the texts and reference books used in the Party's cadres schools as well as other leadership training institutions. Organizational and financial configurations of the economic state were shown by its major functional departments and spending figures. Stated and implied objectives as well as neglected options and the inactivity of the government were also examined to corroborate the finding with regard to the priority aims and preferred means of the Chinese public policy system (Chen 2002a).

Economic State in Transition: A Historical Perspective

The above modelling effort focuses on the situation of the Chinese state during a particular historical period. The central thesis is that the Chinese state was over this period characterized chiefly by its role in economic administration rather than by its welfare function. In other words, the innate character of the Chinese government was to head an 'economic state' rather than a 'welfare state' (of course, not a 'political state' either). The credibility of this position, however, was not self-evident, particularly in view of the unique type of welfare protection which had been long assured some of its citizens (particularly state employees), the still dominant position of the Communist Party (as denoted by the label of a 'party-state'), the legacy of political campaigns waged by the government in the past, and its recently carefully 'balanced' schemes for socioeconomic development.

Here a historical view is crucial for putting all this in perspective. The typical economic state is not a constant and permanent phenomenon. We should not only understand 'what economic state' but also 'why it is'. The 'economicization' or 'over-economicization' of the Chinese state since 1978 should be understood in a sense of 'straightening the crooked beyond the straight' in view of this state's extreme politicization in the past. Reform and 'open door' now seem to be changing it to a more balanced, mixed format, via a process of 'de-economicization' (Chen 2002b). To be sure, the Chinese state is still an economic state rather than a welfare state, even though its organizational structure and economic base (i.e. public ownership system) have undergone dramatic change. Theoretically, Marxist political economy still plays an important part in emphasizing the role of productive force and economic base in determining the superstructure of society. In real life, the Chinese have dreamt, from generation to generation, of being part of an economically strong nation. It is from their painful modern history that the Chinese have learned that they must first make themselves economically prosperous, to stand on their own feet among the nations of the world. Such a determination to use all talents and means to ensure collective success is probably what has made the most fundamental difference when we talk about Chinese achievements compared with other transitional societies in recent years. To develop their economy, the Chinese would leave no stone unturned, including encouraging everyone to 'jump into the sea' (go into business), even at the risk of a rapidly polarizing social reality (Wong and MacPherson 1995).

To fully understand the history and the future direction of the Chinese economic state, therefore, we need to review the rise of the Chinese economic state since the mid-twentieth century. Specifically, we need to understand how the Chinese communist state progressed from a military power to a political state. Next, the far-reaching effects of the Cultural Revolution amid positive changes in the outside world must not be ignored. In this case we need to appreciate how the economic state identity was defined but once lost, and how a misconception of the political roles (e.g., alleged class struggle) as the central function of the state had put the nation on the brink of bankruptcy. The significance of the final transformation from political state to economic state should then be highlighted, matching – in its way – the great postwar progress from warfare states to welfare states in the West.

The tension that has remained between the Chinese state's economic and political functions should still be noted. It should be emphasized that the 'classic' economic state model had rarely been realized anywhere before 1978. Soon after such an identity was recognized, the economic state in China entered a process of rapid change. Indeed, the short period between 1978 and the mid-1980s is worth studying, simply because the economic state had never been so fully appreciated before, even as it was soon to change again, after the CCP's strategic decision to reform the state-owned sector of the economy from 1984. The latter gave rise to a potential trend of 'de-economicization' of the Chinese state by means of economic reform (Chen 2002b), however. A major measure of Chinese economic reform has been decentralization of decision making, serving as a springboard for other associated reforms (Jackson 1992). This decentralization meant the expansion of management autonomy involving basic enterprise organizations (work units) rather than just local authorities. This restructuring reflected the state's resolution to move the country toward 'market socialism' rather than merely a partial reform within the old planned economic system. The systemic changes have affected labour, wages, and even the ownership of the means of production. The change of the socialist infrastructure has been altering the base of the economic state. The consequence of decentralization is that the economic state's administrative control and intervention, at either the central or the local level, has become less and less needed and more and more counterproductive, given the expanding autonomy of the enterprises and diversified property rights structure. A most conspicuous measure passed by the Ninth People's Congress in 1998 was the reorganization of the central government, eliminating a number of economic departments while enhancing the part of social administration including social security and the legal system (SINOVISION News, 10 March 1998). Although social provision still appears problematic in this rapid transition, the economic state is being pushed into a position comparable with that of the welfare state, as regards dealing with the latest challenges. In this regard, the relationship between social and economic developments may best be illustrated and understood by comparing the experiences of the welfare and economic states.

In sum, China's socioeconomic crisis before 1978 and its success over the past two decades can be viewed as a zigzag process of politicization and depoliticization of the 'economic state'. By summarizing the Chinese experience, a lesson on the importance of a GPP pattern in determining the nature of a policy system can be drawn. Without such a historical view, we could not understand China's past problems and current issues, including its lagging behind in political reform. Without understanding the economicization of Chinese GPP in a desperate hope to make up past losses, one could hardly explain why the country would start reform by accepting unemployment and encouraging inequality (Chen 1990). It should be noticed that the changes brought about by the reform are undermining the economic state by creating a trend of 'de-economicization' in the Chinese government. If economic reform and social change are to continue smoothly, another 'transfer' of the country's GPP to a more balanced form of development will be required.

The Relevance of this Work for Ongoing Research and Lesson Drawing

The GPP is a set of master guidelines reflecting general strategies (e.g. overall agendas, emphases and foci, key links and leading approaches) in state policy. It is not necessarily about 'development strategy' since development (more or less strictly defined) cannot be taken for granted as a priority and preference of all states for all historical periods. The study of GPP is particularly valuable for this distinction and, without imposing a narrow (albeit positive) developmental thinking, it is especially sensitive in monitoring a state's potential deviation or isolation from development, and helpful to finding out the factors responsible for it. For instance, without a resolute 'transfer' of state emphasis from the political oppression of 'class enemies' to economic construction, the open and reform policy in China, aimed at development, would be impossible (Chen 2002b). Overseas experts (be their expertise economic, social, and/or political) invited to such a newly opened country as China would soon become very critical about things happening there. However, it is critically important that they appreciate the country's return to development (by giving up some of the ideological concern over capitalism vs. socialism, or whatever), otherwise they would not even be there in the first place. Their technical advice would hardly be relevant and useful without considering China's lost and found, culminating and waning identity, as an economic state. Indeed, as for some other nations in the world, talks on lesson drawing may still be premature and, due to the existence of non-developmental GPPs, developmentalists' dichotomization of the world in terms of 'developing' and 'developed' countries may have been premature. How should selective emphases on political, religious, social, and economic ends and means be constructed to characterize a nation's public policy? And how might such a characterization impact on sectoral policies in respect of poverty, inequality, labour market, housing, health care, pensions, social services, workers' rights, women's issues and so on?

Here the building of a pertinent GPP model could be the key. Since the starting point for lesson drawing in public/social policy is the existence of cross-national differences (cf. chapter 2, this volume), the identification of different GPP patterns in diverse economic, political, social, and cultural contexts has fundamental significance. After all, 'where there is a will, there is a way'. Conversely, if there is no or little will in a state's GPP, then there is not much hope for a nation's lesson learning and advancement.

The economic state model may be helpful for conceptualizing the experiences of many nations other than the welfare states. The Chinese experience may also offer the welfare states some useful lessons. It is understandable that 'developed' nations might be reluctant to learn from 'developing' ones. Yet the development picture has been constantly changing throughout world history; so the 'advanced' nations should not wait until it's too late or until they themselves are outpaced. Indeed, given the mounting troubles of western welfare states, lesson drawing would seem to be not only for China. US experience alone has shown that continued escalation of inequality under the name of equity or inequity need not be accompanied by continued improvement of national economic performance. By this kind of EastWest comparison and lesson drawing, a number of significant lessons can be learned and a more comprehensive view of worldwide development gained (Chen 1999).

China's lesson drawing has been characterized by learning from its own experience in terms of both mistakes and successes. Yet this has also been based on conscious and large-scale learning from abroad, certainly since the foundation of the People's Republic; firstly from the former communist camp (particularly the former Soviet Union) and latterly from the West, with the results being a central command system dedicated to decentralization and then marketization. Given the theme of this volume, most chapters on sectoral policies will focus on current social policy reform in 'socialist market China'. By carefully examining the extent to which, and the ways in which, the PRC has taken, has not taken, and/or may yet take, 'lessons from abroad' in key social policy respects, lesson drawing may become more effective than ever. Without such serious research effort, China may miss out on precious opportunities for learning, or lose out as a result of superficial or bad lessons from home and abroad at any point in time.

For sure, the Chinese used completely to reject the welfare state from a revolutionary communist point of view. For sure, also, some scholars are now apeing the anti-welfare state views of American conservatives/European liberals and completely agreeing with them to 'end welfare as we know it' (although China has not got to the state of welfare as yet) (Liu 2000). In this regard, the quality and 'usefulness' of some of the lessons so far taken, not taken, or still being contemplated must also be assessed with the utmost rigour.

References

Bakunin, Michael (1968), *A Criticism of State Socialism*, Copic Press, London (on behalf of Cuddon's Cosmopolitan Review).
Bakunin, Michael (1990), [1873] *Statism and Anarchy* (trans and ed. Shatz, Marshall S.), Cambridge University Press, Cambridge.

Chan, Cecilia L. W. (1993), *The Myth of Neighbourhood Mutual Help: The Contemporary Chinese Community-based Welfare System in Guangzhou,* Hong Kong University Press, Hong Kong.
Chen, Sheying (1988), 'Community service: a public lecture', *China Civil Affairs Administration,* 1–4, 6 (in Chinese).
Chen, Sheying (1990), 'How to develop social security while developing Guangdong's economy'. *Journal of Zhongshan (Sun Yatsen) University (Social Sciences),* vol. 1 (in Chinese).
Chen, Sheying (1996), *Social Policy of the Economic State and Community Care in Chinese Culture: Aging, Family, Urban Change, and the Socialist Welfare Pluralism,* Ashgate, Brookfield, VT.
Chen, Sheying (1998a), 'Welfare state, economic state, and balanced development', in *Proceedings of 24th Third World Conference,* Third World Conference Foundation, Chicago.
Chen, Sheying (1998b), 'Welfare and culture: conceptualizing social policy of the "economic state".' Paper presented at the *ISA XIV World Congress of Sociology,* 26 July–1 August, Montreal.
Chen, Sheying (1999), 'Beyond welfare state: a cross-national comparative approach to social policy research and teaching', in *NYSSWEA Proceedings,* New York State Social Work Education Association.
Chen, Sheying (forthcoming), *Understanding Chinese Social Policy: Theoretical, Comparative, Historical Perspectives* (unpublished manuscript).
Chen, Sheying (2002a), 'State socialism and the welfare state: a critique of two conventional paradigms', *International Journal of Social Welfare,* 11: 228–214.
Chen, S. (2002b), 'Economic reform and social change in China: past, present, and future of the economic state'. *International Journal of Politics, Culture, and Society,* 15, 4: 569–89.
Chen, Sheying (2002c), 'Social problems of the economic state: historical roots and future directions', *China Report,* 2, 38.
Central Committee of Chinese Communist Party (CCCCP) (1981). 'Resolution on the Party's certain historical problems since the founding of the state'. Cited in Xie, Chuntao (ed.) (1999), *Fifty Years of the Republic: A History with Photographs,* Henan People's Press, Zhengzhou (in Chinese).
Cipolla, Carlo (1980), *The Basic Laws of Human Stupidity,* The Mad Millers, Bologna.
Curry, T., Jiobu, R., and Schwirian, K. (1997). *Sociology for the Twenty-first Century,* Prentice Hall, Upper Saddle River, NJ.
DiNitto, Diane M. (1991), *Social Welfare: Politics and Public Policy,* 3rd edn, Prentice-Hall, Englewood Cliffs, NJ.
Esping-Andersen, G. (1987), 'The comparison of policy regimes: an introduction', in Rein, M. Esping-Andersen, G. and Rainwater, L. (eds.) *Stagnation and Renewal in Social Policy: The Rise and Fall of Policy Regimes,* M.E. Sharpe, Armonk, NY.
Fewsmith, Joseph (1999), 'Elite politics', in Goldman, Merle and MacFarquhar, Roderick (eds), *The Paradox of China's Post-Mao Reforms,* Harvard University Press, Cambridge, MA.
Jackson, Sukhan (1992), *Chinese Enterprise Management Reforms in Economic Perspective,* Walter de Gruyter, Berlin and New York.
Jing, Cao (1999), 'On reversing judgement about June Fourth', *World Journal,* 6 June, A5 (in Chinese).
Johnson, N. (1987), *The Welfare State in Transition: The Theory and Practice of Welfare Pluralism.* Wheatsheaf Books, Sussex.
Jones Finer, C. (1999) 'Trends and Developments in Welfare States', in Clasen, J. (ed.) *Comparative Social Policy,* Blackwell, Oxford: 15–33.
Lindblom, Charles E. (1968), *The Policy-making Process,* Prentice-Hall, Englewood Cliffs, NJ.

Liu, Junning (2000), 'Liberalism and justice: reply to questions', *Modern China Studies*, 4: 50–67 (in Chinese).

Miller, H. Lyman (2000), 'The late imperial Chinese state', in Shambaugh, David (ed.), *The Modern Chinese State*, Cambridge University Press, Cambridge.

Morris, Robert (1985), *Social policy of the American Welfare State: An Introduction to Policy Analysis*, 2nd edn, Longman, New York.

Nathan, Andrew J. (1973), 'A factionalism model for CCP politics', *China Quarterly*, 54: 34–66.

Perlmutter, Felice D. (1997). *From Welfare to Work: Corporate Initiatives and Welfare Reform*, Oxford University Press, New York.

Pye, Lucian W. (1988), *The Mandarin and the Cadre: China's Political Cultures*, Center for Chinese Studies, Ann Arbor, University of Michigan.

Rose, Richard (2001), 'Openness, impersonal rules and continuing accountability: the internet's prospective impact on East Asian governance', paper prepared for a World Bank seminar at the Asian Institute of Harvard University, 1–2 October. *Studies in Public Policy* Number 354, University of Strathclyde.

Schluchter, W. (1981), *The Rise of Western Rationalism: Max Weber's Developmental History*, University of California Press, Berkeley, CA.

Scioli, Frank P., Jr. and Cook, Thomas J. (1975), *Methodologies for Analyzing Public Policies*, Lexington Books, Lexington, MA.

Shambaugh, David (ed.) (2000), *The Modern Chinese State*, Cambridge University Press, Cambridge.

Stone, Deborah (1997), *Policy Paradox: The Art of Political Decision Making*, W.W. Norton New York.

Swaine, Michael D. and Tellis, Ashley J. (2000), *Interpreting China's Grand Strategy: Past, Present, and Future*. RAND, Santa Monica, CA.

Szelenyi, Ivan and Manchin, Robert (1987), 'Social policy under state socialism: market redistribution and social inequalities in East European socialist societies', in Rein, M., Esping-Andersen, G. and Rainwater, L. (eds), *Stagnation and Renewal in Social Policy: The Rise and Fall of Policy Regimes*, M.E. Sharpe, Armonk, NY.

Teiwes, Frederick C. (2000), 'The Chinese state during the Maoist era', in Shambaugh, David (ed.), *The Modern Chinese State*, Cambridge University Press, Cambridge.

Tsou, Tang (1994), *Chinese Politics in the Twentieth Century: Viewed from the Perspectives of Macro-History and Micro-Actions*, Oxford University Press, Hong Kong (in Chinese).

Tsou, Tang (1995), 'Chinese politics at the top: factionalism or informal politics? Balance-of-power politics or a game to win all?' *China Journal*, 34 (July): 95–156.

Walder, Andrew G. (1995), 'Local governments as industrial firms: An organizational analysis of China's transitional economy', *American Journal of Sociology*, 101, 2: 263–301.

White, Gordon (1993), *Riding the Tiger: The Politics of Economic Reform in Post-Mao China*, Stanford University Press, Stanford.

Womack, Brantly (ed.), (1991), *Contemporary Chinese Politics in Historical Perspective*, Cambridge University Press, Cambridge.

Wong, L. and MacPherson, S. (eds), (1995), *Social Change and Social Policy in Contemporary China*, Avebury, Aldershot.

Chapter 4

The Policy Process in Contemporary China: Mechanisms of Politics and Government

Bo Peng

The Context of the Chinese Policy Process

The Monopolistic Role of the State Party and its Power Elite

One of the most important aspects of the Chinese authoritarian regime is the overwhelmingly leading role played by the 'party-state' in the whole policy process. Instead of being at the centre of public debate, policy issues are mostly considered and discussed among party and government organizations, especially amongst a few powerful elites. Furthermore, thanks to the absence of the popular representation characteristic of Western democracy, the Chinese party-state holds a relatively autonomous position in the policy process. The monopolistic role of this party-state and its elite in forming the policy agenda renders the policy process distinctly different from and less transparent than its counterpart in western democracies.

By comparison with the time- and energy-consuming policy debates characteristic of mass media and representative institutions in democratic countries, China's state-led policy process can be time-saving and sometimes more effective. However, because of the monopolistic role of the party-state and the lack of any popular checking mechanism, the process is also more vulnerable to making dreadful mistakes, which can render the policy process awfully inefficient (Hu Wei 1998). It was after some such notorious mistakes in policy making that the issue of Scientific Policy Making became part of the discussion and debate amongst academics and high-ranking officials. Nevertheless, there have been structural obstacles to the pursuit of the scientific policy process, precisely because the monopolistic role of the power elite and the absence of popular involvement are still key problems affecting the Chinese policy process even after 20 years of reform.[1]

In the whole policy process, the CCP (Chinese Communist Party) and government organization has the entire responsibility for policy initiation, formation and enforcement. Hence, the correctness of the policy process depends largely on the efficiency and ability of the power elite and governmental staff. Since the Chinese government is still far from being highly modernized and institutionalized, correct decision making, effective enforcement and scientific assessment in policy agenda remain future targets for administrative reform (Liu 2001). Although there was a shift from political to administrative reform in the 1990s – administrative reform being politically safer than actual reform of the party-state – even administrative reform has been difficult to achieve, in the absence of any macro political transformation.

To repeat, because of the lack of formal institutional channels for the realistic consideration of people's desires, it has been difficult for the government to consolidate its legitimacy via the conduct of effective public and social policy making. In this sort of political system, Chinese politics and society remain separated in a system which has no formal channels and institutions to present people's opinions and requirements. To be sure, the state has a set of methods for successfully highlighting public concerns and encouraging the correct understanding of existing policies. For instance, Chinese news media are still of an admonitory nature in which some information becomes top 'news' not because it is new or of interest to the people, but because it is politically important. By doing this, it is not too difficult for Chinese government to have an impact on public opinion on the policy agenda according to its wish. Another frequently used method is the widespread Study Activities which were very popular and important before reform and also last even nowadays. By institutionalizing the study activity in work units and residential organizations, the Chinese government expresses and explains policy ideas, in order to improves 'correct' understanding on important policies. Nevertheless, this highly autonomous state treats the policy process as a black box closed to outsiders, thus making the process quite difficult to supervise and evaluate. Since the mass of the people lack effective institutional means for expressing their desires, some social problems merely accumulate, leading to popular dissatisfaction and demonstrations[2] and 'illegal' social organizations,[3] both of which are regarded as most dangerous enemies of social stability and state security. Thus it is that some serious social events, such as demonstrations, can become policy initiators – reminding policy makers of the importance of an issue. Even so, the response tends to be more one of fire-fighting than of a long-term strategy for addressing social and economic problems.

Ideological Transformation, the Developmental State and the Policy Process

The reform emerging from the end of the 1970s was aimed at the transformation of the whole economic and political system. To make this reform seem reasonable and to get support from both the political elite and the masses, it commenced with ideological innovations from the very beginning, shifting the major issue of politics from class struggle to economic reconstruction. Since the new political ideology was infused with the efforts of reformers, the foundation of legitimacy of both the Chinese Communist Party (CCP) and Chinese socialism became that of improving the living standards of the people and building a stronger nation state. Anyway, this is not to say that the party-state abandoned its basic, ultimate goal of realizing a communist utopia. Recently, indeed, Chinese President Jiang Zemin delivered an important speech on the 80th anniversary of the CCP, which was symbolized as 'three representatives', which are advanced productivity, advanced culture and the primary interests of people. In it, he demonstrated that the most important goal of party and government was to protect the interests of the largest majority of the people (Jiang Zemin 2001).

Such changes in the foundations of political ideology and legitimacy have affected Chinese politics, including the policy process as a core political issue. Since the legitimacy now stems from concrete economic achievements, rather than from ideological articulation or 'invisible communism' which was the major legitimate resource of the revolutionary regime before reform at the end of the 1970s, the policy process has had to focus on existing domestic and international issues, and policy evaluation is largely dependent on the actual performance of government policy, rather than on its ideological implication. Therefore, in the policy agenda, the rational nature of the policy process has become more prominent than it ever was before reform, and therefore the rational model has become a major research approach for experts studying policy making in China (Lieberthal and Lampton 1992).

Although the *three representatives* emphasizes the interests of the majority of Chinese people, the absence of popular representation means that the policy process is expected to satisfy people, not via beneficiary policies for specific social groups so much as by developing the national economy as a whole, so as generally to improve people's living conditions. It is this developmental nature of the party-state which now dominates the whole policy process. Economic development has become the major index for assessing cadres' performance, with different governmental departments and different levels of government all concentrating on the development goal (Oi 1989; Walder 1998; Shirk 1993).

In short, this shift in mainstream ideology has resulted in the dominance of developmental concerns throughout the governance of China. This has been crucial both for socioeconomic development and for the stimulation of governmental organizations and officials. Nevertheless, in a country without popular representation and accountability, questions of how to link development to people's welfare, and how to protect the interests of weak groups in such a rapidly changing society, continue unresolved.

Governmental Reform and its Impacts on the Policy Process

In the mid-1980s, China's top leader, Deng Xiaoping, introduced reform of the political agenda. As we can observe today, although political reform has not been as successful as economic reform – both political reform and prospects for democratization being hampered by the events of 4 June 1989 – the party-state has never abandoned the slogan of political reform. Moreover, since the introduction of a market economy, and the corresponding social transformation, political and government reform has not only been facilitated by the party-state, but actually required by such a changing society. So, although political and administrative reforms have been kept out of the centre of the party-state's reform strategy since 1989, many concrete changes and measures of reform performance have nonetheless quietly appeared in China.

In the 1980s, one of the major designs for political reform had been the separation of party and government administration. But China stopped this radical reform process after it was convinced that the ruling party might be shaken and weakened once it was to be completely separated from government, which shows that the role of the party-state is still vitally important in Chinese politics even after more than 20 years of reform. Thus efforts were made again to let party leaders at local levels and in work units (*danwei*) be the number one leaders in both party and administrative affairs, and the separation of party and government disappeared from the reform slogans. Although policy makers have tried to integrate the party leadership with professional concerns, the party-state has found this effort to be facing difficulties, because new social demands have put Mao's policy model in a difficult position, wherein the non-professional party cadres hold policy power and are concerned much more about revolutionary purpose than pragmatic economic and social consequence. Even nowadays, while it has been emphasized that the role of the party leadership should be insisted on, the roles of party organizations and 'non-professional' leaders in ideological style have been dealt with less than objectively, in the struggle to maintain cooperation with professional leaders.

Therefore, in matters of political and administrative reform, it is the government organization, by nature more professional, which has been in charge of the most of the policy process. The party gives more space to government in most parts of the process, and the role of party has merely been to supervise this process and, when necessary, to help government in its enforcement – depending on such special policy instruments as propaganda and mass mobilization (Hu Wei 1998).

Since the party-state shows such keen concern over the results of government policy, the relevance of the rational model of policy process becomes ever clearer. Since one of the major tasks of administrative reform was to achieve scientific policy making, which requires regularization and professionalization in the process, many government officials with professional skills have been drawn into the policy process, which was thus conceptualized as technocracy (Liu 2001). Equally, some other sectors such as the research institutions, both in and out of the government system, have become involved in the policy process, especially in policy initiation and assessment. Even so, the new policy process depends more on the investigation and research of *non*-policy makers, especially those staff in charge of policy affairs research within government.

Because of the secular trend in Chinese politics, as a result of reform and the weakening of communist ideology, the interests of different levels and departments of government have become more and more distinct, not to say policy-distinctive. Interest-based considerations and conflicts amongst government organizations can sometimes damage the policy process, even in respect of policies being advocated by top leaders (Huang 1999). Because the changing governmental and official behaviours caused by divided interests have come to threaten the solid party state, it was in this context that central government launched several campaigns, such as *Strengthening Central Authority*, designed to fight against localism, especially at the provincial level and, and to stress politics via the *Three Stresses Campaign*, to bring politics back into the era of the 'economy takes command'. But although the party-state has tried to solve the problem in terms of a policy agenda, this problematic situation looks set to last for some time; in short, until the transformation of this Leninist regime (Winckler 1999).

The Content of the Policy Process in China

Policy Initiation

Policy may be defined as the intentional action of government to improve governance by addressing problems. Thus in the stage of policy initiation, it is very important for government to attain accurate, effective and sufficient information from society and various government organizations. Because of the absence of Western-style institutional approaches of popular expression both in mass media and political representative institutions, it is the party-state which has to try to obtain such information for itself. Without public debate on policy issues – as is quite common in Western democracies – the government has to take responsibility for itself to examine information and identify the real problems. Since China is now experiencing such rapid economic development and social transformation, the party-state's tasks of information collection and problem identification have become correspondingly more demanding. There are several institutional ways and means for the party-state to get the necessary information for policy making:

First, China has developed a set of institutions specializing in policy affairs. From national level to city level, there is a system of policy-focused institutions in the Party and government system. The Policy Research Institute is widely established across many state departments, ranging from party, government, People's Congress to many other locations. Meanwhile, within central government, there exist several other research institutes, such as the development research institute in the State Council, which is also important for information collection and policy initiation.

Second, within the Office Bureau (*Bang Gong Ting*) from the national to the county level, there are numerous officials and clerks in charge of policy initiation. For example, in the Office Bureau of the Shanghai Municipal Government, there are secretaries whose main responsibility is the collection of information from lower levels of government and society, the analysis of problems uncovered and suggestions for policy reform. These all serve to assist the decision making of several mayors in Shanghai.

Third, the party-state has yet another information collection system, the Xinhua News Agency, which is arranged both at national and provincial level. Beside being a public news agency for the masses, the Xinhua News Agency is also responsible for collecting information for policy makers for whom it contributes to an important publication, the Internal Reference, from which many policy initiatives come. Meanwhile, the party-state is still trying to set up some more direct information report systems from local up to central levels, which are designed to be quite separate from the governmental bureaucracy.

Fourth, mass media and academic publications are also utilized for purposes of party-state policy initiation. Although Chinese mass media and academia are much less independent than their Western counterparts, both of them sometimes play a prominent role in policy initiation. There is a famous news programme broadcast by Chinese Central TV, called Focus Talking, which has been concentrating on disclosing social problems, especially scandals involving grassroots government. Although most of its editions are aimed at the local level, it has nevertheless helped to open an information channel for both popular and central government. Certainly its role for maintaining social stability and contributing to policy making has seemed crucial enough to prompt Premier Zhu Rong Ji to pay a special visit to the Central TV studio. Chinese academia is mostly unimportant for policy initiation, but this has not been the case in respect of some very important policy decisions, including policy construction 'The Three Representatives' of the Chinese Communist Party (as explained above). Before this policy was put forward formally by President Jiang

Zemin, it was studied and discussed from different angles by many academics. Such a process amounted both to an academic test of policy impacts and a contribution to further policy formation.

Finally, there are also some informal information 'flow-channels', such as the report system linking sectoral departments to the policy-making centre.[4] It has been advocated that party and governmental officials should periodically highlight local and grassroots organizations for investigation and research. However, now that its information and policy initiative functions have been reduced, most of the investigative and research actions of the top leadership have become a formality, at best paying special attention to particular sectors or localities. Nevertheless sometimes, some trips made to localities by top policy makers have proved essential for important policy initiation. For example, the policy of establishing Special Economic Zones was first stimulated by Yang Shang Kun's visit to south Guangdong (Huang 1999). Deng Xiaoping's trip to the South in 1991 was critical – given the superior authority and influence of Deng and the tremendous impact of his bold words – for urging the power centre to adapt to a more market oriented and open trade policy.

Now as we can see it, policy making in China may be far from pluralism yet there exist numerous policy initiators amongst the top leaders and power elite, government organizations, the mass media and academia. Policy initiation might start from problem solving, as in the cases of unemployment and Falungong; or from the strategic consideration of top leaders with regard to such as Hong Kong policy and the re-strengthening of grassroots CPP organizations. For the most part, the policy initiation process is completed via the combined involvement of different actors, each playing a different role in the various policy agendas. With regard to 'everyday' policy making, in respect of such as social policy, economic policy and ordinary foreign policy, the initiation process mainly occurs within each relevant branch of government. With support from academia, the policy-focused institutions within government are here the major actors; whereas, where policies are called for as a result of urgent social events, the roles of the mass media and the Xinhua News Agency, as an information collector, can be crucial. For some special policy processes, such as CCP reform with regard to the 'Three Representatives', the mentality of top leaders, as well as their close consultants, can play a more important role than ordinary institutions in the initiation of policy. Even so, the presence of such a multiplicity of initiators scarcely means that Chinese policy formation constitutes a pluralistic process. The roles of top leaders and a few of the power elite are always dominant; while the function of government policy institutions, academia and the mass media in policy initiation has always been carefully restricted.

Policy Formulation

The process of Chinese policy formulation can be divided into two parts, policy deliberation and decision-making. Since policy initiation merely provides basic ideas and preliminary considerations about a new policy, it is the policy deliberation process, in which the in-depth study of the problem and the drafting of policy are normally conducted, which is in charge of transferring ideas into comprehensive policy form.

Processes of policy deliberation differ from issue to issue; nevertheless all policy-making institutions depend ultimately on their institutional resources. Such institutions, so important in information collection, also play a crucial role in the process of policy deliberation. Within this party-state system, the Central Party Committee has its own policy research office, focused on researching issues of system-wide significance, especially those related to the security of the party-state. Local party committees, from provincial to city level, also have affiliated policy research offices. However, because issues of party and general politics tend to seem less concrete at the local level, by comparison with those affecting the economy and regular administration, the policy research office at local party level is usually weaker and less involved in the actual policy process than are their counterparts in the central government system. Within the latter, the most important institution for policy deliberation is Office Bureau, which is affiliated to government from central to county level. Its staff devote lots of their time to the processes of policy deliberation, especially in respect of ordinary and technical issues. Within central government, the State Council has its own policy research institutes – such as the Development Research Institute, mentioned above – and many ministries have also established their own policy research institutions, geared to specialized policy research.

In the wake of the reform, to the extent that Chinese policy making had become more and more practical and geared to problem solving, there was heightened demand for specialized knowledge and techniques – and some policy research resources outside the party-state system were also utilized in this process. Among the latter, retired practitioners and academic scholars tend to be the most prominent. Although there remains no institutional way for academics to touch the policy process, some leading scholars are usually invited to the policy deliberation process, most being from the Chinese Association of Social Science and its local branches at provincial level. In addition, some arguments and points taken from academic publications may also be used for policy-making inspiration and to conceptualize ideas prevailing among political leaders.

As we can see now, for ordinary purposes of policy deliberation the party-state normally relies on its own institutional resources, such as the Policy Research Institutes and the Office Bureau, with regard to both party and government systems. To be sure, for some policies with system-wide impacts and top importance to the party-state – such as the new strategy of transforming the CCP by demonstrating 'Three Representatives'– rather more institutions and people are drawn into the deliberation. Usually, however, when an important policy is first initiated by top leaders and a few of the power elite, this amounts merely to a set of rough ideas. Based on these ideas, the policy institute, with help of relevant corresponding academics, then makes a policy draft. Next, this policy draft might be passed on to different parts of central government and to local governments. Meanwhile, some famous academics might participate in debating the policy draft, and some papers published in journals and newspapers might also be drawn into the discussion. The relevant policy institute accumulates all such comments, and then modifies the policy draft. This process of comment seeking and draft modification can be repeated several times, depending on the importance of the policy issue under review. In very important policy cases, the policy draft finally comes to the political bureau of the Central committee of the CCP. If the policy is basically cleared by the

Political Bureau, it will then be submitted to final legitimation organizations, such as the Central Committee of the CCP, the People's Congress, or the People's Political Consultative Conference.[5] Based on comments from the members of these organizations, the draft policy paper will then be modified again before it goes to the final legalization process.

There are different ways of making policy, depending on the issue. The first is to promulgate documents setting out the content of policy. Both in the party and in the government system, this method has been quite a common policy practice for some time. Documents emanating from each level of party and government organization are accorded equal significance in law. Such documents can be about general issues, such as party construction and anti-corruption; but they can also be about mainstream government administration, the latter being termed canonical documents. The second way stems from the tendency towards legalization of the policy process in China, whereby more and more legislative elements have become involved. Here the Chinese party-state finds it more effective to make administrative law to solve problems, rather than just to issue documents without the force of law. As such administrative lawmaking becomes popular in ordinary government administration, so the legislature in China, the People's Congress and its local branches are all playing a more important role in the policy formulation process. This trend became clearer after Li Peng shifted from the position of Prime Minister to the Head of the Standing Committee of the National People's Congress. Nevertheless, although the People's Congress has increased its impact on the policy-making process, and its committees of law, finance and economy are increasingly busy, the role of the Congress in China is still relatively weak, being less independent and influential than legislatures in Western democratic countries.

Usually the final stages of policy making, such as policy promulgation and policy legalization, are treated as the symbols of a new policy, but actually they are not very important in the Chinese policy process, because the real decision making has often been finished long before. Both the policy articulation of the Central Committee of the CCP, and the legalization of policy in People's Congress, are no more than ceremonies to demonstrate a new policy, rather than exercises in final decision-making on it. Up until now, therefore, it is the policy deliberation and decision making taking place before formal policy legalization, which are more important for the study of Chinese policy formation. However, since the Chinese party-state is now trying to reform its democratic system so as to enforce the power and independence of the People's Congress, as well as to build work style (namely to improve working methods and attitudes, as well as being incorruptible) and transform the ways of leadership, this final stage of policy promulgation will presumably become more important.

Policy Implementation

Since the foundation of the PRC, there have been two major tools of policy implementation. The first is bureaucratic hierarchy of the government system. After the CCP shifted from a revolutionary party to a ruling party, its efforts at organizational consolidation proved so remarkable that some scholars characterized communist China by its organizational strength, and perceived its organizational nature as a major character of the Chinese regime (Harding 1981). Since the organizational construction of the government system has been a core feature of the Chinese regime since 1949, policy implementation from the power centre down to local and grassroots levels has been largely dependent on the formal organization system. It was the very importance of this governmental hierarchy which prompted demands for its modernization. Nevertheless, there are some obstacles which the party-state will have to overcome when pushing for administrative modernization. In reality, both the position of the CCP as the ruling party and China's laggard socioeconomic circumstances served to delay administrative reform and ensure inefficiency in policy implementation.

Second, since it is inevitably difficult for government administration alone to conduct policy implementation, the CCP plays a very important role in helping government in this process, when government is not in a position to act effectively on its own. The mechanism of the CCP in policy implementation is different from that of government. Instead of relying on the governmental hierarchy, the CCP largely depends on its own mobilization skills for policy implementation. Thus, during the whole history of the PRC, especially before reform, certain political campaigns were very essential to assist policy implementation (such as Resist American Aid Korea, Combat the Four Evils, Backyard Furnaces, Learn From Dazhai and Daqing, Learn from Leifeng, Support the Army Cherish the People, Barefoot Doctors, Go to Mountains and Countryside, etc.). Although campaigning has been much less important in Chinese politics since the reform, the party still utilizes its mobilizing resources for policy implementation (such as Stern Attack on Crime, Learn from Kong Fansen, Crack Down Fa Lun Gong in the 1980s and 1990s.)

Thus there are two major approaches to policy implementation. For ordinary policy – such as some economic policies, industrial policies and social welfare policies – the government hierarchy plays a fundamental role in its implementation. For other policies of major importance, especially those policies which the government organization has had difficulty in implementing effectively – such as national policy on birth control, reform geared to the household responsibility system, and reforms in agriculture – the CCP utilizes its powerful propaganda machine and its deep-reaching organizational network to help deliver the policy to the grassroots.

However, apart from these two approaches, there is also a newly emerging form of implementation by law, following the trend towards greater legislative involvement in the policy process. Recently this has been further enhanced by the national slogan of Governing Country by Law (rule of law). Although of short duration, this legal approach has been found an effective and sustainable way for policy implementation, and many legislature organizations and law executive institutions have become involved in the process. Nevertheless, this new approach is still in its early stages and can hardly yet be considered a backbone tool of implementation. Indeed, implementation by law in China is still problematic. There remains a long way to go to achieve the rule of law in a country whose legislature is not independent and wherein the practice of law is still far from effective.

In short, although policy implementation has been improved in post-reform China, there are still some problems to be resolved, stemming from the instrinsic difficulties of the authoritarian regime. First, further efforts to modernize Chinese governmental administration are still needed. The problem of 'cellular polity'[6]

(Lampton 1987: 14) works against effective policy implementation, since many policies will be distorted in the transition to local and grassroots levels. Although the party-state has always tried to introduce remedial solutions for this – including setting up performance indicators and assigning supervision teams to the lower levels – policy implementation is still a problem for the Chinese regime to achieve effective governance. Second, the role of the party in policy implementation is still double-edged. While it can be helpful in the implementation of important policies, it also stands in the way of the government's administrative modernization, which hinges on independence with regard to the party-government relationship. Third, since the state has asked governmental departments, local authorities, *danwei* (work units) and other organizations to be responsible for their own profits and losses, the behaviour of governmental department and *danwei* are largely led by their own search for benefits. When any policy (such as environment policy) is incompatible with this basic goal, policy implementation will be affected at various levels when this is transferred from the centre to the grassroots, because local and grassroots officials may distort the policy according to their interests.

Evaluation of the Chinese Policy Process

Strategy Transformation of the Policy Agenda

Since reform, the legitimacy of the Chinese state has been based on effective socioeconomic performance, no longer on the purity of communist ideology through sticking to class struggles. Thus the scientific policy process – including the timely identification of problems for policy initiation, correct decision making in policy formulation, and sufficiently effective policy implementation – has becomes one of the core issues for the Chinese state in its drive to maintain social stability. Thus the Chinese party-state's leading strategy has basically been transformed from one of ideological motivation and revolution to one of pragmatic problem solving (Doak 1985: 138). This change has resulted in some professionalization and regularization of the policy process. As described above, some modern policy-related institutions and methods have been introduced, which are in part changing the nature of the Chinese policy process. Such transformation has been helpful for government, enabling it to arrive at a more effective and scientific policy process, which in turn helps it to maintain social stability and economic development in the face of social and intellectual tensions.

However, although the transformation of Chinese policy strategy has contributed to policy development with regard to ideas and norms, the Chinese state is still confronting structural obstacles in the way of a reasonable and modern policy process. With more and more social issues and tensions arising from the reform process, maintaining social and political stability has become one of the primary tasks of the Chinese government. Indeed, because of the nature of the Chinese society and regime, political and social stability has always been ranked as its first consideration. Thus within the policy process, although problem solving can be helpful for maintaining stability, some reasonable policies might nevertheless have been put to one side, out of an excessive concern for stability and the devotion of too many resources to this end. Thus the prime consideration of maintaining stability can make Chinese policy overpoliticized, which itself can overshadow the modernization of the policy process.

The Institutional Limits of Policy Development

After the ideological constraints on the Chinese policy process had been removed, attention switched to the problem of institutional constraints such as the over-monopolistic role of the party-state, and the absence of policy-supporting democratic mechanisms and the mass media. Although the party-state launched government administrative reform in good time to address this problem (Huang Da Qiang, Chapter 'Public administration in China', Nagel and Mills 1993), after more than 20 years, administrative reform still has a long way to go before it reaches anything approaching Western standards. At the policy initiation stage, the monopoly of the state has some negative impacts. Although the research staff in government and affiliated organizations are much involved in information collection and problem analysis, the widespread community of other information collectors and issues researchers – such as the researchers in universities and research institutes and other non-governmental consultant agencies – is not institutionally included. More importantly, the mass media are not allowed independently to discuss policy-related issues, which has very much limited their capacity to assist in and monitor the policy process. In policy formulation, although there are institutional arrangements for administrative and legislative involvement, actual practice is always different. The over-centralized policy making structure puts policy making in a black box, removed from the supervision of representative democracy, mass media and social organizations as outside scrutineers. Meanwhile, so far as policy implementation is concerned, policy distortion tends to be common whenever policy is carried to local and grassroots levels, and the limited capacity of central government to control policy implementation at these levels makes the situation even worse.

These institutional limits on the Chinese policy process stem from the monopolistic role of the party-state. The Chinese government alone takes much responsibility for the policy process. But being a less developed system, the Chinese governmental organization then has difficulties to do the job, even as many non-governmental organizations are not permitted (owing to the nature of the Chinese authoritative regime) to become institutionally involved in the policy process. Furthermore, because the Chinese government cannot do a good job by itself in the policy process, the party-state has had to utilize alternative resources, such as the leadership of the CCP and the rule of law.

The CCP's Role in the Policy Agenda

As the ruling party in China, the CCP has been playing a positive role in the Chinese policy process, especially during the early stages of communist China. Some scholars still maintain that the party can be a successful assistant for government in policy implementation when the policy is important enough, or when government organization is too weak to conduct it. The advantage of the party in the policy process lies not only in its high authority and ideological strength, but also, more importantly, in its wide- and deep-reaching organizational network which exists separately from the government system. Moreover, the mobilization skills of the party play a very important in some crucial policy processes.

However, the leading role of the party also runs counter to the modernization of the policy process. First, the party's involvement sometimes makes the policy process over-politicized, which can lead to waste or even policy disaster. Second, the party's leading role is also hampering the independent position of government, as demanded for administrative modernization. Whenever the party's involvement tries to eliminate some institutional limits in the Chinese policy process, it tends to increase other institutional obstacles by the same token. If the relationship between government administration and party leadership remains unresolved, the quest for administrative modernization and policy development will still be facing a difficult future.

The Rule of Law as a New Instrument in the Policy Process

Beside the party's involvement, the Chinese party-state has introduced a new method for policy process, which can be called 'the law approach'. This type of effort, under the new strategy of Governing the Country by Law, could more or less resolve problems of policy distortion, and free the centre from its heavy burdens of policy control, such as assigning policy indicators and measurements. Without doubt, Chinese policy development is benefiting from this new strategy of building the Rule of Law. In policy initiation, the rule of law is a useful way of drawing more policy initiators into the policy process, especially those in legislative sectors. In policy formation, it will help legislative departments play a more prominent role, which may obviously help avoid mistakes in policy making. In policy implementation, the Rule of Law can be effective to increase the efficiency of policy implementation and to reduce policy distortion in the course of its delivery to local and grassroots levels.

But, as we can see from Western experience, an effective law-based approach to the policy agenda can be very demanding. For example, the rule of law requires a high cultural agreement between both state officials and the masses. Moreover, the rule of law in China has to be compatible with the outstanding position of the CCP. The rule of law may have a promising future in promoting Chinese policy development, but this depends on whether China can correctly deal with the complicated relationship between the rule of law and the leadership of the CCP.

Conclusion

By shifting the basic political strategy from ideological struggle to economic construction, Chinese reform provided a beneficial base for policy development. Yet, although the Chinese policy process has benefited from system-wide reform, there remain several obstacles for it to overcome. The institutional limits on the policy agenda call for more non-governmental organizations to be involved in the policy process, but active NGOs are sensitive to the very nature of the Chinese political regime. The top consideration given to the maintenance of stability can sometimes divert the policy process, leading to waste and policy mistakes. While the CCP, armed with its mobilization skills and far-reaching organizations, can be a supplementary force in the policy agenda to overcome the institutional limits of policy process, the monopolistic role of the CCP is itself incompatible with the trend towards democracy and administrative modernization in policy development.

Since economic reform and its corresponding social consequences have been providing a friendly political and social background for Chinese policy development, the policy process in China could be facing a promising future. But whether China will achieve a reasonable policy process[7] depends on the efforts made to transform the macro political system. Some hard decisions will have to be taken by the Chinese state, over the dilemma between the rule of party or the rule of law, and between 'revolutionization' and institutionalization.

Notes

1. The so-called Scientific Policy Making was put forward by formal leader of Chinese National Congress, Wang Li in the 1980s. After that, many research papers and articles appeared in newspapers and journals. The discussion of Scientific policy making reminds Chinese officials that correct policy making should be a core issue of Chinese governance. However, the lack of scientific policy making has been an enduring problem in China until now, because it is not only related to the capacity of Chinese policy makers, but also to the basic political structure on which the policy making is based.
2. For example, the issue of laid-off workers in state-owned enterprises has increasingly been causing problems for social stability and political legitimacy.
3. The Falungong is a new, threatening organization. Although its origin relates to many issues, such as fading ideology, and psychological response to rapid social change, its sudden arising and spreading shows that Chinese public policy making should pay more attention to weak groups in society, such as the poor, patients, retired and unemployed people.
4. In the critical time during the policy making before 4 June, the reports from provincial government and sector departments in central government dominated the information channel of those few top leaders as final decision makers.
5. The Chinese People's Political Consultative Conference was first established in 1949, shortly before the foundation of the People's Republic of China. The institute served as Congress before 1954 when the Chinese People's Congress was founded. After that, rather than being cancelled, it continues to be as paratactic organization to government, Congress, judiciary from central to county level. Now its main functions are to unite *democratic parties*, non-party people, and people organization, and to discuss and supervise Chinese politics dominated by the CCP, while holding no institutional power to do so.
6. The 'cellular polity' model shows that, to the extent local and grassroots officials are concerned more about their regional interests, localism and disconnected local parts will challenge the solidarity of the whole polity.

References

Doak Barnnet, A. (1985), *The Making of Foreign Policy in China: Structure and Process*, Tauris, London.

Hamrin, Carol Lee and Zhao, Suisheng (1995), *Decision-making in Dengs China: Perspectives from Insiders*, M.E. Sharpe, Armonk, NY.

Hantrais, Linda and Mangen, Stephen P. (1993), *The Policy Making Process and the Social Actors*, Cross-National Research Group, Loughborough.

Harding, Harry (1981), *Organizing China: the Problem of Bureaucracy, 1949–1976*, Stanford University Press, Stanford, CA.

Huang, Jianrong (1999), *The Applicability of Policy-making Theories in Post-Mao China*, Ashgate, Aldershot.

Lampton, David M. (1987), *Policy Implementation in Post-Mao China*, University of California Press, Berkeley.

Levin, Peter (1997), *Making Social Policy: The Mechanisms of Government and Politics, and how to Investigate Them*, Open University Press, Buckingham.

Lieberthal, Kenneth and Lampton, David M. (1992), *Bureaucracy, Politics, and Decision Making in Post-Mao China*, University of California Press, Berkeley.

Liu, Meiru (2001), *Administrative Reform in China and its Impact on the Policy-making Process and Economic Development after Mao: Reinventing Chinese Government*, Lewiston, Edwin Mellen Press, Lampeter.

Nagel, Stuart S. and Mills, Miriam K. (1993), *Public Policy in China*, Greenwood, Westport, London.

Oi, Jean C. (1989), *State and Peasant in Contemporary China: The Political Economy of Village Government*, University of California Press, Berkeley.

Shirk, Susan (1993), *The Political Logic of Economic Reform in China*, University of California Press, Berkeley.

Tang, Wenfang (2000), *Chinese Urban Life under Reform: The Changing Social Contract*, Cambridge University Press, Cambridge.

Walder, Andrew G. (eds) (1998), *Zouping in Transition, the Process of Reform in Rural North China*, Harvard University Press, Cambridge, MA.

Wei, Hu (1998), *The Process of Government*, Zhejiang People's Publication, Han Zhou.

Winckler, Edwin A. (ed.) (1999), *Transition from Communism in China: Institutional and Comparative Analyses*, Lynne Rienner Publishers, Colorado.

Wong, Linda J. and MacPherson, Stewart (1995), *Social Change and Social Policy in Contemporary China*, Avebury, Aldershot.

Zemin, Jiang (2001), *The Speech at the 80th Anniversary of CCP*, People's Press, Beijing.

Chapter 5

Paradigm Shifts in Social Welfare Policy Making in China: Struggling between Economic Efficiency and Social Equity[1]

Hsiao-hung Nancy Chen

Given the fact that a country like China, the size of whose population is equivalent to a combination of Latin America and sub-Saharan Africa, and that 60 per cent of China's 10 billion population was still living on US$1.00 per day at the dawn of 1978 when the economic reform schemes were first introduced, it is truly remarkable to note that from 1978 to 1995, her annual GDP growth rate reached 8.3 per cent. Her average savings rate (expressed as a percentage of GDP) increased to 37 per cent over the same period. Meanwhile the agricultural sector's share in the overall economy decreased from 71 to 50 per cent, while the proportion of manufacturing and tertiary sectors grew steadily, with structural diversification taking place within those sectors themselves (Figure 5.1). As the World Bank's experts have illustrated so succinctly, China's attempt to complete two transitions at once – from a command to a market economy and from a rural to an urban society – is without historical precedent (World Bank 1997a).

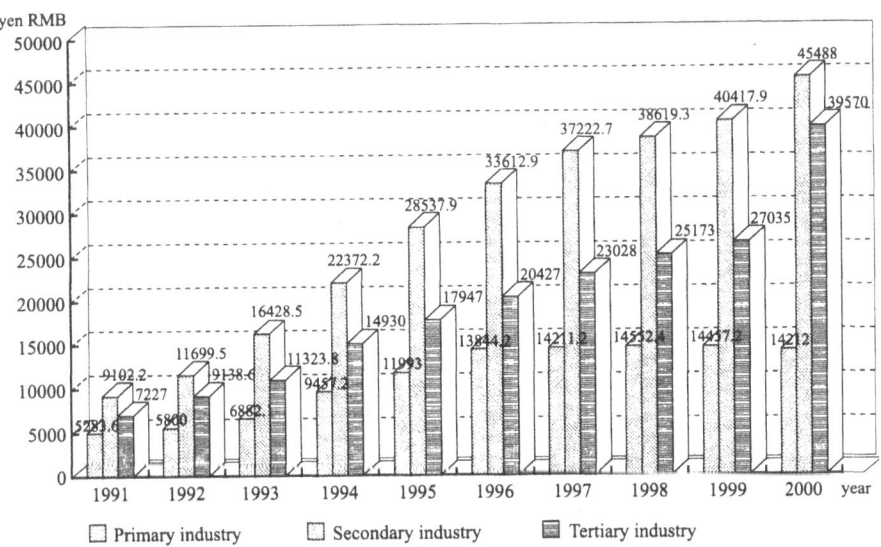

Figure 5.1 Industrial structural change in China 1991–2000

However, despite the impressive economic growth rate China has experienced over the past 20 years, since adopting its open policy, any further economic reform must surely touch on the essence of China's economic system, especially the state-owned enterprise (hereafter referred to as SOE) sector.[2] For it will be impossible to gain economic efficiency without reforming state enterprise pensions, medical care and unemployment insurance systems. Should the existing systems continue, it will be difficult to cut down on the overall costs of state enterprises so as to enhance their market competitiveness. This in turn must impede the country's prospects for further economic development.

It is against this background that this chapter will first outline the characteristics of the Chinese social welfare system prior to 1978, before focusing on the special features of China's wide-ranging endeavours at social welfare reform since then (each of these reforms being explored in greater detail in subsequent chapters of this volume). It will conclude by commenting on some of the salient issues that will have to be resolved in any further reform processes.

Salient Characteristics and Underlying Ethos of the Chinese Social Welfare System prior to 1978

Before plodding into the future prospects for Chinese social welfare reform, it is worth pondering a while on what made the system work as well as it did, prior to 1978, so as to shed light on why the current reform has gone the way it has. To name just a few, the following points are worth making:

1   Urban workers employed in the SOEs enjoyed the fullest welfare of all. Patterned after the Russian model, urban labourers of SOEs, in a sense, were treated as 'labour aristocrats'. The welfare needs of rural residents, by contrast, were taken care of by their Communes before the latter were abolished. For instance, in 1981 when the commune system was still functioning, 71 per cent of all Chinese were covered by medical services. But this proportion had declined to 21 per cent by 1993 (World Bank 1997a).

Different economic structures had already appeared before 1978 in the urban sector, whose employees literally enjoyed no welfare, while their counterparts in the rural sector were also completely left out of the welfare system. One study (World Bank 1997c: 55) showed that out of every 1,000 people, the supply of both doctors and hospital beds in rural areas was 75 per cent short of that in urban areas; and in terms of nurses there was an 80 per cent shortage, compared to urban settings. On the whole, the medical subsidies that rural area received amounted to only one-fifth of those received by urban areas.

2   The 'enterprises' in China, especially the SOEs, were acting as an all-encompassing 'unit', whereby not only the 'full employment' of all their workers was guaranteed but also 'from cradle to grave' welfare was delivered.

Employees in the SOEs enjoyed lifelong employment (job security). In fact, the Chinese communist government all along has taken this as an indicator of 'socialist superiority'.

This practice, nevertheless, was impeding labour mobility between the different types of enterprise as well as affecting the SOEs' market competitiveness.

3   The socialist idea of 'to perform according to one's ability, to each according to his need' cultivated the 'eating from the same big pot' atmosphere, which was detrimental to work incentives and motivation. As a result, there was likely to be much 'redundant labour' in the SOEs. With the advent of the reform, a new type of distribution – distribution according to one's work' – was introduced.

To summarize, the Chinese social welfare system, at the dawn of reform prior to 1978, was one that rendered 'low wage, high welfare', but which was often heavily reliant on government subsidies. Perhaps this also served as one of the main instigators for the later reforms in respect of wages and labour employment.

Special Features of the Social Welfare System Reform in post-1978 China

Table 5.1 Chronological account of key events of the social welfare system reform in China, by different economic planning phases

	6th Five-Year Planning Phase 1981–1985	7th Five-Year Planning Phase 1986–1990	8th Five-Year Planning Phase 1991–1995	9th Five-Year Planning Phase 1996–2000
Old-age insurance system reform	1984 The state, the enterprise and individual are entrusted to share the insurance fee together.	1990 World Bank suggestions adopted: **three-tier protection**	1991 The old-age insurance fund June 1991 Decision of the Reform of the old age insurance system of enterprise workers March 1995 Circular on deepening the reform of the old-age insurance system for enterprise workers **From defined benefit-pay-as-you-go to defined contribution.**	August 1997 Decision on establishing a unified basic old-age insurance system for enterprise workers

Table 5.1 Continued/

	6th Five-Year Planning Phase	7th Five-Year Planning Phase	8th Five-Year Planning Phase	9th Five-Year Planning Phase
	1981–1985	1986–1990	1991–1995	1996–2000
Medical insurance system reform	Prior to 1990: experiment of adopting 'social account' for serious diseases.	1990 Decision on the reform for old-age insurance system for workers. (1) **A combination of social account and individual account.** (2) **Develop and modify the cooperative type of medical system in rural areas.**	December 1994 Jiujiang and Zhenjiang experimental health insurance project.	1996 Decision on health reform and development.
Unemployment insurance system reform	1984 The promulgation of 'labour contract system'.	1986 Promulgation of 'bankruptcy law'.	April 1993 Regulations on unemployment insurance for SOE 'waiting for jobs' workers.	Setting up laid-off workers' re-employment centres to oversee workers' job retraining, etc.
Other social welfare system reform		March 1987 Approval of proposal for implementing social security system in rural areas	January 1992 Basic proposal (trail) on old age insurance in the villages at the country level. February 1992 Decree on labour management in township enterprises. January 1994 Regulations on the support work of the 'five guarantees' in the villages.	
			1994 to 2000 Poverty eradication plan.	

Table 5.1 Continued/

	6th Five-Year Planning Phase 1981–1985	7th Five-Year Planning Phase 1986–1990	8th Five-Year Planning Phase 1991–1995	9th Five-Year Planning Phase 1996–2000
				March 1996 The ninth five-year plan for national economic and social development (1996–2000) 1997 Full-fledged SOEs reform.
				1998 The Ministry of Labour and Social Security was established. March 1998 Continue to reform SOEs and to perfect the social security system. August 1998 'An announcement to establish a unified pension plan at the provincial level.' 1999 'Temporary regulations on collecting social insurance contributions' – **Unifying the Procedures for Collecting contributions.**

Table 5.1 Concluded/

	6th Five-Year Planning Phase 1981–1985	7th Five-Year Planning Phase 1986–1990	8th Five-Year Planning Phase 1991–1995	9th Five-Year Planning Phase 1996–2000
				March 1999 Three regulations: • Temporary measure to regulate the registration of social insurance; • Temporary measure to regulate the declared contribution of social insurance fees; • Measure to supervise and inspect the contribution of social insurance fees.

Source: Compiled by this study.

As Table 5.1 suggests, the all-encompassing reform of the social welfare system currently taking place in China is indeed ambitious. Nevertheless, it is usually easier to say than do. Given the fairly limited budget that has been allocated to the Ministry of Civil Affairs (note that it has always been low – a mere 1.5 per cent of overall national expenditure for nearly 50 years – see Table 5.2), and given the multi-faceted nature of the SOEs' reform, coupled with all the related social security issues thereof, government determination and leadership, management capabilities, workers' mentality are all a *sine qua non* for their materialization. In what follows, we shall reflect critically on some of the salient features as well as on the unsettled issues left by these reforms in the face of China's long-standing socialist history.

The following observations can be made to highlight the features of social welfare reform in post-1978 China:

1. In terms of finance: the 'state' is no longer the sole responsible body. Instead, state, enterprise and individual are all to bear some burden. This is evident from all the recent reforms carried out in respect of China's old-age, medical care and unemployment insurance programmes, whereby a blend of social risk-pooling and a personal account has been introduced.
2. In terms of enterprise management: 'efficiency' not 'full employment' has become the main concern. Thus, 'unemployment' is said to be tolerated and unprofitable enterprises are to be allowed to close down, merge or simply to go

Table 5.2 Expenditures on civil affairs establishments 1950–1996

Year	Expenditure (million yuan)	% in the National Budget
1950	132	1.94
1955	498	1.05
1960	724	1.11
1965	1,079	2.31
1970	653	1.01
1975	1,271	1.55
1980	1,748	1.44
1985	3,001	1.64
1990	5,222	1.54
1991	6,326	1.67
1992	6,296	1.42
1993	6,967	1.40
1994	8,679	1.50
1995	10,320	1.52
1996	12,122	1.53

Sources: K. Zhano (ed.) (1997), *1997 Zhongguo minzheng tongji nianjian (The Chinese civil affairs annual review 1997)*, Beijing: Ministry of Civil Affairs, p. 287. See also Chow (2000:101).

bankrupt. In the process of transformation from a planned economy to a market economy, 'enterprise' is now treated more as a 'production' entity than ever.

3 In terms of the long-lasting dualistic structure: 'more equal' treatment has been allocated to employees outside the SOEs, in both the urban and rural sectors. This has been done mainly because of the following considerations:

(a) to be able to respond to the changing reality: i.e. there has been massive migration from rural to urban areas and between regions;
(b) equal welfare treatment will lead to more labour mobility, which is considered conducive to economic restructuring (at present, most insurance reform, being not portable and thus not conducive to labour mobility, has proven unattractive for people to participate in);
(c) equal welfare for all will certainly also broaden the population base willing to take part in the newly designed system and thus ensure the sustainability of the reform.

4 In terms of 'institution building': a unified 'Ministry of Labour and Social Security' was established in 1998 to oversee matters of social security in respect of all related matters that used to be performed by different branches of the government, such as the Ministries of Labour, Health, and Civil Affairs.

5   In terms of all traditional welfare constituents: the functions of 'family' and 'community' are still much emphasized, even though the 'market' is expected to assume a heavier role.
6   In terms of the crux of welfare system reform: 'social insurance' is still to be the backbone, for all that the importance of both 'social relief' and 'welfare services' programs are not to be neglected.

Remaining Issues to be Tackled in the Process of Chinese Social Welfare System Reform

Ambitious as the reforms may be, the Chinese government and scholars, as well as ordinary citizens, are fully aware of the fact that they will not all be implemented without difficulties ahead. Interestingly, Chinese social security system reform had never attracted much attention from either government or the general public before 1978 or, for that matter, prior to 1990, when the Chinese government decided to speed up economic growth and development after the adoption of the Eighth Five Year Plan for national economic and social development. It was perhaps due exactly to this national endeavour that further economic growth and development was found not to be possible without a strong commitment to reform of the SOEs. For the all-encompassing welfare benefits hitherto delivered exclusively to SOEs' workers had not only created a huge financial burden for the state and the enterprise, but also had become barriers to future reform.

To be more specific, the SOEs during the planned economy era were not profit-seeking economic entities; they were merely workshops there to implement centrally set policies (Chow and Xu 2001). Initial reform measures had been taken as early as 1978 – transforming them from workshops of the government to more independent economic entities (1978–1984). Then, from 1985 to 1992, there were attempts to separate the political part from the enterprise by separating ownership from management.[3] Finally, beginning in 1993, steps were taken to decentralize authority and return profits to the enterprises, turning to taxation instead of profits as a source of government revenue. In short, the power of day-to-day decision-making was devolved down to the individual SOEs, allowing them to retain whatever profits they managed to generate – after they had paid their dues in tax – for further investment. Furthermore, by focusing attention on the large SOEs and thus striving to invigorate the small ones 'by example', it was hoped that a modern enterprise system could be established in China (see below in this chapter for further details). However, it is believed that, before such authentic 'merchandising' can be brought about, the role of the 'state' will still need to be very strong, at least for the transitional period.

It is thus fair to state that the Chinese social security system reform is heavily intertwined with matters of economic reform, and vice versa – the social security system having worked for so long almost exclusively in favour of the SOEs' employees. Without social security reform, economic growth will be impeded; and without economic growth, social welfare reform will be difficult to sustain. However the doubt remains as to whether one can have the pie and eat it at the same time – since the Chinese government is striving so very hard to maintain a balance between stability, development and growth in her socioeconomic reform processes.

In order to answer this question, there are a few urgent issues which need to be resolved, such as:

How is the Role of the 'State' to be Differentiated from that of the 'Enterprise'?

Given the fact that the SOEs account for one-third of China's total industrial output, two-thirds of China's urban employment and half of her total fixed assets investment,[4] one should not be so surprised to learn just how vital the reform of SOEs could be to the success of China's overall economic and social development. Nevertheless, the fact of the matter is that many SOEs are still running on a deficit basis, in the face of ever increasing market competition.

It has been indicated that, in 1992, the percentage of SOEs running on a deficit basis was 26; whereas this was up to 50 per cent by 1996 (Chow and Xu 2001). Being a socialist state concerned not just with economic growth but sociopolitical stability, the Chinese government has often tended to adopt a combination of low-interest loans and subsidies to bail such companies out. Such burdens have usually been transferred to the national banks; a practice which has further slowed down money market development in China.

Given what has been stated, it is abundantly clear that the proper handling of relationships between the state and the bank is another urgent issue for exploration. Suffice it to say that to commercialize the national banks (which now control 90 per cent of China's bank assets and cover two-thirds of its monetary assets), permitting flexible interest rates and strengthening the money market would seem the right directions for China to take in its march to a market economy. Nevertheless, adequate fiscal policy reform is also necessary.

World Bank experts have more than once propounded (e.g. in 1997) that 'shaping a competitive economy requires market forces; however, shaping a caring society requires government leadership'; it has further remarked on the Chinese state as 'both doing too much and too little on wrong things'. In other words, the state is seen as interfering too much in the practices of enterprises – such as appointing managers on a favouritism or reward principle – and yet caring too little for such matters of social infrastructure as education, environmental protection, health and social services. This is reflected in China's not-so-adequate public expenditure structure, where too much government budget has been allocated to the SOEs and too little put forth into the general public's well-being (a mere 5 per cent of total GDP) (see Table 5.3). Such practices are considered incongruous with moves towards a market economy and need to be reprioritized.

Since both efficiency and equity are national development goals in China, the sort of viable 'state cum enterprise relationship' which might be arrived at, has been and remains an urgent question to be addressed. Under its 'focusing attention on large SOEs and invigorating small ones' policy, the Chinese government has so far picked up 1,000 large-scale SOEs (accounting for two-thirds of all state-owned industrial assets, and the majority of sales, taxation and profits) as a focal point for reform, the remaining 304,000 SOEs being left out for various reasons, ranging from low rates of return to internal corruption.

One of the main reasons for picking up the 1,000 large-scale SOEs for trying out the reform has been that large-scale enterprises demand even more diversification of

Table 5.3 Labour insurance and welfare expenditure 1952–1995

Year	Total amount (million yuan)	State-owned enterprises	Collective ownership enterprises	Expenditure by other ownership enterprises	Expenditure as percentage of payroll
1952	952				14.00
1957	2,794				17.90
1962	2,825				13.20
1973	6,691				14.30
1978	7,810	6,910	900		13.70
1979	10,730	9,490	1,240		16.60
1980	13,640	11,930	1,710		17.70
1981	15,490	13,570	1,920		18.90
1982	18,050	15,700	2,350		20.50
1983	21,250	18,270	2,980		22.70
1984	25,770	21,340	4,340	90	22.70
1985	33,160	27,360	5,680	120	24.00
1986	42,010	34,390	7,410	210	25.30
1987	50,870	41,590	8,990	300	27.00
1988	65,310	53,760	11,080	470	28.20
1989	76,800	63,550	12,650	600	29.30
1990	93,790	77,730	15,290	770	31.80
1991	109,470	91,250	17,180	1,040	32.90
1992	130,950	109,580	19,880	1,490	33.20
1993	167,020	138,650	23,860	4,510	34.00
1994	195,810	164,620	24,810	6,380	29.40
1995	2,361.300	198,040	29,450	8,640	29.20

Sources: Figures for 1952, 1957, 1962, 1973: The Chinese Statistical Yearbook Editorial Committee (ed.) 1982, *Zhongguo tongji nianjian 1982*, (*The Chinese statistical yearbook 1982*), Beijing: State Bureau of Statistics, p. 49. Figures for 1978 to 1993: Guo. J. (ed.) *1995, Zhongguo shehui baozhang zhidii zonglan* (*The Chinese social security system summary review*) Shaheshi, Hebei: Zhongguo Minzhu Faziii Chubanshe, pp. 49–50. Figures for 1994 and 1995: Wang. J. (ed.) 1996, *Zhongguo laudong nianjian 1996* (*The Chinese labour review 1996*) Beijing: Zhongguo Laodong Chubanshe, p. 547. See also Chow (2000:108).

ownership, so that the risks being run may be shouldered by shareholders. Moreover, if this is an irreversible trend, delaying such changes will only increase running costs and create more idle assets for the bank. As to the remaining 304,000 SOEs, it is said that government control will gradually be loosened so that mergers, sale, renting out and/or even liquidation may be resorted to. All such measures should help to bring about different forms of enterprise, part and parcel of a market economy.

How to Solve the Re-Employment Problems of the Laid-Off Workers from SOEs

This could be another big challenge for China in the years to come. Though no one really knows exactly how many workers have been laid off by SOEs in China, it could be in the order of hundreds of thousands. Recent statistics indicate that the urban unemployment rate has increased from 2.3 per cent in 1991 to 3 per cent by 1996. This figure is of course an underestimate, due to the fact that, in many cities, workers even if laid-off still keep their work registration with their original enterprises, in the hope of continuing to receive various kinds of allowances. Therefore, the real unemployment rate could be as high as 7.5 per cent in the cities, as indicated earlier. A survey of five major cities – Beijing, Shanghai, Chungching, Shenyang and Guangzhou – demonstrated that adding laid-off and unemployed workers together gave a total of 13 per cent of the overall labour force. If the 'redundant labour' within the enterprises (in approximately 15 to 20 per cent of the state-owned enterprises) is also taken into account, plus the still-growing labour force in the urban sector and migrated labour from the rural sector (80,000 would not be an over-exaggerated estimate), the real unemployment figure could even be as high as 27.78 per cent (Li, Lulu, et al. 2001; Li, Pei-lin, et al. 2000).

Endeavours such as establishing re-employment centres and re-employment service centres have been taken by the government, and at least 5 million people have benefited from some types of retraining. However, bearing in mind the fact that there are more and more people moving into the non-government sector (Table 5.4) more concern should surely be shifting into taking care of their employment welfare needs. After all, China's future lies with vibrant, competitive and private firms in industry and services (Chow and Xu 2001).

Nevertheless, one has to take account of the trade-offs between whether the government ought to try to reform the SOEs first or settle the SOEs' workers first? Figure 5.2 portrays the relationship between economic growth and urban registered unemployment rates, during different phases of China's economic and social development planning period. This would seem to imply that, in pursuing a higher economic growth rate, the country has to tolerate somewhat higher levels of unemployment. The crux of the matter, then, is to what extent such a situation is politically bearable and socially acceptable.

It nevertheless should suffice to state, at this juncture, that there exist strong relationships between the reform of SOEs, labour market formation and income disparity. In certain cities, during the process of reform, if the unemployment rate went too high government would step in and slow down the speed of SOEs' transformation, for the sake of social and political stability. This implies that the state will have to continue providing to her SOE workers huge amounts of wages and various kinds of social welfare, thus continuing to exacerbate the fiscal burden. Further, it is often the case that the government will try to control or even reduce the grain price to subsidize urban residents' consumption. By so doing, not only will

Table 5.4 Changes in the situation of urban employees by type of ownership, 1978–1998 (million persons)

Year	Total no. of urban employees	In SOEs	In collectively owned enterprises	In enterprises with other types of ownership
1978	95.14	74.51	20.48	—
1979	—	—	—	—
1980	105.25	80.19	24.25	—
1981	—	—	—	—
1982	—	—	—	—
1983	—	—	—	—
1984	—	—	—	—
1985	128.08	89.90	33.24	0.38
1986	—	—	—	—
1987	137.83	96.54	34.88	0.50
1988	142.67	99.84	35.27	0.63
1989	143.90	101.08	35.02	0.82
1990	166.16	103.46	35.49	8.33
1991	169.77	106.64	36.28	9.74
1992	172.41	108.89	36.21	11.15
1993	175.89	109.20	33.93	16.34
1994	184.13	112.14	32.85	23.07
1995	190.93	112.61	31.47	29.28
1996	198.15	112.44	30.16	32.81
1997	202.07	110.44	28.83	37.62
1998	206.78	90.58	19.63	48.97

Note: Information not available.
Sources: 'China Statistical Yearbook 1999', pp. 136–7. Also see Chow and Xu (2001:18).

rural residents' income level be decreased, which could lead to massive rural–urban migration but, once migrated into the cities, such people will only be able to find jobs in the non-government sector, which could result in labour market segmentation and accelerate the already dismal income disparities picture.

On this score, a number of related issues also deserve attention. For instance:

(a) How are old/retired workers, who have in the past earned fairly low wages due to socialist ideology, to be compensated?
(b) How are the not-too-well-managed enterprises to be expected to put aside funds for their employees' old age, health and all other kinds of social security benefits?

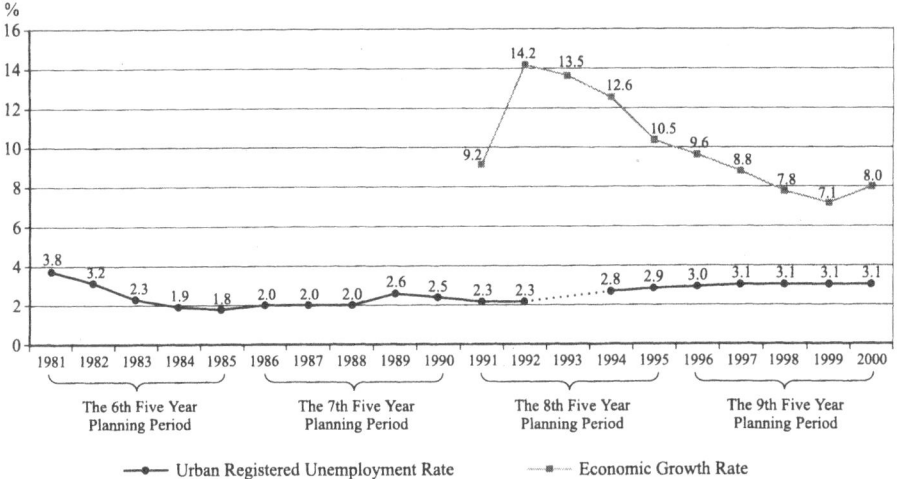

Note: K Data not available
Source: Compiled by this study from various Chinese statistics.

Figure 5.2 Economic growth rate vs. urban registered unemployment rate in China over different planning phases

Will the Dichotomy Existing between Urban and Rural Residents, in Terms of the Welfare Bestowed on Them, Remain?

Given what has been said, the answer is a dire 'yes' at least for the foreseeable future. Otherwise, the 80 per cent of the rural population plus the 20 per cent urban residents' problems could augment the complexities of the reform efforts and lead to further instability in society. This perhaps is why the Chinese government in recent years has worked so very hard in areas such as outlining poverty lines, establishing community centres and easing its tight population migration policy in the urban sector, as well as strengthening its 'five guarantee' system (i.e. clothing, food, housing, medical and funeral services) in the rural sector (see other chapters in this volume).

From a 'System' Perspective, what will be some of the Prerequisites Needed should China Decide to Adopt the Three-Tier Social Insurance Protection Proposals Recommended by the World Bank (1994)?

In other words, are the current social welfare reforms aiming at a universal or selective social welfare system? Is China indeed financially ready to afford a system beyond basic needs satisfaction?

First and foremost, the government has to decide which level of basic protection to all can and should be easily financed. Would it be more appropriate, given China's present stage of economic development, to render to all citizens just a basic needs satisfaction?

Table 5.5 Social insurance coverage 1986, 1989, 1992

Types of workers	No. of workers (million)		
	1986	1989	1992
Total labour force	512.89	553.33	594.30
Urban workers	132.90	143.90	156.30
State-owned	93.30	101.10	108.89
Collective ownership	34.20	35.00	36.20
Individual ownership	4.80	6.50	8.40
Others	0.60	1.30	2.80
Township workers	79.40	93.70	105.80
Village workers	379.90	409.40	438.00
Workers covered by social insurance	103.83	126.77	140.87
% of labour force covered	20.25	22.91	23.70
% of city workers covered	78.11	88.10	90.13

Note: It was reported that the income and the expenditure of the Social Insurance Fund for 1993 were 42,000 million and 38,000 million yuan respectively, leaving a surplus of 4,000 million yuan. The total accumulation of the Fund stood at 25,000 million yuan at the end of 1993, with 8,000 million yuan invested in government banks, 3,100 million yuan used by local finance, 1,600 million yuan put in special financial accounts, leaving 12,500 million yuan (Zhongguo shehui baozhang zhidu zonglan, p. 83).

Sources: Guo. J. (ed.) 1995, *Zhongguo shehui baozhang zhidu zonglan (A summary review of the Chinese social security system)* Shaheshi, Hebei: Chinese Democracy and Legal System Press, p. 336. See also Chow (2000:113).

Besides, one has to bear in mind how many enterprises in China actually have the ability to grant their employees second-tier supplementary insurance (see chapter 10 in this volume) and the likely gap that might open up between the well- and the not-so-well-managed enterprises. Research (e.g. Li, Pei-lin et al. 2000) has revealed that, in 1997, total expenses for an enterprise – adding together pension, medical and unemployment costs – could amount to as much as 30.4 per cent of a worker's total wage. If the present base for all social security is not broadened to cover the whole population, the burden for SOE workers must, one way or another, be shared by the rest of the population, thus creating another kind of inequality. In addition, aside from the not-so-well-developed insurance market, how many individuals in China can really afford to purchase their own insurance in the market? Might a contribution-based system create even more social inequality, be this personal, regional, and/or sectoral?

Two other related issues also warrant consideration: First, what model might fit China the best: Defined benefit (pay-as-you-go)? Defined contribution? Or a combination of the two? The individual account system introduced so far has often been criticized as something 'nominal' rather than 'real', partly because of the long tradition of Chinese socialist workers' 'eating from iron rice bowl' mentality and partly due to the fact that, for the not so promising SOE workers, there exists literally no money to put into their individual accounts.

Second, what should be the relationship between social insurance programme reform and other welfare schemes? To effectuate the 'equity' goal, current insurance-based reform – if meant to be comprehensive – ought certainly to be expanding its scope to incorporate the social relief and social welfare services.

Issues of Management:

(a) Adequate insurance fund management deserves particular attention. Past experience from other countries has demonstrated that while huge social security funds may be helpful in achieving the goal of massive infrastructure building, they might also create inflationary pitfalls due to mismanagement. Some studies (e.g. Chow and Xu 2001; Chow 2000) have shown that resistance to change of the SOEs can sometimes come exactly from the government itself. Aside from corruption, national banks that have over-loaned to SOEs, and state enterprise managers operating as vested interest groups, may all pay lip service to all kind of reforms, without genuinely backing them.
(b) Whether or not the country should adopt a unified reform system or allow the system to vary according to different places' needs, is another issue worth looking into. Adopting different systems for different areas may be more adjustable to reality, yet applying a unified system can often broaden the insurance base and thus encounter less resistance to the reform of the SOEs on a nationwide scale.
(c) The lack of a private sector (third sector). A stronger civic society also needs to be encouraged, to strengthen and make up for the areas left by the state and the enterprises. But this, unfortunately, is one area of reform the existing government seems quite reluctant to contemplate.

Concluding Remarks

Of course, there are numerous other issues that Chinese social security reform has to tackle, such as her ageing population, her one-child policy and its consequences for intergenerational transfer, her relative early retirement age (50-55 for women and 55-60 for men), appropriate coverage as well as whether payments/benefits should be geared to number of years worked or wage-related (i.e. geared to the highest or average wage over the overall working life of the recipients). Some of these issues are technical in nature, others are more ideological and structural.

For instance, the population aged 65 and over has already reached 6.96 per cent (revealed by the Fifth Census) of the total population, as of 2001. It is forecast that, by the year 2020, the aged will account for around 11 per cent of the total population. How will this trend affect China's social welfare policy? The relative ratio of workers to retirees today is 10 : 1 but, given the ageing trend, the ratio will soon become 6 : 1 – and it should further reduce to 3 : 1 by 2050. This undoubtedly implies that future generations will have to shoulder heavier burdens in respect of pensions cover, especially in a country like China that has experimented with a one-child policy for more than 20 years.

Next, will the insistence on a 'publicly owned enterprise' ideology be at odds with the reform goals, with regard to 'privatization'?

In addition, how is the balance to be achieved between economic efficiency and social equity, as so vividly portrayed in China's tenth five year economic development plan promulgated on 5 March 2001? This tenth five year economic development plan envisaged an average growth rate of 7 per cent for the next five years. By 2005, the contribution of agriculture, manufacturing and the service sectors to GDP are estimated to be 13 per cent, 51 per cent and 36 per cent respectively; whereas they are expected to account for 44 per cent, 23 per cent and 33 per cent of the labour force respectively.

Under the banner of 'Development is a Immutable Truth', the theme of continuous SOE reform, along with social security system reform, is again being stressed. Besides emphasizing that for those SOEs that are not running well, merger, sell out or liquidation measures may be adopted, for large-scale SOEs, a system of shareholding is to be encouraged, as is the separation between politics and enterprises in general. Employment certainly ranks as a top priority, side by side with wage reform, housing reform and community-provided services. But the bottom line once again is really that of how best to strike the balance between growth, development and stability?

Finally, the implications of joining the WTO and its likely impact on social welfare reform should also be assessed. From 11 December 2001, when China joined the WTO, a worldwide labour standard is certainly to be applied to her enterprises. On the one hand, this may put off some outside investors that in the past might have tried to take advantage of China's less strict labour/welfare standards, and this may slow down her overall economic growth rate somewhat. On the other hand, it may expedite the process of China's joining the world system by mapping out her socioeconomic system including welfare reform schemes.

In conclusion, this chapter has envisaged that China, like other areas and countries trying to promote social welfare, is confronting a series of challenges and dilemmas in her processes of reform. All are challenging the wisdom of China's decision makers. And the odd thing is that they have to solve the problem of SOEs inefficiency and the social welfare reform all at the same time.

It is, however, interesting to reiterate that even if the nature and levels of problem are different due to the divergent development stages and social structures of each country (see chapter 2 in this volume), when we compare China's social welfare reform experiences with those of other countries, issues embedded in the process of reform turn out to converge somewhat. Perhaps for a latecomer like China, there will be the advantage of learning from such forerunners to assist her own painstaking and still evolving processes of reform.

Notes

1   The author wishes to thank Professors Catherine Jones Finer and Jane Lewis for their valuable comments for revision of this paper since the occasion of the Workshop at St Antony's College Oxford on October 19–20 2001. Thanks must also be extended to Drs. Li-way Chang and Meng-ru Shen for their assistance on computer graphics. The author, nevertheless, bears sole responsibility for whatever shortcomings this paper may contain.
2   As of today, there are mainly four different types of enterprise in urban China: (1) State owned enterprises, (2) Collectively owned enterprises, (3) Individually owned

enterprises, and (4) Enterprises with other types of ownership such as joint ventures, shareholding corporations, foreign-funded enterprises and enterprises funded by residents from Hong Kong, Macao and Taiwan. In 1980, SOEs constituted 75.98 percent of China's total enterprises, it declined to 28.24 percent in 1998. In contrast, collectively owned enterprises' percentage as of the overall enterprises increased from that of 23.54 percent to 38.41 percent whereas individually owned and other types of enterprises' share in total enterprises grew dramatically from that of 0.49 percent to 40 percent for the same period, demonstrating the fact that along with economic reform, various types of ownership and managerial firms are flourishing.

3   Note that, in the Chinese context, 'red' in terms of ideological identity had often been regarded as more important than 'expertise' in management. In other words, as long as top managers were loyal to the communist ideology, it didn't matter whether the enterprise was running properly (making a profit) or not. Whereas, with the advent of reform, there were attempts to separate the two, by appointing someone to be the real manager in a modern sense, while perhaps keeping someone else still to oversee the purity of employees' thoughts in the SOEs.

4   In terms of the percentage share of SOEs in her gross output by industrial subsector, SOEs of China is indeed ubiquitous. They range from oil, tobacco, water supply, logging, coal, gas utilities, transportation machinery, chemicals, beverages, food processing, printing, textiles, rubber products, paper, lumber, metal products, plastic, leather, garments to furniture, etc.

References

Aaron, Henry J. (1998) 'The Chinese social insurance reform: personal security and economic growth', Paper presented at the International Symposium on establishing a market-oriented social security system in Beijing, China.

Chow, Nelson W.S. (2000), *Socialist Welfare with Chinese Characteristics: The Reform of the Social Security System in China,* Centre of Asian Studies, University of Hong Kong.

Chow, Nelson and Yuebin Xu (2001), *Socialist Welfare in a Market Economy,* Ashgate Aldershot.

Chow, Xiao-chun and Lin Wang (1994), 'Social protection: economic analysis and system suggestions', (I), (II), *Reform,* 5:17–28, and 6:64–78 (in Chinese).

Chu, Li (1994), 'Social protection system reform under market economy', *Sociological Studies,* 5:7–10 (in Chinese).

Feng, Tung-chien (1995), 'The process of reforming Chinese old-age insurance system'. Paper presented at the Contemporary Chinese Affairs: Taipei, Taiwan (in Chinese).

Ger, Yen-feng (1998), 'Social protection issues along reform and development processes' (I), (II), *Sociological Studies,* 1:98–110, and 9:93–100 (in Chinese).

Goodkind, Daniel, Truong Si Anh and Bui The Cuong (1998), 'Vietnam's old age security system: recent transformations and their implications for upcoming changes in China'. Paper presented at the International Symposium on establishing a market-oriented social security system in Beijing, China.

Kuo, Shi-tzn (1994a), 'Medical insurance and its international comparison', *Sociological Studies,* 3:106–12 (in Chinese).

Kuo, Shi-tzn (1994b), 'Old-age insurance system and its international comparison', *Sociological Studies,* 5:32–41 (in Chinese).

Kuo, Shi-tzn (1995), 'Social welfare and its international comparison', *Sociological Studies,* 2:67–78 (in Chinese).

Kuo, Shi-tzn (1996a), 'Some thoughts on how to promote old-age insurance policy', *Finance Studies*, 12:28–32 (in Chinese).
Kuo, Shi-tzn (1996b), 'On financing the old-age insurance system', *Economic Reform and Development*, 6:31–3, 38 (in Chinese).
Li, Jinyan (1998), 'Social security reform in China: a tax lawyer's perspective'. Paper presented at the International Symposium on establishing a market-oriented social security system in Beijing, China.
Li, Haizheng and Morozek, Janusz (1998), 'Financing a social security for China: who will pay?', Paper presented at the International symposium on establishing a market-oriented social security system in Beijing, China.
Li, Lulu, Wang, Fen-yu et al. (2001), *Urban Labour Mobility in China: Employment Model, Occupational Career and New Migrants*, Beijing Publishing Company, Beijing (in Chinese).
Li, Pei-lin, Chang, Yi and Chao, Yen-tung (2000), Employment and System Change: Job Searching Processes of Two Special Groups, Zhechiang People's Publishing Company, Hangzhou (in Chinese).
Sung, Xiao-wu (1998), 'On social protection system reform', *Modernization Studies*, 14, Foundation for Promoting Chinese Modernization, Taipei, Taiwan (in Chinese).
Tang, Chun (1998), 'The last social safety net: a framework of the minimum living protection system for Chinese urban residents', *Chinese Social Sciences*, 1:117–128 (in Chinese).
Work Bank (1994), *Averting the Old Age Crisis: Policies to Protect the Old and Promote Growth*, Oxford University Press, New York.
World Bank (1997a), *China 2020: Development Challenges in the New Century*, World Bank, Washington DC.
World Bank (1997b), *China 2020: Old Age Security: Pension Reform in China*, World Bank, Washington DC.
World Bank (1997c), *China 2020: Financing Health Care: Issues and Options for China*, World Bank, Washington DC.
West, Loraine A. (1998), 'Demographic underpinnings of China's old age pension reform'. Paper presented at the international symposium on establishing a market-oriented social security system in Beijing, China.
Yang, Ying (1993), 'Major reforms on Chinese social protection system'. Paper presented at the Workshop on National Development and Cross Strait Relations, Taipei, Taiwan (in Chinese).
Yan, Ying (1998), 'The pay-as-you-go pension vs. the private pension system – on China's social security reform'. Paper presented at the International symposium on establishing a market-oriented social security system in Beijing, China.
Yin, Jason Z. (1998), 'Social security management: Is privatisation better choice for China?' Paper presented at the International symposium on establishing a market-oriented social security system in Beijing, China.
Yuh, Shou-tung (1996), 'To construct an adequate social protection system with Chinese characteristics' *Economic Problems*, 5:2–7 (in Chinese).
Zheng, Gongcheng (1998), 'The rational choice of social security system in China'. Paper presented at the international symposium on establishing a market-oriented social security system in Beijing, China.

PART 2

POLICY SECTORS UNDER SCRUTINY

Chapter 6

Policies Geared to Tackling Social Inequality and Poverty in China

Xinping Guan

Introduction

Over the past two decades, one of the most significant socioeconomic trends in China has been mounting social inequality. Official statistics, scholars' researches and people's life experiences have shown that income distribution in this country has been shifting away from the traditional equal pattern to an increasingly unequal one. In recent years, more and more social researchers have focused on this issue, trying to find out the causes, mechanisms and possible consequences of this process.

As a result of the trend towards increasing inequality, poverty has become a serious social problem. Although there has been an economic boom lasting for about two decades, and average income has increased considerably, some groups are still in a lower income status and thus in a poor living condition. Since this poverty problem threatens political stability, both directly and indirectly, the government has paid a lot of attention to it in recent years, and various economic and social attempts have been made to solve this problem. Scholars have also been very active in this area. There have been numerous academic efforts to measure the economic and social gaps between groups, and to arrive at explanations for the extent of poverty in contemporary China.

Both social inequality and poverty have special meaning for social policy researchers. While many economists try to account for social inequality and poverty as being a consequence of economic system reform and rapid economic growth, social policy researchers have to respond to such questions as:

- How have the past two decades of social policy reform – i.e. reforms in such areas as social security, health policy, education, housing and personal services – contributed to issues of social inequality and poverty?
- How might these issues influence the further reform and development of social policy?
- How might we arrive at a 'good' social policy system, capable of solving problems of inequality and poverty in the future market economy in the context of globalization?

In this paper, we will outline and account for general trends in social inequality and poverty in China, discuss their possible influences on China's social policy, and analyse the Chinese government's responses to these issues so far.

Social Inequality

General Trends

Gini coefficient. Over the last two decades of the twentieth century China experienced a rapid increase in social inequality, along with its rapid economic growth. Just before this period, the Gini coefficient[1] was estimated as low as about 0.31 in 1978 (Li et al. 1995). According to most researchers in this field, however, the Gini coefficient, after about 20 years, is now estimated at about 0.45, higher than for most developed countries and many developing countries. The highest estimation is even 0.49 (S. Li 1998; Fan 1999, etc.). In the last decade, the scale of China's income inequality has been growing simultaneously in three directions: inequality between regions, rural-urban inequality, and inequality within rural and urban areas.

Inequality between regions. The big gap between regions within a country is the most significant phenomenon in China's social inequality, by contrast with other countries. In 1998, average income within the richest big city was 480 per cent of that in the poorest city, and the average income gap between farmers in the richest and poorest provinces was 440 per cent (Zhu and Ruan 1999). Another research finding has indicated that, whereas in 1980 the Gini coefficient for regional difference was just 0.14, by 1995 this figure had become 0.23, about 64 per cent higher (P. Zhang 1999) than in 1980.

Rural-urban inequality. Inequality between urban and rural residents is also very pronounced. According to one estimate, the rural-urban income gap was 260 per cent in 1998, even higher than the figure of 246 per cent for 1997. (Ru et al. 1999:11). Another estimate shows the 1998 figure to be as high as 371 per cent (Zhu and Ruan 1999).

Social inequality within rural and urban areas. Income inequality within urban and rural areas is also becoming more pronounced. According to some research, the Gini coefficient for rural residents in 1982 was about 0.22, but had grown to 0.41 by 1994. The Gini coefficient for urban residents was 0.19 in 1986, but had grown to 0.37 by 1994 (Li et al. 1995). These gaps have continued to grow in recent years, especially in the urban areas (see Table 6.1).

Table 6.1 Urban inequality 1990 and 1998

Year	Income ratio of the top 20% to the bottom	Income share of the bottom 20%	Income share of the top 20%	N
1990 (%)	420	9.0	38.1	1082
1998 (%)	960	5.5	52.3	2148

Source: Xu, Xinxin and Li, Peilin, '1998–1999: An analysis and forecast of China's employment, income and Information Industry' in Ru et al. (1999:35).

Explanations

Market transition: economic system reform. Many researchers believe that the rapid growth in income inequality is a product, to a large extent, of the economic system reform which began at the late 1970s, and especially of the rapid moves towards a market economy since 1992. In its early stages, however, the economic reform had not given rise to a big growth in income inequality. Because almost all kinds of labourers benefited from the reform and economic development, albeit to different degrees, the early reform did not result in such privatization and unemployment, and neo-liberal reforms had not extended to such areas as social welfare. The early reform even had a reverse effect on income distribution, especially before the mid-1980s, because some previous lower groups (e.g. farmers and urban non-state labourers) benefited more from it. Similar effects have been observed in other transitional countries in their early stages of reform (Sun 1995; Chen and Lu 1999; Guan 1999, etc.). However, nobody doubts the contribution of economic reform to the rapid widening of inequalities since 1992.

Marketization has had some important effects leading to an increase in inequality. First, it creates stronger competition in economic activity, and thus causes income differentiation between labourers. Second, it causes higher urban unemployment, because companies, including state companies, have perforce become profit-seeking organizations. Third, it causes structural changes in China's social stratification, with some new richer classes getting a much higher income from their control over property and management (Lu et al. 2001).

Globalization: the open-door policy. Until recently, most Chinese researchers focused on internal factors when trying to explain China's growing social inequality. Outside influences have been underestimated, or even neglected. Stimulated by China's entry into the WTO, however, some researchers are now turning their attention to these outside factors. Researchers here have found that the non-linear character of the growth in income inequality cannot be explained just by domestic economic system reform from the late 1970s. Trying to explain the rapid growth in the Gini coefficient in the 1990s, we find that it has paralleled the growing trend in China towards a foreign-orientated economy (Guan 2000, 2001; Ye 2001).

This foreign-oriented economic strategy, characterized by the enlargement of foreign trade and foreign investment, began from the early 1980s, but developed especially rapidly after 1992, as shown in Tables 6.2 and 6.3.

Table 6.2 Annual average foreign capital into China (billion US$)

Years	Total	Loan	Direct Investment	Others
1979–91	6.13	4.06	1.80	0.27
1992–98	46.75	10.63	34.61	1.52

Source: Calculated from the data in Chinese Statistic Yearbook (1999), Chinese Statistic Press.

Table 6.3 Annual average foreign trade (billion *yuan*)

Years	Total Foreign Trade		Export	
	Yuan	% of GDP	*Yuan*	% to DGP
1985–91	407.07	27.6	198.52	13.5
1992–98	2031.82	36.6	1082.91	19.5

Source: Calculated from the data in Chinese Statistic Yearbook (1999), Chinese Statistic Press.

The data in Tables 6.2 and 6.3 show this rapid increase in foreign trade and foreign investment after 1992, especially the tremendous increase (1,923 per cent) in direct foreign investment. Other data show that over the period 1989–1998, the extent of foreign-invested enterprises had increased 12 times, and the total employees they accounted for had increased 12.5 times. So far, up to mid-2000, there have been 353,704 foreign-invested enterprises in total, originating from 180 countries and regions. Contracted foreign investment has been US$641.7 billion, and actual foreign investment has been US$327.7 billion. From 1993, China has been the biggest foreign capital receiver among all the developing countries. Currently, about 400 of the 500 world biggest transnational corporations have enterprises based in China. Foreign-invested enterprises now account for almost one half of total international trade in China, and employ about 10 per cent of Chinese non-agricultural labourers (all the above figures from Zhan 2000; China News Agency 2000).

By making such a huge investment, transnational corporations and other international investors are in effect leading the Chinese economy into the globalized world economic system. At the same time, however, as a result of the foreign-oriented nature of this economic transition, China's income distribution and inequality has inevitably been affected more than ever by this globalization.

The effects of the foreign-oriented economy on income inequality in China can be summarized as follows:

- The unequal distribution of the foreign investment between different regions exacerbates differential economic growth rates, thus resulting in enhanced income gaps between regions.
- Entering into the globalized world economy, Chinese enterprises are bound to encounter more and more international competition in trade and international investment. To increase exports and attract more investment, China, like so many other developing countries, has to try to keep its labour cheap. At the same time, to reinforce its competitiveness in the sphere of high-tech economics, the Chinese government and Chinese companies are bound to pay 'international prices' when competing with developed countries for higher-educated people. Such a 'dual-competition' feature of China's international competition strategy has had a fundamental impact on its inequality parameters, and will have even more effect after entry into the WTO.

Political and ideological factors. Both academic researchers and the ordinary public have observed that political power can play a role in enlarging income inequality. In the current political system, the groups within or close to political power can find it easier to have economic privilege, legally or illegally, whereas powerless groups are liable to gain much less from the economic transition process. The government hopes to rein in this trend via some stronger disciplinary measures to control bribery and other abuses of power. But the bribery of officials and its impact on social inequality is still seen a big problem by researchers and public opinion.

A fresh political issue related to inequality is the government's attitude towards the private economy. For most of the previous half century, private economy was unacceptable politically and ideologically in this socialist society. After the reform, however, the private economy has, step by step, secured economic and political room to develop. Now, the private sector has been authorized politically, and even the owners and executives of private business are allowed to join the Communist Party. Under this policy, the private sector looks to have a favorable political environment, and should thus be developing fast as a result. Officials tend more to emphasize the private sector's contribution to the high economic growth rate, rather than to discuss its negative aspects. In academic circles, so far, there are few researchers to be seen pronouncing in public about this policy's negative effects with regard to social inequality.

In the three decades prior to reform, egalitarianism was dominant in China. It was seen as the significant characteristic of a socialist society. But from the early stages of the reform, this so-called 'extreme egalitarianism' was officially criticized. It is now an official principle of policy making that economic efficiency should take precedence over equity. In the past two decades, it is this latter principle, and the government's changed attitude towards egalitarianism, which have been accepted to a large extent by the public. However, there have been some reverse trends in public opinion in recent years, as inequality has been seen to go too far.

Poverty

Related to social inequality, the poverty problem is currently another 'hot topic' among scholars and the public. Because of China's 'dual system', i.e. the huge gap between the rural and the urban economy and society, the concept of poverty has quite different meanings when applied to rural and urban societies.

Rural Poverty

General trends. In the first three decades of the People's Republic, rural poverty was not seen as a big problem because income was fairly equal among farmers, although as whole they were comparatively poor. As a result of the 'family responsibility system', which characterized the first round of rural economic reform beginning from the late 1970s, most of the former poor villages and farmers had become better off, and thus the rest were seen as being in poverty. In the mid-1980s, it was estimated that there were about 125 million farmers in poverty, who were unable to become better off by their own efforts. Assistance from the outside was badly needed.

From the mid-1980s, a big anti-poverty programme began in rural areas, which had two significant features:

- targeting regional poverty, i.e. aiming to increase regional economic growth, rather than helping individual poor families directly;
- strengthening poor farmers' economic capability by investing in infrastructure and providing loans in support of their economic activity, instead of just providing social relief.

As a result of governmental efforts in the 'first-round' anti-poverty programme of 1986–1992, in which about 400 million *yuan* was put into the poverty regions per year, the number of poor villagers had been reduced to 70 million by 1992. From 1993, a new round of anti-poverty strategy began, aimed at eliminating all absolute poverty in China before the end of the twentieth century. While the above-mentioned features were still adhered to, there were also some new emphases in this latter round which lasted for eight years, including:

- More financial resources were made available: over 25 billion *yuan* were provided by governments per year for economic development and poverty relief in the poverty regions (Gao Hongbin 2001).
- Financial assistance was extended to remote poor villages and poor families, even while most government financial resources were still being invested intensively in 'growth poles' and in public projects;
- More social projects, mainly in basic education, were included – by comparison with the first round – although the number was still insufficient to meet the needs in education development.

By the end of 1999, the government declared that the goal of eliminating absolute poverty had been basically reached. In reality, this official goal had only been partly reached, because there were still about 37 million farmers in poverty according to China's official rural poverty line (annual income 600-800 *yuan* per capita). It is estimated that, if measured by international standards, i.e. US$1 per capita per day, there would be more than 150 million people in poverty (S.Wang 1999). The poorest were the farmers in the remote villages, mainly in the western provinces, where natural conditions are extremely bad, and the economic and social infrastructures are so lacking that farmers are not able to become better off by themselves without assistance from the outside.

Current problems and policies. Although the Chinese government's anti-poverty strategy of the 1990s was successful to a large extent, there remain serious problems in the rural poverty regions. The following are the most serious:

- Although most farmers have an income over the subsistence level, their income is still quite unstable. If government assistance should stop, many of them are highly likely to fall into poverty again.
- Social services – especially education and health services – are quite poor in most of the poverty villages.

To solve these problems and enlarge the 'fruits' of the anti-poverty strategy of the 1990s, the government has launched a new round of 10-year anti-poverty action (2001–2010) from mid-2001. As far as this policy is concerned, the new action is basically to follow on from that of the 1990s, except that the new round also has the following three features:

- Central government's financial resources will be concentrated more in the mid and western provinces, and more targeted on the poverty counties, which are fewer in number, but poorer in economic condition.
- Financial assistance will be further concentrated on productive projects, at both community and family level, and still less on simple living allowances.
- Social projects, i.e. education and health services, are to receive greater emphasis.

Urban Poverty

General trends. Urban poverty is a new topic in China, by comparison with rural poverty. Before the reform, most urban residents were quite equal in income. Besides, thanks to the full employment policy, which was seen as one of the basic features of the 'socialist planned economic system', the unemployment rate was very low.[2] However, after the reform, especially since the mid-1990s, urban poverty has become a serious problem.

There have been many estimates of urban poverty rates in recent years, ranging from 5 per cent up to more than 15 per cent, according to varying standards (absolute vs. relative) and modes of measurement (Guan 1999). But so far the official poverty lines, which are based on certain 'operational measurements' – i.e. the standards adopted for official poverty relief programmes – are still very low. So far, the lowest poverty rate estimate offered by poverty researchers is 5 per cent, but in nearly all cities government poverty rates for the social assistance project, e.g. the MLS, are less than that. Besides, only urban residents with urban household registration are included in such a measurement in the current poverty studies. The so-called 'floating people', who are working and living in cities and towns without permanent urban household registration, are not included. If this big lower-income group of about 80–100 million were included, the urban poverty rate would be much higher.

Explanations. Urban poverty is more complex to account for than rural poverty. Briefly, the growing urban poverty rate is to be accounted for by reference to a series of economic and social factors:

(a) Economic factors: Basically, most urban poor families are poor because of their main member's (mainly the husband's) unemployment or low income. As a result of the transition to a market economy and the open-door policy, many urban enterprises have encountered strong competition from two quarters: newly developing foreign-invested companies and rural industry. Some less-efficient urban enterprises, mainly state- and collectively-owned, have thus fallen into bankruptcy. Those not so far bankrupted, have had to increase efficiency and reinforce competitiveness by cutting down on their payrolls of redundant employees, in order to survive in the face of stronger market competition.

There are two kinds of unemployment in China's urban economy. The first one is registered unemployment, including those who are fired completely by their employers, who then register with the government unemployment services. (Some of these can get benefits from the official unemployment insurance programme.) This kind of 'official unemployment rate' is quite low, i.e. below 3.5 per cent in the 1990s. However, there is another kind of unemployment called 'laid-off workers', which means that the workers have lost their jobs, but are still members of their enterprises, and so still have rights to some living subsidy and welfare benefits from their employers. Due to its complexity and constantly changing nature, there are no accurate official statistics available on this laid-off rate at the national level. Nevertheless, according to official sources (National Statistic Bureau 2000), the total number of laid-off workers was 6.5 million at the end of 1999. Up to the end of 1999, according to some researchers, the accumulated number of laid-off workers was about 20 million, of whom about 7 million had not then been re-employed (Yang and Wang 2001). However, the actual number of the laid-off may be underestimated by official statistics, because many workers who were not registered in the 're-employment service centres' were not officially counted in. Put the two kinds of unemployment together, i.e. the laid-off and the registered unemployed, and actual urban unemployment rates should be roughly 5–8 per cent over recent years.

(b) Social factors: Social factors related to growing urban poverty include the decline of social security benefits and other social services in urban areas. As a result of the moves to reform social security, government has abandoned its previous full responsibility for guaranteeing stable employment, pensions and health services for state workers. Although some new patterns of social insurance have been designed to replace the old arrangements for pensions and the health service, employees now have to share with their employers to pay for the social insurance programmes. For many less-prosperous enterprises, such additional costs will be making their business more difficult, and some employers are even refusing to pay for such insurance, with the result that some retirees cannot get pension benefits. More seriously, since many cities' municipal governments have not yet implemented the new medical insurance programme, designed by central government in 1998, many employees cannot have their medical bills reimbursed, and actually have to pay by themselves for the ever-higher medical costs caused by the ever-increasing prices of medicine and hospital services. In this situation, medical cost is a significant factor causing some people in low-income groups to fall into actual poverty. A similar situation is also true of housing, education and other public and personal services, which were traditionally welfare services, but which have now become, to varying extents, commercial or semi-commercial services.

General features of urban poverty. According to some researchers, the current population of the urban poor includes three sub-groups. The first group is the traditional 'three Nos', those who have no income, no working ability (e.g. the disabled or the elderly) and no family support. This type of poor people is seen as the traditional urban poor, because they have been treated as the urban poor and have received governmental social relief since the early stages of the urban social assistance system in the 1950s. The second group includes those who are poor because they do not have stable jobs, have been on low incomes for a long time, or have more dependent family members. They are usually in chronic poverty. The third group is called 'new urban poor', which includes the urban unemployed and laid-off workers, and low-income workers in state and collective enterprises. These can lose their jobs or salaries as a result of the reform of urban enterprises, leading to bankruptcy or the laying-off of workers.

Of the three groups, the first is the traditional urban poor of Chinese cities and towns. The second group was regarded as urban poor until quite recently, although these kinds of difficult people have existed for a long time. The third one is the new group in urban China: resulting from urban economic reform and the economic transition from a centrally planned to a market economy and from a closed economy to an open one. It is this last group which has been the biggest in recent years. According to research carried out in Wuhan, a big city in central China, this 'new urban poverty' accounts for about two-thirds (64.2 per cent) of all urban poor people, defined in terms of the beneficiaries of the Minimal Living Security (MLS), in 1997 (Poverty Study Team of Wuhan University 1999) That means that the current urban poverty problem in China can, to a large extent, be attributed to the economic reform and transition process.

As a result of this increase in the 'new urban poor', urban poverty, taken as a whole, has some new characteristics. First of all, urban poor people are a fluctuating population. Most of them, especially the able-bodied workers, fall into poverty just because of some temporary disadvantage, such as being laid-off or having their salary reduced. Most of them, though losing job opportunity temporarily, still keep their motivation for work, and thus may easily become better-off within a short time, once they get a new job or their enterprise recovers profitability. Nevertheless, according to official statistics, laid-off workers totalled 6.57 million at the end of 2001, by comparison with 6.25 million in 1999 (National Statistic Bureau and National Commission of Planning and Development 2001).

Anti-poverty policies. Anti-poverty action in urban China began in the early 1990s, in the areas of employment services, social insurance and social assistance.

(a) Employment services: Although the traditional governmental policy of assigning all urban labourers a job (in the centrally planned period) was abolished in the1980s, the government still has a policy of helping urban labourers, especially laid-off workers, to get new jobs in the labour market by providing services for job seekers. There are various programmes in operation in cities and towns, but these are more often undertaken by local government. They include: creating more job centres in urban areas and investing in the information system; providing training programmes for laid-off workers; encouraging those laid-off to accept informal employment, including self-employment and working in 'community services'. However, achievements are still limited, especially in respect of providing training programmes for laid-off workers. Although re-employment rates are higher in cities with a booming economy – mainly as a result of their higher economic growth rates – laid-off workers are still very difficult to place in employment in most other cities.

(b) Three 'security lines': To alleviate urban poverty, certain social security projects have been established, of which the three 'basic security lines' – unemployment insurance, living allowances for laid-off workers and the Minimal Living Security System – are the most important.

Unemployment insurance: Beginning in the late 1980s, this project is to provide benefits to the registered urban unemployed person. Based on contributions from both the employers and the employees, the unemployed – once registered in a social insurance agency – can get unemployment benefit for as long as 3 to 24 months, according to the number of years he/she has paid insurance contributions. However, since most urban job losers do not choose to be registered as unemployed, the official 'registered unemployment' rate is quite low (see above), and the actual coverage so far remains small.

Living allowance for laid-off workers: This is a temporary benefit for laid-off workers, mainly of state enterprises. After being laid off, the workers are organized into 're-employment service centres', which help them secure new jobs by providing job information and training, and also by providing them with a basic living allowance. However, because the enterprises are required to share the costs for this allowance, some badly placed enterprises find it impossible to contribute to a 're-employment service centre', or hesitate to provide all their laid-off workers with the living allowance. According to official statistics, about 95 per cent of laid-off workers entered into the re-employment centers, of whom about 95 per cent received a living allowance, averaging 323 *yuan* per month, in the first half of 2000. (Z. Lu 2000). But according to some researchers and reporters, the actual beneficiaries are far fewer than official statistics would suggest. According to a recent report of the Xinhua News Agency, some laid-off workers in a city in Anhui Province could only get 100 *yuan* per month, much less than the local official standard of 207 *yuan* (Huang and Zhou 2002).

Minimal Living Security (MLS): Because the old urban relief programme could not deal with the enlarging poverty problem due to its very narrow coverage, the new programme of MLS was designed to replace it. Whereas the old social relief programme had just covered the 'Three Nos', the new MLS is to provide cash benefits for all those households with urban resident registration whose per capita income fell below a certain standard. Pioneered in just some big cities, such as Shanghai, in the early 1990s, this new anti-poverty programme had been established in almost all cities before the end of 1998. It is so far the most stable anti-poverty programme, targeted directly at the urban poorest. Yet, because it was until recently financially supported by local (municipal and district) governments, the coverage was very small, and many urban poor were still not getting benefits by the end of 2000 (In 2000, the national average coverage was just about 1 per cent of all the urban residents). In 2001, thanks to the participation of the central government, the number of beneficiaries increased rapidly. Up until October 2001, the beneficiaries numbered 7.15 million (about 2 per cent of the total urban residents) and this number may have reached 11.89 million by the end of 2001. In the first 10 months of 2000, total government expenditure on the MLS was about 3.2 billion *yuan*. The government plans to enlarge the coverage of the urban MLS to about 15 million, or about 5 per cent of the urban population by the end of 2002 (Social Relief Section of the Civil Affairs Ministry 2001).

Although it would be a big achievement if this goal could be reached, there remains another problem to be resolved, namely the lower benefits level. Currently, the average standard for all the cities' MLS lines is just 146 *yuan* per capita, and in the first 10 months of 2001, the national average monthly benefit was just 66 *yuan* per capita (Social Relief Section of the Civil Affairs Ministry 2001).[3] Moreover, no plan has so far been reported to raise MLS standards in China's cities. Without a rise in the MLS criteria and an increase in average benefit levels, the MLS cannot do much to help poor people out of poverty. It can only provide basic living standards to its beneficiaries, i.e. basic food and clothes. Their needs in education, medical care and other departments, will continue to go unmet.

New Developments and Problems in Recent Years, in Response to both Inequality and Poverty

As social inequality has been getting more serious and the poverty rate has been increasing, the Chinese public has begun to object to there being any further increases in either inequality or poverty. Given this situation, the government has had to make some changes in its economic and social policies from the late 1990s, including:

- Reinforcing the anti-poverty strategy in both rural and urban areas. In rural areas, the government programme has been increased to a large extent. In 1999, for example, central government's financial support to the poverty regions was increased to 24.8 billion *yuan*, much higher than that for the 1980s and early 1990s. In urban areas, the government has made a great effort to secure all the laid-off workers' basic income maintenance. At the same time, as required by central government, most cities have enlarged their social assistance coverage and their average payments to the urban poor in 1999.
- Launching the 'Great Development in the Western Part' strategy, which means more attention being paid to poorer western provinces. One of the important aims of this strategy is to narrow the economic gap between the western and eastern parts of this country. However, since the relevant policy details are still in the process of formulation, it is too early to foretell how many benefits are likely to be shared by the west's people in the coming 'great development' strategy.
- Loosing the control over the urban household registration system, and allowing more rural labour to enter into cities and towns. Without doubt, this change will help to reduce the big gap between rural and urban residents.

Yet despite the above-mentioned changes, the basic principle of social policy remains unchanged. In short, policy making is still shaped by the aims of economic efficiency and political stability, rather than the goal of social equity and equality. The government's hesitation to accept social equity as the first foundation of its social policy arises mainly from its worry about the possible harmfulness to China's economic competitiveness in the international market.

Possible Challenges Facing Chinese Social Policy after Entry into the WTO

China is now to enter the WTO, and some Chinese scholars have begun to pay attention to the social implications of this move. The importance for social life of entering into the WTO seems, if anything, more complicated than that for economic life. A detailed analysis would require more empirical data, but some general issues can be identified, as shown below.

Social Inequality in China

Although there will be quite a lot of uncertain factors about Chinese economic development which may have a bearing on social inequality after entry into the WTO, the 'dual-competition' feature of China's international competition strategy will have a fundamental impact on its inequality prospects. As the biggest developing country, China's economic competition with other countries will become stronger simultaneously in two directions after entry into the WTO. One direction will be to compete with developed countries in high-tech industries. This is actually a competition for highly educated professionals, which involves providing them with ever-higher incomes. As such, it involves a 'race to the top'. However, the other competition will be with other developing countries in the international market for a larger share of international investment and trade in labour-intensive industries. To win this competition, both China's own labour-intensive industries and those of its international competitors will be striving to keep labour costs down. This, therefore, could be a 'race to the bottom'. As a result of stronger competition in both these directions, an increase in social inequality would seem inevitable, so long as no more measures of social protection are implemented in the future.

Further Basic Problems for China's Social Policy

First of all, China's social policy after entering into the WTO will depend on the government's ability to balance its policies in two directions at the same time: to accelerate economic growth and to maintain social stability. The government will face challenges, however, in both these directions after entry into the WTO.

On the one hand, China will be involved in fiercer international economic competition. Considering its ambitious economic strategy to catch up with the developed countries, maintaining a high level of economic efficiency will be a first consideration of government. As a result, social justice may be consigned to a secondary position for some time. Even if government social policy were to be based merely on considerations of social stability rather than social justice, the intensity of pressure from international economic competition may, even so, not allow it enough room to balance its economic and social goals.

On the other hand, as a result of increased social inequality, there may well be a stronger negative response to 'liberal reform' on the part of ordinary people, especially the worst-off groups. In this context, the possibilities for further reform of the social welfare system will depend on the government's ability to maintain effective social control. Yet, considering this country's socialist and egalitarian traditions, the short-term room for manoeuvre may not be large.

Meanwhile, China's social policy, although still regarded as a domestic concern of the government, will be more subject to international intervention. Such intervention may come in two varieties: ideological influences from other countries, and international concerns for 'fair competition' in the economic marketplace. Since any changes in social policy may have an effect on the economic environment, these traditional 'domestic affairs' are liable to become more of a focus for international attention in this era of globalization.

The Need to Establish a Basic Standard for Social Protection among Developing Countries

Since the decline of social welfare in both developed and developing countries has been caused, to a large extent, by these countries' ever-closer international interaction in a globalized world economy, any effort to improve social welfare could not succeed if taken merely as a 'domestic action' by single countries. Some attempts at international action have already been proposed by scholars and governments in developed countries. But such proposals have so far been refused by the developing countries. Thus fierce debates have continued for years between developed and developing countries over these issues, amongst which the most important issue has to be the dispute over the issue of the 'Labour Standard' in the WTO.

Developed countries' efforts to force developing countries to accept a basic labour standard, by linking this to international trade requirements, has so far been seen as a protectionist device and thus been rejected by the latter. Most, if not all, developing countries consider that accepting the Labour Standard will raise their labour costs and thus reduce their economic competitiveness with developed countries. The developing countries' attitude towards the Labour Standard rests on the basic idea that, since developed countries and developing countries are competitors in a globalizing world economy, the latter have to hang on to the relative cheapness of their labour forces as being one of their few comparative advantages in the global competition. Nevertheless, there may be different ways of solving this problem, by reconsidering the dynamics of the developing countries' international competition.

In the globalizing world economy, there are two kinds of international competition open to the developing countries. One is that with the developed countries in the high-tech economic sectors, which can be called 'longitudinal competition'; another is that among other developing countries, mainly in their labour-intensive sectors, which can be called 'latitudinal competition'. For a developing country, the longitudinal competition takes place mainly in its high-tech sectors. Actually, in the high-tech sector 'cheap labour' is by no means an advantage. It is rather a disadvantage because it will cause 'brain drain', and thus weaken competitiveness. For a developing country, therefore, labour costs are meaningful for competitiveness only with regard to latitudinal competition; i.e. in the competition with other developing countries, this being mainly in the labour-intensive sectors.

In the labour-intensive sectors, furthermore, although having cheaper labour might strengthen competitiveness in a single country, it could nevertheless fuel a 'race to the bottom' competition so long as many developing countries are pursuing the same approach. All developing countries will thus be losers in this 'zero-sum game', and the only winners will be the transnational corporations and other international investors. Briefly, globalization pushes the developing countries into a situation of 'prisoner's dilemma', in which any country's attempt to keep its labour cheaper by reducing social protection may be followed by other countries. In consequence, the labour forces of all the countries are liable to be harmed, with no country gaining an advantage in the international competition.

Nevertheless, in this situation no single developing country is in a position to insist on a high level of social protection for itself, or even to keep its previous social welfare arrangements unchanged when others are cutting down on welfare provision. Thus the only way to escape from this dilemma is to set up a basic social welfare standard and international coordination mechanism in social protection among the developing countries to counter such a 'race to the bottom' competition.

In short, when we shift focus from 'the longitudinal competition between developed and developing countries' to 'the latitudinal competition among developing countries', a regional, or even worldwide standard of social protection becomes meaningful for developing countries. Only by means of some such joint effort can developing countries retain adequate means of social protection while maintaining, or even strengthening, their economic competitiveness *vis-a-vis* developed countries.

This approach may help the Chinese government to escape the 'social protection dilemma' associated with entry into the WTO. It may be especially meaningful for China as the largest developing country because, by the same token, China should be able to wield important influence in support of there being a system of international cooperation in social protection. After all, China is a socialist country and should play a leading role in propelling international social efforts towards social protection in the interests of workers.

Notes

1. After the early 1990s, more Chinese social researchers tend to apply the Gini coefficient to measure the extent of income inequality, which ranges from 0 to 1 from the absolute equal to totally unequal, and it is universally accepted that a society will be seen as quite unequal when the Gini coefficient is above 0.4.
2. Actually, there was no 'unemployment rate' in China's official statistics before the early 1990s.
3. The amount a beneficiary is paid by the MLS is between his/her existing family income and the MLS standard. For example, in a city with a MLS standard of 200 Yuan p.c., a family of three with a total family income of 500 Yuan will just get another 100 Yuan paid by the MLS.

References

Bai, Shuqiang (2000), *Global Competition*, China Social Science Press.
Chen, Zhao and Lu, Ming (1999), 'The enlarging income inequality: An international comparative analysis', *World Economic Studies*, 3.
Chen Zhaofang (1999), 'Economic globalization's development and the impact on developing Countries', *Wuhan University Academic Journal*, 4.

Chen, Jian (2000), 'International trade and labour standard: A discussion of focus issues in the WTO', *International Trade*, 6.
Cheng, Yan (1999), 'Economic globalization and the changing perspectives', *World Economy and Politics*, 6.
China News Agency (2000), 'China Has Utilized Foreign Capital More than US$320 Billion in the Past 20 Years', from the web-page of china.com, 8 September 2000 [http://finance.china.com/zh.cn/news/4/20000908/244756.htm].
Deacon, Bob, with Michelle Hulse and Paul Stubbs (1997), *Global Social Policy: International Organizations and the Future of Welfare*, Sage, London.
Ding, Yifan (2000), *Great Waves: Economic Globalization and the Challenge to China*, China Development Press.
Duoji, Cairang (2001), *The Researches and Practices of China's Minimal Living Security Systems*, People's Press.
Fan, Xinmin (1999), 'A review of China's urban inequality studies', *Social Studies*, 3.
Fu, Zhengping (1999), 'A comparative analysis of advantage in competitions', *International Trade*, 8.
Gao Hongbin (2001), 'China's anti-poverty and development programmes: focus on the west and middle regions', reported by Xinhua News Agency (Reporter: Dong, Jun), 19 June.
Guan, Xinping (1999), *Urban Poverty in China*, Hunan People's Press.
Guan, Xinping (2000), 'China's social policy: reform and development in the context of marketization and globalization', *Social Policy and Administration*, 34, 1.
Guan, Xinping (2001), 'Globalization, inequality and social policy: social protection in China on the threshold into the WTO', *Social Policy and Administration*, 35, 2.
Guo, Liancheng (2000), 'An analysis of economic globalization's positive and negative effects', *World Economics and Politics*, 8.
Huang, Fanzhang (2000), 'Several viewpoints about economic globalization', *World Economics and Politics*, 10.
Huang, Quanquan and Zhou, Limin (Xinhua News Agency) (2002), 'Security is just a book value', 13 January.
Jiang Shixue (2000), 'Economic globalization's impacts on the developing countries', *World Economic Studies*, 4.
Lei Da and Yu, Chunhai (2000), 'An institutional analysis of economic globalization', *World Economics*, 4.
Lenski, Gerhard (1984), *Power and Privilege: A Theory of Social Stratification*, University of North Carolina Press, Chapel Hill.
Li Benhe (2000), 'Globalization's multiple impacts and China's countermeasures', *World Economics and Politics*, 1.
Li, Kunwang and Liu, Zhongli (2000), *Economic Globalization: Process, Trends and Countermeasures*, Economic Science Press.
Li, Peilin (ed.) (1995), *Social Stratification in the Market Transition in China*, Liaoning People's Press.
Li, Qiang (1993), *Social Stratification and Mobility in Contemporary China*, China Economics Press.
Li, Qiang, Hong, Dayong and Song, Shige (1995), 'Analysis on Income Gap of China's Social Groups', *Science and Technology Review*, 11.
Li, Shi (1998), 'China's economic transition and changes in income distribution', *Economic Research*, 4.
Li, Xuczcng, and Cheng, Xuebin (1997), 'A quantitative analysis of the interest gaps among Chinese urban social strata', *Chinese Social Sciences*, 6.
Li, Yining (2000), 'Globalization and China's economy', *World Economics and Politics*, 6.
Li, Zhuo (2000), 'The international coordination for competition policy', *Economics Review*, 2.

Lin, Yifu, Cai, Fanf and Li, Zhou (1999), 'Comparative advantage and developing strategy', *China Social Sciences*, 5.
Liu, Ding (1999), 'The core elements of economic globalization and its impacts on employment', *Southern Economics*, 11, 12.
Liu, Minghui, and Chen, Junhui (1998), *Social Security Theories and its Reform Practices*, Northeast Finance and Economic University Press.
Liu, Ruizhong and Zhang, Xinhua (1989), 'China: a welfare state with low income', *China: Development and Reform*, 6.
Lu, Aiguo (2000), 'Globalization and capitalist world economy: a review of the economic globalization studies', *World Economics*, 5.
Lu, Tong (2000), 'Conflicts in the process of economic globalization: from the Seattle conference', *World Economics and Politics*, 2.
Lu, Xueyi, et al. (2001), *An Analysis of Social Strata in Contemporary China*, Social Science Literature Press.
Lu, Zuxian (2000), 'The average living allowance for the laid-off workers in state enterprises increased to 323 yuan per month', *Guangming Daily*, 1 September.
Massey, A. (1997), *Globalization and Marketization of Government Services*, Macmillan Press, London.
Mu, Huaizhong (1998), *Studies on the Proper Level of Social Security in China*, Liaoning University Press.
Mu, Jifeng, Feng, Zongxian and Guo Genlong (2000), 'Fiscal and tax policies and public expenditure in the context of globalization', *World Economics*, 5.
National Statistic Bureau, (2000) *Statistic Bulletin of Economic and Social Development in the People's Republic of China – 1999*, 28 February.
National Statistic Bureau and National Commission of Planning and Development (2001), *Statistic Bulletin of China Labour and Social Security – 2000*, April.
Poverty Study Team of Wuhan University (1999), 'Urban poverty and anti-poverty policies: Wuhan's case', *Economic Review*, 4.
Research Group in the Institute of Foreign Economic Studies (2000), 'Economic globalization's five challenges to Chinese government', *References in Economic Studies*, 86.
Ru, Xin, et al. (eds), (1999), *China in 1999: Analysis and Forecast of Social Situation*, Social Science Literature Press.
Social Relief Section of the Civil Affairs Ministry (2001), *Current Situation of the Urban Minimal Living Security*, Workshop Paper, 15 November.
Sun, Liping (1995), 'The new development in foreign sociology on market transition and income distribution', in Li, Peilin (ed.), *Social Stratification in the Market Transition in China*, Liaoning People's Press.
Swaan, A. (1994) *Social Policy beyond Borders*, Amsterdam University Press, Amsterdam.
Tian, Xiaoxia and Tao, Ranfeng (2000), 'A theoretic review of the explanations of capital's outflow', *Economics Information*, 1.
Townsend, Peter, with Donker, Kwabena (1996), *Global Restructuring and Social Policy*, Policy Press, Bristol.
Wang, Lie (ed.) (1998), *Globalization and World*, Central Compilation and Translation Press.
Wang, Ping (2000), 'Globalization's impacts on Latin American economy', *Latin America Studies*, 1.
Wang, Shaoguang (1999), 'The challenge of inequality', *Management World*, 4.
Wang, Xuexiu (1997), 'The debates on labour standards', *International Trade*, 3.
Wang, Yi (2000), 'Globalization and governments in developing countries', *Open Door Review*, 9.
Wang, Zixian (2000), 'Guided by competition advantage', *International Trade*, 1.
Xiong, Yuegen (1999), 'The relationships between state, market and welfare: rethinking Western social policy theories development', *Sociological Studies*, 3.

Xu, Dianqing, et al. (eds), (1999), *Social Security Reform in China*, Economic Science Press.
Yang, Gang and Wang, Lijuan (2001), 'New century and new poverty: urban poverty in China', *Economic Reform*, 1.
Ye, Rong (2001), 'The open-door policy and income inequality', *Shan'xi Statistics*, 2.
You, Hongbing (1998), *A Study of Income Inequality in China*, China Economics Press.
Yu, Keping (ed.), (1998), *Socialism in the Global Age*, Central Compilation and Translation Press.
Zhan, Yi (2000), 'Foreign-invested enterprises contribute one half of China's foreign trade', *Guangming Daily*, 4 February.
Zhang, Hanlin and Liu Guangxi (1999), *Economic Globalization, WTO and China*, Beijing University Press.
Zhang, Jikang (2000), 'The internationalized industries in the economic globalization and their unbalanced development', *World Economics and Politics*, 5.
Zhang, Ping (1999), *The regional inequality among the farmers and their non-agricultural employment*, Economic Research, University of Chicago Press.
Zhang Shi Peng and Yin Xuyi (1998), *Capitalism in the Globalization Era*, Central Compilation and Translation Press.
Zhang, Youwen (2000), 'Entering into WTO and China's globalizing development strategy', *World Economic Studies*, 5.
Zhang Ziangchen (2000), *The Politic and Economic Relations between Developing Countries and WTO*, Law Press.
Zhao, Haili (1999), 'A comparative study of public expenditure in welfare between China and other countries', *Financial and Economic Studies*, 11.
Zhu, Xinwu and Ruan, Dawei (1999), 'The big income inequality and its negative impacts on China's economic development', *Statistic Research*, 10.

Chapter 7
Reflections on Inequality and Poverty in China

David Piachaud

China and the United Kingdom have much in common. Both have governments that are, at least in some vestigial sense, socialist in their goals. In both countries there has over the last two decades been substantial economic liberalization. Both have a long-standing and continuing concern with inequality and poverty. There are of course huge differences. China with a population of over one billion is huge compared with the United Kingdom. Income levels in Britain are on average far above those in China. While China remains a predominantly rural, agricultural economy, Britain is urbanized and post-industrial with services accounting for more employment than manufacturing and agriculture being only a tiny part of employment and output.

With the new Labour government elected in 1997 there has been a renewed interest in poverty and inequality. The divisive years of harsh economic liberalism under Mrs Thatcher's Conservative government have been replaced by a concern with social justice and extending opportunities to all segments of society. Most specifically, Prime Minister Blair set out the target of abolishing child poverty in a generation and policies to achieve this are on course; both selective and universal benefits have been increased, in-work benefits have been increased to encourage the move from welfare dependence into paid work, and causes of long-term poverty such as teenage pregnancy and poor education have been tackled.

In this context, the renewed British concern with poverty and inequality has a number of features of particular significance:

- First, poverty is clearly being defined in relative terms as being below a proportion of average income level – half of mean income or 60 percent of median income being the most commonly used definitions.
- Second, there is increasing attention to the dynamics of poverty based on long-term longitudinal data. Persistent poverty is a more serious policy concern than short spells of low income.
- Third, there is growing recognition of the inter-relationship of social problems. Poverty is associated with poor education, poor health, worklessness, poor physical environment and many other features of social disadvantage; at the same time poor education, poor health and worklessness contribute to poverty. Improving opportunities is not therefore a simple thing requiring only one policy instrument; it requires wide-ranging changes.
- Fourth, there is acceptance of the need to promote social investment and that this

should have priority over cutting taxes. This contrasts with the Thatcher years when the scale of the public services was seen as a major problem.
- Fifth, there is a shift of emphasis from alleviating poverty to trying to prevent poverty. Tackling child poverty both alleviates and prevents poverty since the experience of child poverty makes later poverty in adulthood much more likely.

Yet despite (or perhaps because of) the number of policy initiatives, there remains considerable confusion about the goals of policy. How far should poverty be given priority over tackling inequality? Is the objective to increase equality of outcomes or equality of opportunity? These are questions to which there are no consistent answers.

Many of the questions facing policy makers and policy analysts in the United Kingdom are similar in nature, if different in scale, to those that arise in China.

The rest of this chapter focuses on the evidence, discussion and policy issues raised in Xinping Guan's important and stimulating chapter on 'Policies Geared to Tackling Social Inequality and Poverty in China' in this volume.

The Measurement of Poverty and Inequality

Guan argues that 'the concept of poverty has quite different meanings when applied to rural and urban societies' (above, page 75). This is at the same time true and misleading. It is true that prevailing and expected standards are very different in rural and urban societies. It is misleading in that rural and urban societies cannot be separated in a clear, distinct way. Most obviously, people move from rural to urban areas and some move back again. There are also important transfers of resources which make comparisons between the two types of society difficult to make. Second, there is not a clear-cut division: there are small urban areas and big villages in rural areas, so that no precise dividing line is possible. Third, and perhaps most importantly, there is increasing communication across and about different areas. In an increasingly global world, there is growing knowledge even in the remotest villages about what is happening in distant cities and far-off countries. With cheaper travel and the electronic media it is harder to separate rural and urban societies. Expectations and standards may differ between rural and urban societies but as economic development occurs these differences are likely to diminish. Concepts of poverty that can apply across the whole of China, indeed across the world, are more and more necessary.

In measuring urban poverty the exclusion of those without urban household registration raises a real problem. The estimate of 80–100 million 'floating people' is a huge number to exclude in counting poverty. Because of the advantages associated with urban registration, such as access to services and housing, these floating people represent a serious and a new form of poverty.

The evidence for the growth of inequality that is presented by Guan is based on changes in Gini coefficients – a measure of how far the distribution of incomes differs from total equality. However, in Britain, comparisons between Gini coefficients has made clear how sensitive this measure is to the definition of income used. First, there is the question of the income unit used: the more extended the unit, the less will be the inequality recorded. At one extreme, a whole nation might be treated as one big family in which case it might be assumed that all income was shared and there was no inequality. At the other extreme, if every individual were treated as a separate unit then small babies would have zero money income and inequality would appear to be very high. Thus in comparing Gini coefficients it is necessary to be clear that the same units – families or households – have been used. A second source of apparent, but misleading, differences in Gini coefficients is if different time periods are used for measuring income. For instance, in Britain there is more inequality in weekly income than in annual income. The third possible distortion concerns the definition or measure of income used in different surveys: the inclusion or not of production for own-consumption and benefits in kind may artificially push Gini coefficients up or down. In short, great care is needed to make valid comparisons over time.

These problems may apply to comparisons of income inequality between regions or between rural and urban areas. An added problem arises if the composition of the populations compared is changing. If for example the best-off rural residents move to urban areas, and nothing else changes, then the measured gap between rural and urban areas would increase. Even bigger problems arise when comparisons are made with other countries. For example, Guan points to a bigger gap between regions than exists in other countries (above, page 72). Yet because China is a very large country, a bigger gap between regions is only to be expected. There is, for example, a larger gap between regions across the whole of Europe than there is between regions in Britain alone. Thus great care must be taken in cross-national comparison to ensure that like is being compared with like.

Anti-Poverty Programmes

The mid-1980s anti-poverty programme in China aimed at increasing regional economic growth rather than trying to help individual poor families directly, and aimed at strengthening economic capability rather than just providing social relief (above, page 76). This shift in emphasis towards poverty prevention away from alleviation has much to commend it and is characteristic of social policy reforms in many countries. The general shift from 'passive' to 'active' labour market policies is one sign of such a shift. So too is the recognition that social conditions – especially those of the poorest – depend on the state of the economy. The amounts available from social relief are generally small, compared with the extra income that results from increased employment and earnings.

China's current 10-year anti-poverty action for 2001–2010 has three main features:

- more targeting of resources on the poorest provinces and counties;
- a concentration on productive products at community and family level;
- a greater emphasis on social projects.

Such a programme has clear advantages over more general poverty relief. But the British experience suggests there can also be problems. First, there may be difficulty in identifying the appropriate 'targets' – and there is certainly a cost in collecting and analysing the information needed to target accurately. Second, the greater the degree of targeting, the more this may create adverse incentives: if the province, community or family does more for itself then it will lose state support. Third, in selecting social projects it is important to identify those that are sustainable and will contribute to development, rather than simply meet immediate needs, however pressing these may be. With limited resources, the needs of the very sick or very poor are urgent and genuine, but those needs have to be weighed against the need to improve the social infrastructure and assist development, which may appear less urgent and unlikely to yield immediate benefit.

Economic Reform

In common with many countries, China is concerned to catch up with the developed world. To do this, priority has to be given to economic efficiency. Since the start of economic reform, Guan states: 'It is now an official principle of policy-making that economic efficiency should take precedence over equity' (above, page 75). A conflict between efficiency and equity has been stressed in most western neo-classical economies over the last 50 years. Efficiency and equity conflict, it was argued, so the government must decide, on political and social welfare grounds, what balance to strike between the two objectives. Now, however, the inevitability of this conflict is being questioned.

What is not being questioned is that some degree of inequality is necessary for there to be appropriate incentives in the economy. Nor is it being questioned that some inequalities of income are fair because they compensate for more unpleasant tasks or longer hours of work. But, in other ways, inequality may harm efficiency and less inequality may assist efficiency. A more equitable education system that ensures a basic education for all may contribute to economic growth. Similarly, an equitable health care system may add to the efficiency of the labour force. Furthermore, just as promoting equity may increase efficiency, so policies promoting efficiency may contribute to equity. Better quality services and products are of benefit to rich and poor alike. Very often it is the poor who suffer from the worst quality of services and products, in effect adding to inequality.

Probably the most important factor in maintaining income and preventing poverty is employment. This underlies the British Government's goal of 'Work for those who can'. Achieving macro-economic stability and a steady growth of the economy is crucial to relieving poverty. Thus Britain's onetime full employment policy used to be an effective anti-poverty strategy. Unemployment is not necessarily a cause of poverty, if social security benefits are set at high levels, but in most – if not all – countries increases in unemployment have caused increases in poverty. The ending of the full employment policy in China may contribute to economic growth, but it threatens to result in greater poverty.

Because of market competition, it has been necessary for many Chinese enterprises to lay-off workers. However the laid-off workers retain some rights to benefits from their previous employer. By contrast, those who are officially unemployed have access to the unemployment insurance programme. The 'laid-off workers' present a problem, both for economic efficiency and for poverty. For economic efficiency, enterprises must be able to reduce their employment without continuing costs of labour. To prevent poverty, those laid-off must have access to adequate income until they can obtain new employment; this requires income protection for *all* those effectively unemployed, together with retraining or work programmes that will assist their future employment.

It is appropriate that sharing the cost of unemployment protection should add to the cost of employment – it is in effect an insurance premium. But how this cost should be divided between employers and employees is not clear-cut. Employers should pay if employment is viewed as a permanent, lifetime commitment, with social insurance to protect them against the risk of not being able to maintain that commitment. Employees should pay if employment is only a limited-duration commitment, with social insurance a mechanism to protect themselves against the risk of future unemployment. In either case there seems no reason why government funds should protect urban workers, when the same protection is not available in rural areas. To subsidize social protection solely in urban areas, can only serve to increase urban-rural inequality.

In terms of future poverty and inequality no change seems more important than a reduction in the control exerted by the urban household registration system. Guan states: 'Without doubt, this change will help to reduce the big gap between rural and urban residents.' The impact of such a change is not, however, simple. Some will gain, others lose. Migration should help the individuals who migrate. An increased supply of labour in urban areas should result in lower urban wages. In rural areas a decreased labour supply should lead to higher wages. Thus inequality should in principle be reduced. However this analysis ignores the effects migration might have on growth in urban and rural areas. The loss of many of the better-educated and most enterprising young people to the cities – as typically happens with free migration – may boost urban growth and slow economic growth in rural areas. Thus the long run effect may be to increase rather than decrease inequality.

The impact of economic development on inequality depends crucially on the pattern of that development. Guan describes a two-track form of development:

> One direction will be to compete with developed countries in high-tech industries. This is actually a competition for highly educated professionals, which involves providing them with even-higher incomes. As such, it involves a 'race to the top'. However the other competition will be with other developing countries in the international market for a larger share of international investment and trade in labour-intensive industries. To win this competition, both China's own labour-intensive industries and those of its international competitors will be striving to keep labour costs down. This, therefore, could be a 'race to the bottom'. (above, page 82).

As Guan concludes, 'an increase in social inequality seems inevitable' but he then adds 'so long as no more measures of social protection are implemented in the future'. What must be questioned, on the basis of experience in other industrialising countries, is whether in practice measures of social protection are likely to be adequate to off-set a growing inequality in original incomes. The combination of (1) a high-tech sector in which earnings are at least partially influenced by the international labour market for the most highly skilled and creative scientists, engineers, designers and entrepreneurs and (2) a labour-intensive sector competing internationally to have the lowest labour costs will produce a 'highly unequal society'.

Such a polarizing society is not, however, inevitable. Nor may it be desirable. It not only represents a threat to social stability, it is also questionable as a route to economic efficiency and growth. Just as there is 'appropriate technology' that reflects the relative scarcity of physical capital in a developing economy such as China, so to there is 'appropriate human capital' which reflects the state of economic development. A relentless pursuit of the most advanced 'high-tech' products is not always a wise economic policy. An example of this was the development by Britain and France of the supersonic passenger aircraft Concorde. This development was certainly high-tech, but was not on any reckoning a wise economic investment – huge amounts of tax revenues were used to subsidize very rich air-travellers. Training people in skills that are only likely to benefit a rich minority is likely to lead to greater inequality and out-migration, which benefits rich nations at the expense of the poor.

Issues for China's Social Policy

Guan states that:

> China's social policy, although still regarded as a domestic concern of the government, will be more subject to international intervention. Such intervention may come in two varieties: ideological influences from other countries, and international concerns for 'fair competition' in the economic marketplace (above, page 83).

It does seem most probable that there will be more international intervention in China's social policy. (This volume itself illustrates the point). This influence is not, however, clear in its direction. In terms of ideology, a US-dominated 'liberal' economic perspective receives much public attention. However there are other ideological approaches which dominate thinking in continental Europe, and in much of East Asia, which involve a much less restricted role for social policy. In terms of international competition there have been many fears that there would be a 'race to the bottom' with social protection being cut back to keep down costs and maintain competitiveness. Yet, so far, this has not generally occurred. While there may be increasing global competition, governments have been reluctant to reduce social protection. This may be attributable to internal political factors such as pressures and demands for maintained or improved social protection. But it may be the result of a realisation that much social expenditure is a sound economic investment, contributing to the quality of human and social capital.

Guan's analysis is particularly interesting and important in relation to standards of labour protection. He writes:

> No single developing country is in a position to insist on a high level of social protection for itself, or even to keep its previous social welfare arrangements unchanged when others are cutting down on welfare provision. Thus the only way to escape from this dilemma is to set up a basic social welfare standard and international coordination mechanism in social protection amongst the developing countries (above, page 84).

The need for a basic standard of social protection is compelling. How can one poor country compete effectively in international markets if another poor country has lower labour standards? One example of this is child labour. Many developing countries either lack legal protection for children or, more commonly, fail to enforce it effectively. This is often justified on the grounds that stopping child labour would worsen the conditions of the poor children. Yet if some countries exploit children how can other countries afford to protect them? Therefore a common internationally enforced standard of protection seems highly desirable.

What is more contentious is how extensive international labour standards should be. It is desirable that no workers should work in conditions that are unhealthy or unsafe, that all should have well-protected employment rights and that all should enjoy decent levels of pay. Yet these desirable goals cannot all be achieved merely by passing national or international laws. There must be clear political and economic priorities. It is better to have effectively enforced standards relating to some goals, such as eliminating child labour, than to have wide-ranging but unenforced standards that in reality achieve nothing. The best is often an enemy of the good, and this is particularly true of labour standards.

One lesson above all is clear from the British experience, and is borne out by Guan's discussion of inequality and poverty in China. Social policies cannot be considered in isolation from economic policies if poverty and inequality are to be reduced. It is common for social policies to be expected to deal with the casualties of economic policies – policies often introduced with little concern for their consequences for poverty. Such an approach is likely to lead only to more poverty and inequality and to ineffective social policies. If inequality and poverty are to be effectively reduced they must be central concerns of both economic and social policy. The damaging division between economic and social policy must be broken down.

Chapter 8
Labour Market Construction and Labour Mobility in Urban China

Fenyu Wang and Yandong Zhao

Introduction

The objective of China's reform of its labour employment system is to build up a well-developed labour market and achieve an effective allocation of labour resources by means of market regulation. Labour market construction leads directly to free labour mobility, which is the key to ensuring the healthy and sustainable development of the labour market. The degree of freedom of labour mobility has, therefore, become an important index for assessing the development level of the labour market. For labour mobility is not only a key to employment efficiency but also an expression of social equality. In this sense, we hold labour mobility research to be of strategic significance, both theoretically and practically. For some years, Chinese researchers have produced vast amounts of literature on labour mobility, including occupational mobility, in urban China; on new migrants from rural areas to the cities; and on unemployed and laid-off workers. But most of these studies focused only on a single dimension of labour mobility.

The Survey of Occupational Mobility and Migration (SOMM) research project aims to present a broader and deeper picture of China's labour market construction and labour mobility by means of a scientific social survey, to discuss the experience gathered in this labour market construction and to review the social problems arising from it. We selected 7,835 households by random sampling in Beijing, Zhuhai and Wuxi, three typical Chinese cities in terms of labour mobility. In November to December 1998, the survey was conducted in these sample cities by trained interviewers. Some 7,326 questionnaires were completed and successfully recovered. The response rate was 95 per cent.

In our study, labour mobility was discussed in three dimensions: (1) mobility between different occupations, industries and work units within the urban areas, (2) the mobility of rural labourers to cities, and of urban labourers to other cities, and (3) the mobility of labourers from one employment status to another. Such a set of classifications permits an intensive and comprehensive review of labour mobility in urban China today.

Development of the Labour Market and Occupational Mobility

Historical Development of Labour Market Construction

Before China introduced its policy of reform and opening-up in the late 1970s, the employment of labour had been a task of government, which made all the decisions and dealt with all problems in the field. Such a united management of the labour market proved more and more inappropriate, given the progress of China's economic reform and the resulting pressures on employment. Accordingly, after a few reforms and trials, China has finally consigned its labour employment to market regulation. From Table 8.1 below, we can see clearly that, with the development of the socialist market economy, the annual employment growth rate in the state sector has been declining since 1994 (the collective sector had begun to decline from 1992), while the growth rate of non-state economic sectors has been increasing ever since 1990.

Table 8.1 Annual employment growth by ownership in China: 1990–1997 (%)

Sectors	1990	1991	1992	1993	1994	1995	1996	1997
State	2.4	3.1	2.1	0.3	-0.3	0.6	-0.1	-1.8
Collective	1.3	2.2	-0.2	-6.3	-5.4	-4.2	-4.0	-4.4
Non-State	24.2	31.7	30.6	90.1	39.4	17.4	7.4	13.1

Source: National Bureau of Statistics 1997:15; 1998:130–131.

Accordingly, changes have also taken place in methods of job attainment over recent years. This can be seen from how people get their first job in life. From the 1950s to the 1970s, the largest proportion of urban residents got their first job by government assignment. However this proportion has decreased sharply since the 1980s. By 1998, the proportion of such labourers in the three sample cities had dropped to only 10-15 per cent. Meanwhile, the proportion of labourers who got their first job via labour intermediaries has grown dramatically since the 1980s, nearing 20 per cent by 1998.

There remains, however, a significant 'institutional vacuum' between the breakdown of the traditional employment system and the formation of the new one. That is why we see in Figure 8.1 that social contacts such as relatives, friends and acquaintances have played such a major role in job attainment over recent years. From 1995 to 1998, nearly half of the sample labourers got their jobs through such informal channels. This illustrates very well the significance of informal institutional factors. As sociologists have suggested, the economic system is 'embedded' in social networks and social institutions (Granovetter 1973, 1995). Moreover, the result also reminds us of the urgency of labour market construction, so as to render it the major channel for labour resources allocation.

The development of labour market construction so far is also borne out by the increase in the rate of return to education. As sociologists and economists have asserted, investment in human capital can only be beneficial in a market society (Xu 1986).We found in our survey that the income gaps between labourers of different

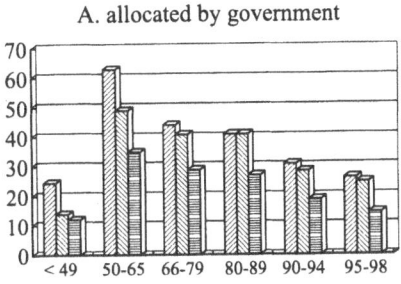
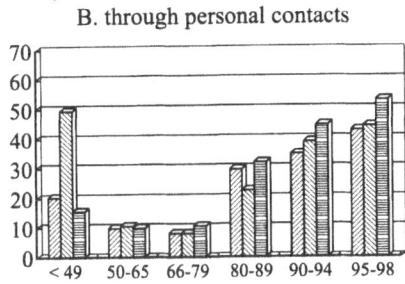
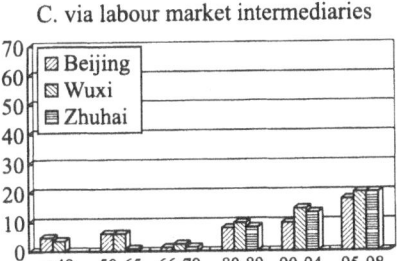

Figure 8.1 Changes in methods of getting the first job 1949–1998

educational qualification were evident and widening, by comparison with previous surveys. According to the survey conducted by Zhao Renwei and associates (Zhao et al. 1999), the wage gap between people with college education and those with only a primary school education stood at 19 per cent in 1988 but at 42 per cent in 1995. We discovered an even higher proportion of 93 per cent in this regard in our own survey. This is not only in sharp contrast to the pattern of job payment in the 1980s – characterized by 'high incomes for manual labourers but low incomes for mental ones' – but is also an incarnation of the achievements that China has made in labour market construction.

Increasing Occupational Mobility: Achievements and Shortcomings

A direct result of labour market construction is the increase in total labour mobility and the acceleration in the frequency of labour mobility. Under such circumstances, a labourer's scope for changing job is very much subject to the structure of the labour market. Before China initiated its economic reform and opening-up policy in late 1970s, labour mobility between different work units and economic sectors was strictly controlled by the state, giving rise to a very low rate of job change. From Table 8.2, we can see that, before the 1970s, labourers in the three sample cities switched to a different job only after an average period of 15 to 20 years, whereas by the 1980s the figure had dropped to 10 years, and by the 1990s to only 5 years.

Table 8.2 Average years between job changes in different eras

Year	Beijing	Wuxi	Zhuhai
Before 1949	20.5	18.8	29.6
1950–65	26.7	22.8	21.3
1966–79	16.8	16.5	14.1
1980–89	10.4	9.6	9.2
1990–94	5.2	6.1	5.7
1995–98	4.8	6.6	5.1
Total	13.0	11.8	8.7

However, though much progress has been made in labour market construction, we have to recognize that the rate of labour mobility in China is still relatively low, especially when compared with that of developed countries. Some 30 per cent of labourers in our three sample cities had never changed jobs in their entire careers (a figure similar to the 34.9 per cent for Yokohama, Japan, in the 1970s, but much higher than the 13.9 per cent for Detroit, USA, for 1970).

After dividing the respondents into different age groups and making further comparison, we found that the number of job changes of Chinese labourers was much less than that of their peer groups in Japan or America (See Table 8.3). Another discovery of our survey was that some of the current social institutions, including China's household registration system, personnel filing system and social security system, still pose considerable obstacles to the free flow of labour. All of which shows that there is still a long way to go before Chinese labourers can change their jobs without restriction.

Table 8.3 Means of job changes in labourers' careers for different age groups

	Cities and Countries				
Age	Beijing	Wuxi	Zhuhai	Japan	USA
< 24	0.45	0.55	0.40	2.1	4.4
25–29	1.08	0.76	0.82	2.7	6.2
30–34	1.07	1.29	1.38	3.1	7.4
35–39	1.14	1.27	1.56	3.5	7.4
40–54	1.24	1.47	1.58	4.2	10.0
55–64	1.38	1.74	1.43	4.9	11.0
> 65	1.67	2.11	2.79	–	11.2

Note: The data for Japan and the USA are cited from Hashimoto and Raisan (1985).

Mobility of Labourers according to Employment Status: Unemployment, Lay-off and Re-employment

Another direct result of labour market construction is that the past invisible unemployment of the era of the planned economy becomes increasingly visible in the forms of unemployment and lay-off, an issue of major concern to the Chinese government of today. Our survey explored the mobility of labourers from one employment status to another.

According to the survey, we estimated the proportion of laid-off workers to the entire local labour force, in the three sample cities in 1998, to be as follows: 6.6 per cent for Beijing, 5.6 per cent for Wuxi and 4.7 per cent for Zhuhai; and the proportion of unemployed workers: 12 per cent for Beijing, 10 per cent for Wuxi and 13 per cent for Zhuhai. Comparing with official statistics published by the Chinese government, the laid-off rate in our survey is at the same level as the official figure, while the unemployment rate is about four times the government's figure. The reason for this gap lies in the different statistical methods employed. When defining 'unemployed workers', the government takes into account only those unemployed workers who have registered at local labour departments, whereas our survey included all the people without a job at the survey time, though they are able and willing to work. Based on our survey, we feel safe to say that the unemployment rate published by the Chinese government is too low to cover the real level of unemployment in China.

Laid-off Workers

Basic features. We discovered in the survey some basic features of laid-off workers. First, the number of laid-off female workers is larger than that of male workers. In Beijing, laid-off female workers are roughly twice as many as laid-off male workers. Second, 70 per cent of all the laid-off workers surveyed fall into the age group 26 to 45, with some 60 per cent of the laid-off in Beijing and Wuxi aged from 36 to 45. Third, most of the laid-off workers in the three sample cities are in manufacturing industry, which evinces a lay-off rate of over 60 per cent in Beijing and Zhuhai and nearly 80 per cent in Wuxi. Fourth, more than half of the laid-off workers surveyed have only a junior high school education. Finally, while many of these laid-off workers are experienced, their experience is limited to a very narrow field – nearly 60 per cent of them had never changed their jobs, or had only changed once, before being laid off.

Difficulties of re-employment and 'hidden' employment. From the descriptions above, we can see that these laid-off workers face an unfavourable situation in the competition for re-employment. Facts have repeatedly proved this in spite of the favourable policies and measures that the government offered for laid-off workers. We found that most of those surveyed had not yet got new jobs during the time of our survey, given a jobless rate of 63 per cent for Beijing, 55 per cent for Wuxi and 80 per cent for Zhuhai. In fact, only about 30 per cent of laid-off workers recorded since 1992 had found regular work by the end of 1998. We also found that over half of laid-off workers remained unemployed for an average period of eighteen months to two years in Beijing and Wuxi, and for nearly three years in Zhuhai. The reasons for this phenomenon are diverse. Objectively, many laid-off workers are at a disadvantage in the labour market competition, due to general inferiority in age, education and work experience. Subjectively, quite a number of them intend to keep in contact with their previous work units so as to continue to enjoy the welfare benefits – such as medical care, pensions and lay-off allowances – although many work units now no longer provide such welfare. But for this reason, they are reluctant to sever relationships and get a new job elsewhere.

The contradictions between old and new labour employment systems have led to the universal existence of 'hidden' employment, or in other words, to quite a number of workers retaining their relationships with their previous work units while finding jobs elsewhere for extra income. The proportion of such laid-off workers accounted for some 27 per cent in Beijing, 31 per cent in Wuxi and 14 per cent in Zhuhai. Such 'hidden' employment is undoubtedly a rational choice for laid-off workers, since they can not only continue to get welfare treatment from their previous work units,[1] but 'also gain extra money' from their new jobs. However, it is their previous work units who have become the 'losers' in this game, to the extent that they have to continue to provide their laid-off workers with welfare treatment. Since most of these work units are state-owned, this phenomenon helps to explain, partially, the loss of state assets.

Implementation and evaluation of the re-employment policies

(a) Re-employment centres: Re-employment centres are quite common in Beijing and Wuxi. According to our survey, 27 and 34 per cent of the laid-off workers surveyed in Beijing and Wuxi respectively said they had been aware of the centres in their previous work units, though another 15 per cent had been unaware of their existence. However, due to worries that they might lose connections with their previous work units, only 16-22 per cent of the laid-off workers surveyed in late 1998 registered in re-employment centres and thus severed their relationship with their previous work units.

(b) Employment training: Employment-oriented training has proved unsatisfactory in China, according to our survey. Even in Beijing, the city with the highest re-employment training rate in our survey, only 6 per cent of the laid-off workers surveyed said they had actually experienced re-employment training. We found that most of the trainees were under 25 and had worked in state enterprises before. Our survey also showed that three-three-fourths of the trainees underwent short-term training with the training fees being provided by their previous work units, while the remaining fourth received their training in re-employment centres outside their previous work units.

Unemployment

Basic features of the unemployed. Our survey shows the basic features of the unemployed to be somewhat similar to those of laid-off workers. First, the number of unemployed women workers is larger than that of men workers. Second, most of the unemployed workers surveyed were 26 to 45 years old. Third, most of the unemployed workers in the three sample cities had had junior high school education or less. Fourth, 60-70 per cent of the unemployed had worked in one to two work units in their previous careers. Finally, the reasons for their unemployment were diverse. About 35 per cent had been fired by their work units. 37 per cent had resigned or left before the labour contract expired. A further 11 per cent had withdrawn from private business owing to poor economic performance. And another 7-12 per cent had never had a job before.

Difficulties over re-employment. Most of the unemployed surveyed had remained jobless for more than a year before being interviewed. In Beijing, over half of the unemployed found new jobs after a period of continuous unemployment of more than 15 months; in Wuxi, it was after a period of more than 17 months; and in Zhuhai, more than 22 months. The difficulties that they face in securing employment seem overwhelming.

In the eyes of the unemployed, their own lasting unemployment is due to their low level of education, poor technical skills and expertise, and relatively old age. Yet 20-25 per cent of the unemployed attributed their prolonged unemployment to 'having no favourable social connections'. Only 5-6 per cent of the unemployed attributed their protracted unemployment to the fact that 'to find a job is really difficult'. From this we can see that the cause for their prolonged unemployment is understood as largely lying within themselves.

Evaluation of re-employment policies

(a) Unemployment registration: Unemployment registration is an important means for the government to monitor labour employment and take corresponding action. However, the general level of unemployment registration is very low, according to our survey. Actually, fewer than 22-24 per cent of the unemployed were registered at relevant labour departments. Most of those who registered were relatively young, had received a relatively high education, were keen to find jobs through government channels and to enjoy unemployment insurance granted by the government.

(b) Job assignment by the government: Only 1-2 per cent of the unemployed surveyed said they had been provided with job assignments by the government. And only half of these assignments proved successful. In other words, half of the assignees had rejected the jobs allocated by the government. This rejection rate may be partially attributable to over-expectation on the part of the assignees. But in any case, the job assignments or opportunities being offered by government still lag far behind actual needs.

(c) Employment training: A small proportion of the unemployed were found to have received employment training, a proportion similar to that among laid-off workers. Most of the employment trainees were found to be young and of relatively high educational level, partly because these were people who believed the training might result in higher pay in the future. However, the high cost of training remains a major obstacle to its take-up, which is especially the case for the training provided by private companies. Though the employment training offered by the government or state enterprises costs less, its effectiveness lags far behind the expectations of the trainees. This has partly explained why few workers experienced re-employment training after unemployment.

Geographical Labour Mobility: Influence of New Migrants to the Cities

Geographical mobility of labour has become more and more pronounced with the progress of labour market construction. This floating population can thus account for an increasingly large part of a city's total population. According to our survey, floating migrants constitute 8, 12 and 50 per cent of the population total in Beijing, Wuxi and Zhuhai respectively.

Basic Features of the Migrants

First, most migrants surveyed in Beijing were single young men, while in Wuxi and Zhuhai women migrants take the lion's share. Second, most of the migrants were found to be 20 to 25 years old when they first migrated. In Beijing, they were currently aged 29 on average, in Wuxi 30, and in Zhuhai 26 on average. Generally speaking, migrants are a little younger than the generality of local residents. In this sense, they help to alleviate local problems arising from an ageing population. We also found in our survey that 24-39 per cent of the migrants were single, a figure much higher than that for local residents. In general, single female migrants were much more common than single male migrants.

Employment and Working Conditions of the Migrants

We found in our survey that, contrary to 'common sense', geographical labour mobility was generally *intentional*. In other words, rural-urban labour mobility is not completely 'blind', as has been suggested by many before.[2] We found that about half of the migrants had relatives, 30-40 per cent had townsmen or fellow villagers and 15-20 per cent had friends, schoolmates or other acquaintances in the cities they moved to. Those migrants who did not know anybody in the cities they moved to accounted for less than 20 per cent. In Beijing, about 75 per cent of the migrants had found their jobs before they actually moved to the city, while in Wuxi the figure stands at 60 per cent and in Zhuhai 40 per cent – still a big number. We also found that 70-75 per cent of them began their jobs within a month after they moved to the cities. Most of them got their jobs through relatives, friends and other acquaintances, or direct recruiting fairs. Therefore, we can conclude that rural-urban mobility is generally geared to a clear destination and is well prepared.

Most of the rural floating migrants work in secondary and tertiary industries. To be exact, most migrants in Beijing work in the building industries (here mainly referring to males) and the service industries. In Zhuhai, most of the migrants work in manufacturing, with female migrants playing a bigger part. And in Wuxi, most of the floating population works in manufacturing and the service industries. Here we would like to point out that the job pattern of migrants is, in some cases, the same as that of the local laid-off or unemployed workers in the cities. Therefore, competition between these two groups of people in some fields of work has become inevitable. The result has shown the migrants to be in a better position in this competition, because they are generally younger, their education level is roughly the same and they are more tolerant of poor working conditions. No wonder some urban laid-off or unemployed workers have declared that the migrants in the cities have 'snatched the "rice bowl" from their hands'. Actually, 50 per cent of the laid-off or unemployed workers surveyed in Beijing agreed with this remark, while in Wuxi and Zhuhai the figures stand at 43 and 35 per cent respectively.

However, the treatment that the migrants have received is far from fair. Their general pay level is relatively low. For example, the wage per hour of the male migrants in Beijing is 27 per cent lower than that of fixed local residents while in Zhuhai it stands at 51 per cent lower. What is worse, the wage per hour of the female migrants is 41, 22 and 58 percent lower than that of local female residents in Beijing, Wuxi and Zhuhai respectively. To earn more money, these migrants have to work extra hours. According to our survey, the average weekly working hours of the male migrants in Beijing, Wuxi and Zhuhai were 61, 53 and 59 hours respectively. Their working hours are far longer than those of local residents and, of course, far longer than what is stipulated in the Labour Law.[3]

Future of the Migrants

We found in our survey that most of the migrants did not regard their living conditions as bad, although they have to work long hours, receive low pay, live in poor houses and lack social security. Over half of the migrants surveyed believed they had a better life compared with ordinary Chinese families. In Wuxi and Zhuhai, many new migrants spoke positively of their living conditions. We think that this phenomenon stems from the fact that most migrants do not compare their living conditions with those of local residents in the city but rather with those in their home towns. Therefore, they are inclined to feel content with their conditions, which are actually seen as bad in the eyes of local urban residents.

However, there was another phenomenon worth our notice. In Wuxi and Zhuhai, we came across many migrants who had lived in these cities for over ten years. In contrast to the new migrants, these people did not speak highly of their living conditions, which may indicate that these migrants no longer regarded themselves as migrants and had therefore begun to compare their living conditions with those of local urban residents. This finding prompted other questions, such as how did all these migrants think of their future? Will they, as many once believed, return to their home towns after they have earned enough money? We carried out a special investigation in this regard.

First, we found that some 50 per cent of the rural migrants planned to stay on in the cities instead of going back home in the future. Those who expressed a willingness to return to their home towns eventually accounted for less than 10 per cent. Second, we found that only 7 per cent of rural migrants in cities were still keeping close contact with their hometowns.[4] Third, we found that even the farmland, which has long been viewed as the very 'apple of the eye' of the farmers, is no longer a strong attraction to these rural migrants. We asked a hypothetical question 'Suppose the government were to take back your land as the cost of your residency in the city, would you still choose to live in the city?' Most rural migrants answered 'yes'. If the government really intended to practise this 'exchange urban residency with farmland' policy, our estimation is that one-fourth of the rural migrants in Beijing might possibly leave the city, but the figure would probably be much lower in Wuxi and Zhuhai.

From what is described above, we may conclude that if the migrants have the right to choose, they would be inclined to stay in the cities instead of going back to their villages. Therefore, clear information is presented here to city planners – they can no longer treat the rural migrants as 'migratory birds' in cities but have to prepare for the possibility of their permanent residence there. Consequently, the management pattern for these migrants must be improved: their access to better infrastructure and services should be assured, and they should be provided with the same rights as the urban local residents. The development of a new management system that could help the rural migrants to be better incorporated into the urban world has become an urgent task of policy makers.

Institutional Supports for Labour Market Construction

Reform of the Social Security System

The analysis above shows that China's labour market has enjoyed an impressive achievement, the market mechanism has been established, and the free movement of labour between different professions, industries, occupations and regions has been greatly improved. However, market establishment is not an isolated process; it needs the coordination and supplementation of a series of necessary institutional reforms. Among them, the re-establishment and improvement of the social security system is the most urgent for securing the development of the current labour market.

So far, China has still not established a national medical and pension security system. Meanwhile, the development of commercial social insurance organizations is at an elementary stage. Most urban employees still rely on their work units to obtain most of their security items. This 'Unit Security' model not only leads to huge inequalities in the provision of security and welfare among different units, but also becomes one of the institutional obstacles hindering further labour mobility. Employees cannot find a security network outside their units except via the informal support of families, relatives and friends. So, once the security mechanism of their units goes wrong, employees and their families can find themselves in a very difficult situation. The unemployed will suffer the most as a result.

For those laid off or unemployed, their working units still, so far, take responsibility for their social relief and security. Included are direct approaches such as pension distribution, regular allowance and temporary allowance;[5] and indirect approaches such as investment in projects for unemployment insurance and local welfare provision. However, such combinations of security mechanisms have had rather a limited coverage. Some 60 to 80 per cent of the unemployed respondents in our survey claimed that they had never received any relief from either their employers or any other source. Laid-off workers might still be being taken care of by their former work units, which makes their situation seem a little better; yet many of the enterprises they have been relying on have themselves already been suffering serious financial difficulties, or have even closed down.

In any case, laid-off workers and the unemployed get very small sums of relief from either their work units or the government. For the month before our survey, the reported rates of relief received by laid-off workers averaged 237 RMB in Beijing,

202 RMB in Wuxi and 381 RMB in Zhuhai. Unemployment relief, which was 217 RMB, 174 RMB and 432 RMB in the three cities respectively, was thus not that much different from the relief received by the laid-off. The unemployed in Beijing and Wuxi had mainly come from state-owned enterprises (SOEs). Most of them could obtain medical and pension security from their former work units. Again, three-quarters of the unemployed in Beijing and two-thirds in Wuxi still had access to medical security. Their former work units also guaranteed the distribution of their pensions. In Zhuhai, where private enterprises have taken a relatively higher percentage of the labour market, only one-third of the laid-off can still get medical security from their original units. But the unemployed face an even more serious situation: 85 per cent (Beijing and Wuxi) to 98 per cent (Zhuhai) of them cannot enjoy any form of medical security and 60-70 per cent of them have not made any preparation for their old age.

One of the direct impacts of this imperfect social security system on the re-employment of the laid-off is the prevalent phenomenon of 'hidden re-employment'. Some of the laid-off become so-called 'double institutional people'. On one hand, they are still connected to their old institution and enjoy its social security; on the other hand, they can obtain income from other jobs outside the old institution. Though 'hidden re-employment' has various shortcomings, it is very difficult for government and enterprises to implement effective measures because of the imperfect social security system.

Finally, the effect of social security can be shown clearly from the attitude of the laid-off to various re-employment policies and their answers to the question: 'under what condition would you agree to cancel the labour relationship with your former unit?' Some 43-54 per cent of the laid-off thought it acceptable to 'cancel the labour relationships with the original units, but still to enjoy the secured medical and pension insurance'. When choosing the preconditions for cancelling their labour relationships, 27-56 per cent of the laid-offs think 'guaranteeing medical and pension insurance' should be a precondition for cancelling the labour relationship. Thus, social security turns out to be one of the most important factors that the unemployed consider when trying to find new jobs. If such social security issues cannot be solved appropriately, re-employment policies could be doomed to failure.

Rights Protection for Labourers

It is absolutely necessary to implement effective regulation of the market during the process of improving labour market mechanisms. In July 1994, the *Labour Law of People's Republic of China* was approved on the Eighth Session of the Eighth National People's Congress. This provided legal security to ensure the healthy development of the labour market in China. In our survey, we inspected the implementation of the labour rights and interests of employees as regulated under this Labour Law and other laws.

Daily work hours, weekly average work hours and compensation for extra work hours are all clearly regulated in the Labour Law. The results of our survey showed state-owned enterprises (SOEs) to have the best record on implementation of the work time-related regulations in the three cities. About 60 per cent of state-owned unit employees work from 40 to 44 hours each week; whereas the situation of collective, private and foreign-invested enterprises is not so satisfying. In Wuxi, one-quarter of collective enterprise employees work more than 55 hours a week. In Zhuhai, the situation of collective enterprises is better, but more than half of the employees of private enterprises there work more than 55 hours a week.

When it comes to the signing of the work contract, the labour contract system is the core, the implementing precondition and the basis of the Labour Law. Among the total sampled in our survey, about half of the employees had signed a labour contract with their employers. However, if those working in government departments and institutions are excluded (most of whom had not signed labour contracts, because they had no need for their security to be protected by them), the percentage signing contracts was much higher. Therefore, it could be said that the implementation of the contract system has been successful to a certain extent. However, it should still be noticed that it is the state enterprises that tend to be able to implement the contract system well. Non-state sectors, especially private and collective enterprises, seem unable to implement the contract system satisfactorily. The number signing labour contracts for private enterprises only amounts to 11 to 36 per cent of that for state enterprises.

Finally, we inspected the development and effect of labour unions. At the end of 1998, there were around five million sub-labour unions under the direction of the All-China Federation of Trade Unions and around 90 million labour union members in China (National Bureau of Statistics 1999).The relationship between labour union and government was so subtle that some researchers even argue that the labour union has become a kind of quasi-governmental organization and has lost its original function (Liu 1999). However, according to the results of our research, we argue that the establishment of the labour union in enterprises has had definite positive effects on the protection of the rights and interests of employees. The results of our logistic regression analysis indicated that 'whether the units have the labour union or not' has had obvious effects on employees about whether they sign labour contracts or not, whether they receive medical care and pension security or not, irrespective of the ownership, type, size and length of establishment of their units (see Table 8.4). The units with labour unions obviously pay more attention to the protection of labourers' rights and interests than those without labour unions.

We should pay more attention to the low percentage of labour union establishment in rural collective and private enterprises. Our survey found the percentage of labour union establishment in these enterprises to be manifestly lower than that in other types of enterprises. Other results have shown the labour rights and interests protection situation in rural collective and private enterprises to be the very worst. Therefore, we should speed up labour union establishment in these enterprises, to ensure the protection of employees' rights and interests through legal means. The market is not 'omnipotent'. Indeed, the legal regulation of the market is indispensable for maintaining the principle of social fairness and thence improving the efficiency of society as a whole.

Table 8.4 Impact of an individual's unit characteristics on the signing of labour contracts and the social security obtained: logistic regression

	Medical security (1 = provided by units)	Pension (1 = provided by units)	Signing of labour contract (1 = signed)
Establishment of labour union (1 = Established)	1.380 ***	0.949 ***	1.395 ***
Unit ownership (1 = State owned)	0.908 ***	0.675 ***	–
Period of the unit establishment	-0.184 **	-0.168 ***	-0.134 ***
Unit size	0.001 ***	–	–
Type of unit (1 = governmental and civil units)	–	–	-1.428 ***
Residency (1 = urban)	1.664 ***	1.695 ***	0.660 ***
Working years	0.019 **	0.046 ***	-0.033 ***

Notes: 1. The coefficients in the table are all Exp(B)s.
2. $* p < 0.05; ** p < 0.01; *** p < 0.001$, the coefficients that have not reached the significance of 0.05 were not listed in the table.

Negative Side Effects of Labour Market Development

Urban Poverty

Most people have the impression that China's poverty is concentrated mainly in rural areas. But in recent years, urban poverty and the emergence of 'new urban poverty groups' have become a noticeable social problem. In our study, we found that the laid-off, unemployed and rural-urban migrants account for the major part of the urban poverty-stricken population. In Figure 8.2 we see that 70 to 90 per cent of poor urban people are laid-off, unemployed and rural-urban migrants. The implication of this result is that, if we can provide sufficient help to the laid-off and migrants, the urban poverty problem will be greatly mitigated.

First, let us take a look at the situation of the laid-off and unemployed. As we mentioned earlier, many of these have no jobs, and therefore no salary or income. The current social security system cannot completely cover them. Therefore, their lives have been extremely difficult. Our survey shows that 55-70 per cent of the unemployed depend on the incomes of other family members, 6-11 per cent of them depend on family savings, and 5 per cent rely on pensions and on the support of relatives and friends. More seriously, most of them have heavy family burdens. Taking the unemployed as an example, three-quarters of them are married and more than half have children to bring up. Furthermore, one-quarter of the unemployed have no other income earners in their families, any more than do one-seventh of the laid-off. All of these can thus be regarded as the 'high risk population' of urban areas, who need help more urgently than anybody else.

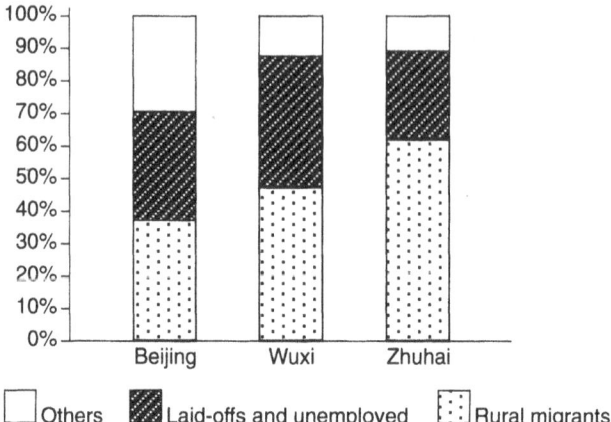

Figure 8.2 The structure of urban poverty population

So, compared with the individuals and families who have jobs, the laid-off, unemployed and their families suffer more difficulties. One month before the survey, the average individual income of an unemployed person in Beijing was only 210 RMB (including those who had no income at all). In Zhuhai it was 263 RMB, in Wuxi it was less than 200 RMB. The average income of an employed person is 5 times that of an unemployed person, and 2.5 times that of a laid-off person. We can also see this trend from the differences in family income. The average annual income gap (average annual income of a family with employed members minus the average annual income of a family without such) between families with unemployed members and families without, ranges from 6,700 RMB in Zhuhai to 11,000 RMB in Beijing.

Let us next take a look at the rural-urban migrants. From Table 8.5 we can see the income gap between migrants and urban dwellers and the rate of poverty. The data in the table obviously show rural floating migrants to have lower incomes than urban dwellers, and a higher rate of poverty. The poverty rate among floating migrants was three times that of the local people of Beijing, and nearly twice that of local people in Wuxi and Zhuhai.

We should be aware that differences in the mechanisms of getting social security and welfare between rural and urban populations were not considered in Table 8.5. If that factor were taken into account, the income gap between them would be much larger. Only about 20 per cent of rural floating migrants can enjoy medical security in the three cities. In Wuxi, 12 per cent of them are entitled to pension cover, while in Beijing and Zhuhai the percentage is only 1-2. The housing condition of floating migrants is also very depressing. In Beijing and Zhuhai, seven out of ten rural floating migrant families live in a low standard of accommodation such as shared apartment, work-shed or hostel. If this issue does not receive enough attention, new 'slums' or 'shed families' could emerge in Chinese cities in the future.

Table 8.5 Mean annual household income (in *yuan*: total, per capita and per adult equivalent), poverty incidence and poverty gap

		Total household income (mean)	Income per adult equivalent	Income per capita (income)	Poverty incidence (% of households)	Mean poverty gap	N
Beijing	Non-floater	22,012	12,867	7,751	8	25	1,629
	Rural floater	12,684	8,105	5,794	25	31	312
Wuxi	Non-floater	17,629	10,017	5,884	5	29	1,628
	Rural floater	11,728	7,381	5,069	13	28	481
Zhuhai	Non-floater	32,288	18,075	10,636	9	36	908
	Rural floater	13,503	8,846	6,456	15	28	776

Notes: The table refers to the 'economic household', i.e. includes incomes from persons located elsewhere who pool and share resources with interviewed household.

Equivalence scales based on the age composition cannot be applied here as we do not have any demographic information about the household members located in the place of origin. We therefore use the simple measure of taking the square root of the number of household members.

Poverty incidence (headcount index) is the percent of households having per capita income below the official poverty line, which was 2520 yuan per year in Beijing; 1800 in Wuxi; and 2640 in Zhuhai.

Mean poverty gap is the difference between the poverty line and mean income of the poor households (in percentage of the poverty line).

Increasing Social Inequity

One of the 'side effects' of market reform in China has been increasing income inequality. We calculated the level of income inequality of the residents in the three cities. In our samples, the 10 per cent of residents with the lowest incomes had only 2 per cent of the total income, while the 10 per cent of those with the highest incomes enjoyed more than 28 per cent of the total income. Take Zhuhai, the city with the highest inequality rate of the three sample cities, as a detailed example. The 10 per cent of Zhuhai residents with the lowest incomes have only 1.5 per cent of the city's total income; the 50 per cent of the people with the lowest incomes only accounted for 20 per cent of the city's total income; and the richest 10 per cent of residents received 33 per cent of the total income of all dwellers.

We have no intention of declaring that an increase in income inequality is bound to signal some deterioration in social fairness. After all, one of the targets of reform in China is to break down egalitarianism, so as to let some become richer earlier. All we wish to claim here is that people's 'bottom-line' tolerance of income inequality must be considered and studied, rather than taken for granted. When perceived levels of inequality are too much for the people, they will have a strong feeling of being deprived, which may lead to latent problems in social stability and development. Therefore, it remains an urgent job for the Chinese government to adjust income distribution appropriately, so as to maintain social equity in this emerging market society.

In the above analysis of income inequality, we did not include the inequality caused by different social security systems. In fact, the result of this research shows that the different social security and welfare entitlements an individual might get from his/her unit could also be an important cause of social inequality – one which was often ignored in the past. In this research, we found there to be an obvious 'accumulating effect' to the welfare and security provided by the units. That is to say, if an employee can get medical security from his/her unit, then the possibility is very high for him/her to have a stable work contract, get a house with allowance, and enjoy other kinds of welfare such as a retirement pension. However, those employees who cannot get such security will very likely be unable to get any of the above social benefits and welfare. This result can be demonstrated via the correlation coefficient matrix concerning the welfare and security that people received (see Table 8.6). The very strong correlation coefficients among various welfare and security items imply that there exists a relationship of 'everything or nothing' between them. This kind of 'everything or nothing' phenomenon in social security and welfare distribution not only leads to social unfairness, but also results in a specific kind of danger. A destitute class, deprived of any social security, might emerge. If this class should overlap with the above-mentioned groups of urban poor, poverty will thus be 'stabilized' and become a serious threat to social stability.

Table 8.6 Correlation matrix between social welfares and securities that an individual obtains

	Medical security	Pension security	Labour contract	Housing hours	Work
Medical security	1.00				
Pension security	0.62***	1.00			
Labour contract	0.28***	0.33***	1.00		
Housing	0.03	0.03**	-0.01	1.00	
Work hours	0.39***	0.41***	0.19***	-0.04**	1.00

** $p < 0.01$ ***: $p < 0.001$ (two-tailed test).

Another indication of social inequity is discrimination in the labour market, especially discrimination against women and rural floating migrants. It has been discovered that, holding other things constant, the average salary per hour of women is 10-15 per cent lower than that of men. That is to say, even though the education level, labour ability and working experience might all be the same, a female employee's income could be about one-tenth lower than her male counterpart simply because of her sex. Furthermore, women are more vulnerable than men when laying-off or unemployment is in question. Among the urban unemployed, the percentage of women is higher than that of men (the rate for women in Beijing being 41:59, Wuxi 45:55 and Zhuhai 48:52). Meanwhile, it is also very obvious that rural floating migrants suffer their own discrimination. Quite apart from the salary discrimination mentioned above, migrants also face many other kinds of unfair treatment. Most obviously, they can actually be excluded in advance from access to many work opportunities. In many cities, local governments set various admittance limitations on industries and occupations for floating populations. When their children go to school, they have to pay higher fees than others. Even so, 40–56 per cent of migrants claim that their children are further discriminated against when being enrolled. More unfairly, when urban employment becomes worse, migrants often become the targets of the government and are forced to go back to their home towns. In that way more jobs can be offered to the laid-offs and unemployed among urban dwellers.

Concluding Remarks

Recent years have witnessed a rapid development of labour market institutions in China. This can be shown clearly from our research: the rapid expansion of non-state-owned economic sectors has become an active force to provide new jobs; the traditional planning system has become less and less important for people trying to get jobs; the labour market is playing a more and more important role, indicating that labour mobility is increasing in frequency and total amount.

However, we should also realize that, even when the labour market is developing rapidly, the traditional household registering system, personnel file system and social welfare and security system still greatly limit the free flow of human resources in China. The result is that current social labour mobility in China is still lower by comparison with developed countries, with regard to both total amount and frequency. Therefore, to speed up the reform of the household registering system, the personnel archive system and the social welfare and security system is a precondition for improving the labour market mechanism and giving sufficient play to its function of allocating labour resources.

In order to ensure the healthy development of this labour market, it is essential to establish an efficient, unified social security system with extensive coverage. Currently, the most urgent point is to change the traditional social security system provided by work units, and to transfer this 'unit security' system to a single 'social security' system.

A well-developed labour market also needs effective regulation, which should be an important function of government. Currently, the implementation of the Labour Law should be strengthened to really safeguard the rights and interests of labourers. This may include: (1) standardizing the labour employment system for non-state-owned departments in the fields of work time, labour contract and strengthening the labour union construction of the non-state-owned departments; (2) clearing up the discrimination in the labour market in respect of e.g. sex and household registering discrimination.

Sufficient attention should also be paid to the new poor groups in urban areas. Currently the urban poverty issue specifically comes across as consisting of the poverty of the laid-off, the unemployed and rural floating migrants. Improving the living conditions of these groups of people must obviously be an urgent task of government. Detailed solutions include (1) creating more jobs and developing the training system for the laid-off and the unemployed, and improving their living conditions; (2) changing the management pattern for floating migrants, and changing 'management of labour' to 'management of resident', so as to provide them with equal access to services as urban dwellers; (3) improving the urban 'unemployment registration' system, especially for those who have been unemployed for a long time, so that the government collects information on 'real unemployment rates', and can respond with proper policy adjustment.

Notes

This report is based on the Survey of Occupational Mobility and Migration (SOMM), a joint research conducted by the National Research Center for Science and Technology for Development (NRCSTD), China, and the Fafo Institute for Applied Studies, Norway, in three cities of China in 1998. The Norwegian Government (Royal Ministry of Foreign Affairs and NORAD) made the project possible by providing the necessary funding. The Chinese research team members are as follows: Wang Fenyu (team leader), Li Lulu, Ge Yanfeng, Fan Lihong, Wang Junfeng, Deng Xueming, Ju Wenxhong, Yuan Fang and Zhao Yandong.

1. We should also be aware, however, that many laid-off workers in China cannot get any actual welfare support from their previous enterprises, since these enterprises are not making any profit.
2. While speaking of the rural floating population, the Chinese government once used a special term *mangliu* (blindly floating population), which did not disappear until the late 1980s. This term reflects, in a sense, the policy makers' general perception of the rural floating population in the past.
3. See the next section of this chapter for further description of legal work hours approved by Chinese Labour Law.
4. Indicated by three variables: (1) whether they are willing to go back to the home town in the future, (2) how often they return to the home town, and (3) the frequency and amount of their remittance to their family or relatives.
5. According to the regulations of government, when a worker is laid off, he/she should get regular allowance from his/her previous work unit. However, since many state enterprises are not making a profit, their workers could only get a temporary allowance from time to time.

References

Granovetter, Mark (1973), 'The strength of weak ties', *American Journal of Sociology*, 78: 1360–80.
Granovetter, Mark (1974), *Getting a Job*, Harvard University Press, Cambridge, MA.
Granovetter, Mark (1995), *Getting a Job*, rev. edn, University of Chicago Press, Chicago.
Hashimoto, Masanori and John Raisan (1985), 'Employment tenure and earnings profiles in Japan and the US', *American Economic Review*, 75, 4 (September): 721–35.
Liu, Aiyu (1999), *Laodong Shehuixue Jiaocheng [Introduction to Labour Sociology]*, Beijing University Press, Beijing.
National Bureau of Statistics (1997), *China Statistics Annals 1997*, Chinese Statistics Publishing House, Beijing.
National Bureau of Statistics (1998), *China Statistics Annals 1998*, Chinese Statistics Publishing House, Beijing.
National Bureau of Statistics (1999), *China Statistics Annals 1999*, Chinese Statistics Publishing House, Beijing.

Walder, Andrew (1986), *Communist Neo-traditionalism: Work and Authority in Chinese Industry*, University of California Press, Berkeley and Los Angeles.

Xu, Jiayou (1986), *Shehui Jiecenghua he Shehui Liudong [Social Stratification and Social Mobility]*, Sanmin Publishing House, Taipei.

Zhao, Renwei, Shi Li and Siqing Li (eds) (1999), *Zhongguo Jumin Shouru Fenpei Zaiyanjiu [Re-studying the Income Distribution of Chinese Residents]*. Chinese Finance and Economics Publishing House, Beijing.

Chapter 9

The British Labour Market and Labour Market Policy in Comparative Perspective

Jochen Clasen

Introduction

Any assessment of British and Chinese labour markets and labour market policies is faced with the problem of comparability. As the chapter by Wang and Zhao in this volume clearly illustrates, the Chinese labour market is going through a period of rapid development. Significant ruptures have occurred within a very short period, with vast differences in the emergence of market-based employment relationships between rural and urban areas and between employment in state, collective and non-state sectors. By contrast, due to early industrialization and urbanization, the British labour market can be regarded as one of the most established in the world. As a consequence, this chapter does not engage in a systematic comparison between the two countries. Instead, drawing on some of the aspects emphasized in the chapter by Wang and Zhao on the emerging Chinese labour market, it reflects on the British situation within a European context. These aspects include hidden unemployment, labour mobility, flexibility, social security support for the unemployed and employment training.

Some Aspects of the British Labour Market

Following the first oil price shock and economic recession in the early 1970s, the UK belonged to a group of European countries with high unemployment rates. This only changed after 1993 when rates began to fall slowly but steadily. By 2001 unemployment had reached the lowest levels since the early 1980s, representing less than 5 per cent of the workforce. A similar trend of declining unemployment in the second half of the 1990s occurred in other, mainly smaller, European countries such as Denmark, Ireland and the Netherlands, while the larger economies of Germany, France and Italy struggled to bring unemployment figures down to any significant degree (Eurostat 2001).

British labour force participation and employment rates also rose in the 1990s. However, overall trends obscure a decline in male and steeply increasing female labour force participation. Much of the latter is part-time work, which often means half-time work or fewer hours. With 40 per cent the UK has the second highest female part-time employment rate in the EU. This share has not changed significantly since the mid 1970s. For men, part-time rates are well below EU average, and so are temporary contracts for both British men and women, having increased only very little in the 1990s (European Commission 2001).

Uniquely within the EU, British men have been consistently more affected by unemployment than women. This has to do with the decline in predominantly male types of employment, such as manufacturing, and the growth of, predominantly, female types of employment in services (Rowthorn 2000). Weakening trade union influence in the 1980s and relatively little employment protection in the UK are but two factors which explain why this general trend has been more pronounced in Britain than in other European countries.

The employment gap between the South and the North of the UK has narrowed (Jackman and Savouri 1999). Nevertheless, the rate of unemployment had declined to below 3 per cent in the South-East of the UK, but remained over 9 per cent in the North-East. Spatial disparities within regions and between urban and rural areas remain characteristic for the British labour market. While overall employment grew by 1.7 million jobs between 1981 and 1996, Britain's 20 major cities have lost 500,000 jobs (Turok and Edge 1999).

Chapter 8 of this volume points to the existence of 'hidden' employment in urban China, with substantial numbers of laid-off workers maintaining their links with their previous employers while earning additional income from new jobs elsewhere. While these forms of hidden employment might also be found in the UK, hidden unemployment is a more characteristic feature of the British labour market. Indeed, the number of working-age people neither in employment nor registered as seeking a job has grown in the 1990s. Normally, when employment increases the number of those out of work but not unemployed, i.e. the economically inactive, falls. However, while male unemployment declined after 1993, male inactivity continued to rise, from 1.5 million in 1990 to 2.3 million by 1998. Between the mid-1970s and the mid-1990s male non-employment (excluding students) climbed from about 8 per cent to 22 per cent; and there is a clear positive association between regional unemployment and male inactivity (Gregg and Wadsworth 1999).

By the end of the 1990s, 28 per cent of men over 50 were economically inactive, compared with 7 per cent in the mid-1970s (Dickens et al. 2000). But inactivity also rose strongly for younger age groups. This is reflected in a substantial increase in sickness rates in Britain, reaching 7 per cent by the end of the 1990s and thus the highest rate of working age sickness in the EU (2.1 per cent in Germany; 0.3 per cent in France). Indeed, since the early 1990s there have been more economically inactive than unemployed men in Britain, with the gap widening throughout the 1990s, reaching a ratio of 2:1 by the end of the decade. This dramatic development is obscured by the sharp increase in female labour force participation, with both trends broadly offsetting each other, leaving aggregate inactivity fairly stable (Gregg and Wadsworth 1999).

Many European countries have witnessed a polarization between work-rich two-earner and workless (no-earner) households since the 1980s (Gregg et al. 2000a). However, the incidence of workless households in the UK rose very steeply after the early 1980s, to 19 per cent of all working age households by 1996. Since then the rate has declined somewhat, but not by much (Gregg et al. 2000a). Also, the UK has by far the highest rate of workless households amongst households with children across the OECD. Nearly 20 per cent of all British children grow up in households with no adult in paid employment. Finally, there is a strong correlation between poverty and workless household rates.

Labour Market Insecurity and Unemployment Protection

Although the average job tenure has dropped significantly since the 1970s, chapter 8 of this volume indicated a low level of labour mobility in Chinese urban labour markets. How does this compare with the developed British labour market? In the UK, the average job tenure was 8.3 years in the second half of the 1990s, with 18 per cent of tenures lasting less than one year. Perhaps surprisingly, on average these figures changed little between the mid-1980s and the mid-1990s (OECD 1997: 14). But this masks differences between different labour market groups. Increasing average job tenures for women with dependent children indicate that mothers have gained from improved maternity rights. By contrast, for male workers over the age of 50 the average job tenure dropped significantly during the late 1980s and 1990s (Gregg et al. 2000b). In comparison with other European countries job tenure is very short in the UK, and more similar to that in the USA, Canada and Australia. This is probably influenced by weaker employment protection measures and labour law regulations in the UK compared with the rest of Europe, apart from Denmark.

Overall, the short average job tenure in the UK corresponds with relatively high levels of job insecurity. Employees in other European countries with high job turnover rates and short average tenures, such as Denmark, seem much less worried about job security. Even in Spain, where more than a fifth of the workforce changes jobs within six months, employees feel less insecure in their jobs than in the UK (OECD 1997). The International Social Survey Programme (ISSP) suggests that between 1993 and 1996 job insecurity in the UK increased to a level which was higher than in any other European country, with similar levels recorded only in France. Other survey data confirm a steep increase in perceived job insecurity in 1992 in the UK and high levels since then, even though unemployment started to decline (Spencer 1996).

Thus, high levels of job insecurity in the UK cannot be explained merely with reference to short average job tenure rates or levels of unemployment. Weak protection against unemployment might be coupled with a good protection during unemployment. This is the case in Denmark, a country which provides high levels of income replacement during unemployment. As a result, the connection between unemployment and poverty is not very strong (Hauser et al. 2000). By contrast, short average job tenures in combination with weak social security support during unemployment might explain high levels of employment insecurity in Britain.

Wang and Yandong point to an 'imperfect' social security system for the unemployed in urban China. A minority of laid-off workers are in a favourable position due to the ties which they maintain to their previous employment, facilitating access to pension entitlement and other allowances. However, between 60 and 80 per cent of workers surveyed claimed not to have received any benefits from this or other sources. The inadequate support provided by unemployment protection in China is one of the reasons why recent labour market developments have coincided with growing urban poverty. By comparison, the British system of income maintenance during unemployment seems comprehensive and generous. However, within a European context, this impression is quickly dispelled and the connection between unemployment and poverty is stronger than in other EU countries.

One reason for this is the deteriorating system of unemployment benefits. A succession of small but cumulatively significant restrictions and cuts characterized unemployment benefit policies in the 1980s (Atkinson and Micklewright 1989). As a result, access to benefit entitlement became more difficult while the real value of unemployment benefit fell in relation to average earnings from 16.4 to 12.6 per cent between 1978 and 1990 (Bradshaw 1992). This trend is also reflected in a summary measure of benefit entitlements (of 18 separate gross replacement rates covering different lengths of unemployment spells, two earnings levels and three household types) published by the OECD (1998: 24). This measure shows a long-term decline in benefit generosity in relation to earnings which started in the mid 1970s and was more pronounced than in any of the other 14 European countries covered.

In the 1990s unemployment policy became increasingly driven by the notion of motivating individual job seekers to be more active in their job search and to make attitudes 'more realistic' in terms of wage expectations, which were too high (Deacon 1997: 38). A stricter benefit regime had to be created in line with increased flexibility in the labour market, later complemented by the improvement of in-work benefits, which was an attempt to make lower-paid employment, subsidized by social security benefits, more attractive for claimants with families. These have to be seen in the wider neo-liberal policy context of the time (Wood 2001). Driven by a strong free market ideology, actively supported by employer organizations interested in improving competitiveness by lowering labour costs, and relatively unhampered by institutional impediments, parliamentary obstacles or legal constraints, Conservative governments in the 1980s and 1990s were able to proceed further and faster with labour market deregulation than other European countries. The role of trade unions was substantially weakened. By 1994, the UK had no regulation of working time or wage levels, no legal protection for those hired under fixed-term contracts and no right to representation at the workplace. It scored zero – lowest among EU and EFTA countries and alongside the US – in a composite index of labour market standards, covering regulation of working time, minimum wages, employment protection, employee representation and fixed-term contracts (OECD 1994: 154).

By the mid-1990s Labour had accepted the principle of subsidizing low wages through social security benefits (Grover and Stewart 2000: 242) and the need for a deregulated and flexible labour market. A consensus had emerged around the problem of 'welfare dependency' (Finn 1998: 112). It underpinned the 'stricter benefit regime' introduced by the Thatcher and Major governments as well as the Labour Party's acceptance of the need to put more duties on unemployed people. Unlike previous Labour Party policy, the Blair administration accepted that the provision of social security can have detrimental effects on individual behaviour. Benefit fraud and unemployment traps, for example, became problems perceived as attributable to the impact of welfare systems on job seekers, and the effect of long-term unemployment as detrimental on job search and employability.

The share of unemployed people in receipt of insurance-based benefits has never been very high in the UK, but declined steadily, from about 50 per cent of all registered unemployed receiving contributory-based benefits in the 1970s to around 15 per cent by the late 1990s (DfWP 2001). The Jobseeker's Allowance (JSA), introduced in 1996, blurred the distinction between insurance-based and means-tested support. It substituted the previously dual benefit structure for unemployed people with a unified system. Contributory unemployment benefit was replaced by the contribution-based JSA which reduced the entitlement period for contributory benefits from 12 to 6 months. The addition for an (adult) dependant was abolished and lower benefit rates were introduced for claimants under the age of 25. Those who had exhausted contribution-based JSA, never qualified for it, or needed additional support, could apply for income-based (i.e. means-tested) JSA.

Since the JSA, unemployed benefit claimants have been required to sign a 'Jobseekers Agreement', specifying the detailed steps intended to take to look for work. The definition of 'actively seeking work' also changed and more compulsory interviews were also introduced, at 13 weeks (at which point some voluntary schemes are made available), 6 months (Restart interview), 12 months, 18 months and 2 years. At these stages different schemes became compulsory and different types of help available.

The level of JSA is extremely low in comparison with unemployment benefit levels in other European countries. However, depending on the family context and other potential sources of household income, unemployed people might receive premiums (families, lone parents) and can apply for additional means-tested benefits. The rates of Council Tax benefit and housing benefits, for example, can exceed JSA-based support. However, the European Community Household Panel (ECHP) shows that the risk of poverty among unemployed people in the UK is extremely high (Gallie and Paugam 2000: 385). In a recent study, Gallie et al. (2001) confirmed this cross-sectional evidence with longitudinal information. The first three waves of the ECHP (1994–1996) show that the level of income poverty was far higher than in any other of the 11 EU countries covered.

Labour Market Training and Other Active Policies

Wang and Zhao indicate that the number of unemployed workers in urban China who had received employment training is below 10 per cent. This is extremely low in comparison with unemployed workers in Europe, including the UK, where efforts in the area of active labour market policies have recently been stepped up. However, there are important differences between British labour market policies and those pursued by other European countries.

Relying traditionally on a voluntarist approach to training, steeply rising unemployment in the early 1980s prompted a range of programmes to be put in place or expanded (King 1995: 135; Meager 1997: 72). However, after Margaret Thatcher's third general election victory in 1987, labour market policy was scaled down significantly. Only increasing unemployment in the early 1990s led the government to introduce some rather small-scale temporary job programmes, such as the *Employment Action* (1991) and the *Community Action* schemes (1993). By the mid-1990s the Major government was also experimenting with employment subsidies on a limited scale. Introduced in 1993, *Workstart*, for example, was piloted in four areas. It provided subsidies for taking on unemployed people who had been out of work for more than two years. However, evaluations indicated poor labour market integration rates, as well as deadweight and substitution effects. This reinforced the government's scepticism about large-scale subsidy programmes which were regarded as distorting market forces.

A more significant step towards a more explicit workfare regime taken by the Major government was *Project Work*. Introduced on a trial basis in two localities in 1996, this was a compulsory work-experience scheme aimed at people under the age of 50 who had been out of work for at least two years. For the first 13 weeks claimants were given intensive job-search guidance, followed by a mandatory period of up to 13 weeks' work experience. Hailed as a great success in the 1996 Conservative Party Annual Conference (apparently a 20 per cent higher rate of leaving the unemployment register than in control areas), it was to be expanded to another 28 areas, and its nationwide introduction was announced as an answer to Labour's New Deal programme in the run-up to the 1997 general election.

Employability became a buzzword in the second half of the 1990s, and the central focus to Labour's supply-side oriented labour market policy (Philpott 1999). It refers to attitudes to work, expectations regarding employment and wages and the behaviour of jobseekers and employees as major determinants of employment chances (Peck and Theodore 2000: 731). The Labour government proclaimed that increasing employability would help people to gain skills and qualifications, fight systematic disadvantage among specific groups, and increase the pool of employable labour available and thus contribute to non-inflationary employment growth. To some extent, this corresponded with the European and international discourse on making social protection systems more 'employment friendly' (OECD 1994; European Commission 1998). However, the shift in Labour's position towards the link between social protection and labour markets appears to have been more influenced by the USA, at least in terms of conceptual debates on welfare rights and obligations (Deacon 2000; Walker 1999; Peck and Theodore 2001).

Central to Labour's election plans in terms of welfare reform after 1997, the New Deal programmes did not alter benefit levels but considerably increased the conditionality attached to benefit receipt. Successively introduced since 1998, there are separate New Deal programmes for different groups of unemployed people (for details see Millar 2000; Trickey and Walker 2001). The 'flagship' is a compulsory scheme for all people between 18 and 24 years of age who have been unemployed and in receipt of benefit for six months or more. The programme consists of three stages. The four-month 'gateway period' provides individual 'intensive' job-search assistance. The second stage consists of one of four options: subsidized work in either the private or the public sector, participation in education or training and the option of becoming self-employed. All options involve at least some degree of training and skill acquisition. Unlike any previous programmes, the take-up of one of the four options is compulsory. Failing to enter unsubsidized work after completion of one of the options, further guidance and, if required, training follows (the 'follow-through' stage).

Another compulsory programme is the New Deal for long-term unemployed people who have been unemployed for two years or more and, in some pilot areas, also those out of work for 12 or 18 months. It consists of a period of intensive job reorientation followed by referral to training or work-experience places. The four other New Deal programmes are generally on a voluntary basis. However, a trend towards a more prescriptive approach is detectable in two of them. The New Deal for lone parents is aimed at lone parents whose youngest child is five years old and enrolled in primary school, but others may also take part. Participation is voluntary, but since April 2001 the work-focused interview for all new lone-parent claimants (with children over five) has become compulsory. The New Deal for partners of unemployed consists of personal advice and assistance with work for the potential second earner in an unemployed household. It has also recently become compulsory for partners under 25 without children.

Both of these schemes indicate a widening of labour market policy to groups who are not necessarily registered as unemployed. The same applies to the New Deal for disabled people which is targeted at all working-age disabled or sick claimants and consists of personal advice and assistance (for details, see Stafford 2002). Finally, the voluntary New Deal for those over 50 was launched in April 2000. It is aimed at those who have claimed JSA or Incapacity Benefit for at least six months. It offers personal advice and assistance, training grants and employment credits which allow participants to accept lower wages.

However, the notion that the New Deal has created a new labour market policy regime in the UK needs to be qualified. OECD data indicate that in 1990/1 the UK was devoting 0.6 per cent of GDP to active programmes, which compares to an unweighted average of 0.77 per cent for 21 OECD countries. The trajectory of British efforts in this area was downwards, from 0.7 per cent of GDP in 1985 to 0.4 per cent of GDP in 1996 and 0.37 per cent in 1997/1998 (OECD 1998). By comparison, in the same period average spending in OECD countries rose from 0.7 per cent to 0.9 per cent of GDP. This upward trend included countries with high and stagnating unemployment (Germany, France), as well as countries with declining unemployment rates (Denmark, the Netherlands). Measured as spending per person unemployed, British expenditure declined even more quickly.

Unfortunately OECD data do not distinguish spending on job-search activity from administrative costs. Nevertheless, the increase of total administrative costs from 22 per cent (1985) to 43 per cent (1996) of total expenditure on active labour market policy in the UK is conspicuous. The latter figure was far above the EU average (19 per cent) at the time. In the same period, expenditure on training measures remained below the EU average, and spending on job creation in the public sector dropped significantly from 25 per cent (1985) to 2 per cent in 1996, which was the lowest in the EU (bar Luxembourg) and far below the EU average of 15 per cent.

Within the New Deal programmes spending is heavily weighted towards the young unemployed, representing about 70 per cent of total expenditure. It is unclear whether this emphasis has paid off. The decline of youth unemployment had already started before the New Deal was launched, and it is difficult to disentangle the favourable economic climate from any contributions the New Deal might have made to falling unemployment. In any case, the positive macroeconomic context meant that the anticipated outlay for the first years of the programmes (£5.2 million) was lower than initially anticipated.

But even the level of resources which was planned for the New Deal would not have substantially changed the scope of British labour market policy. The OECD

(1999) points out that the share of spending on active labour market policy in the UK rose from 27 per cent in 1994 to 31 per cent in 1997. However, real term spending on active labour market policy remained low and fell more sharply in the 1990s than in any of the other 20 OECD countries, with only the USA, Japan and Greece spending less than the UK (Robinson, 2000). In other words, the rise in the relative share of resources devoted to active measures is a result of the decline in (passive) social security spending on unemployed people from £10.4 billion (12.3 per cent of total social security expenditure) to £6.1 billion (5.2 per cent) in the same period between 1994 and 1997.

The New Deal has not altered this picture. It raised total spending on active labour market policy by merely one-tenth of a percentage point of GDP. Since this was well below expenditure levels earlier in the 1990s (Robinson 2000: 18), it did little to reverse the trend of declining expenditure on active measures. In other words, the suggestion that the New Deal represents a radically different approach to active measures, at least in spending terms, is clearly inaccurate. The UK has remained a very modest spender on active labour market policy.

On the other hand, the New Deal is but one element in the package of increasing labour market participation and 'making work pay'. In fact, rather than labour market policies, the minimum wage and tax credits are much more central to the government's welfare-to-work reforms. The UK government's forecast for 2001/2, for example, was to spend £900 million on the New Deal but 'an extra £6,000 million on increased benefits and tax credits aimed at low-income families' (Robinson 2000: 25). Whether by design or by accident, the emerging strategy, then, seems to be one which is less based on training and more on relatively cheap job-search-focused programmes to move people into regular employment and to subsidize especially employees with families so that their net income is above the poverty line (ibid.). The incomes of those in work are enhanced by the introduction of a minimum wage, and a range of tax credits. The National Child Care Strategy combines guaranteed nursery places for all four-year-olds with subsidies for child care at the beginning and end of the school day and in the holidays. From 2003 a new Integrated Child Credit will be introduced which aims at pulling together all of the financial support for children that is currently paid through welfare payments, in-work benefits and tax credits into a single instrument, with the same rules and administration.

Conclusion

A direct and systematic comparison of labour market developments and policy changes in unemployment support and labour market policy between the UK and China seems futile. Not only is the size of the countries very different but the constitutions of national labour markets are at opposing ends of a continuum. The British labour market is one of the oldest in the world. Political attempts to regulate or influence the interplay between labour demand and labour supply have perhaps been less intensive than in some other European countries, but they rest on a long history. By contrast, the Chinese labour market is still in a process of development and subject to strong geographical, occupational and other disparities.

Refraining from a systematic comparison, this chapter thus drew on some of the characteristics which were highlighted in Chapter 8 in this volume (hidden unemployment, labour mobility, flexibility, social security support for the unemployed and employment training). These aspects were used to guide the discussion of the British labour market and contemporary labour market policies in a comparative European context.

The chapter indicated aspects of policy continuity within labour market and benefit policies in the 1990s. This included the emphasis on reducing social security spending and the concentration of resources on those in 'real need', as well as the belief in the beneficial effect of deregulated labour markets, and a more explicit responsibility on the part of job seekers. But there are also discontinuities. The New Deal extended compulsory 'workfare-like' elements (Trickey and Walker 2001), particularly for younger people and long-term unemployed. It included groups who were previously not targets of labour market policy (lone parents, disabled people, partners of the unemployed). It also connects labour market policies with a wider welfare-to-work strategy which aims to move people from benefits into employment by a mixture of incentives, opportunities, encouragement and compulsion.

However, representing largely a supply-side instrument aimed at raising the employability of registered job seekers, the New Deal has not increased the level of spending on active labour market policy in the UK. Also, within the range of programmes, the relative significance of training and skill enhancement is rather modest. Unlike elsewhere in Europe, there is no trend towards establishing an intermediary labour market or expanding job creation. Whether such an approach will be sufficient to provide effective labour market integration in regions of cumulative labour market disadvantage (high levels of unemployment and inactivity) remains questionable without targeted demand measures (such as urban regeneration and job creation for less skilled people).

In order to improve the labour market participation rates of some groups (lone parents, disabled people) a more substantial effort might be needed which would match the political rhetoric. Access to training and education for these groups has remained rather limited, and other policies to help facilitate transition to work insufficient. The minimum wage will have benefited many lone parents and the number of lone parents receiving in-work subsidies almost doubled between 1996 and 2000. However, the effect is often marginal due to the reduction in other means-tested benefits (e.g. housing support) and a shortage of affordable childcare (Dean 2001).

Within a European context, the UK system of unemployment support seems an excessively means-tested system. Tax credits can help to weaken unemployment traps but potentially open up poverty traps if low-paid subsidized jobs do not function as stepping stones but as the baseline for people trapped at the bottom end of the labour market. Also, potentially a new cleavage in terms of the level of social protection might emerge between relatively better-off benefit recipients in work, and others who have to rely on increasingly residual social security support outside paid employment. It is a poignant reminder, and an important point to make in the context of emerging labour markets such as the Chinese one, that equally successful economies in Europe, such as Denmark or the Netherlands, have enacted similar active labour market policies to those in the UK, without dispensing with their more adequate levels of unemployment protection.

References

Atkinson, A.B. and Micklewright, J. (1989), 'Turning the screw: benefits for the unemployed', 1979–1988, in A. Dilnot and I. Walker (eds), *The economics of social security*, Oxford University Press, Oxford.
Bradshaw, J. (1992), 'Social Security', in D. Marsh and R.A.W. Rhodes (eds), Milton Keynes *Implementing Thatcherite Policies: Audit of an Era*, Open University Press.
Deacon, A. (1997), 'Welfare to Work: Options and Issues', in E. Brunsdon, H. Dean and R. Woods (eds), *Social Policy Review 9*, London: Social Policy Association, pp. 34–49.
Deacon, A. (2000), 'Learning from the US? The influence of American ideas upon "new labour" thinking on welfare reform', *Policy and Politics*, 28, 1: 5–18.
Dean, H. (2001), 'The family policy trilemma: the consequences for low-income families in liberal welfare regimes', paper presented at the European Sociological Association, Helsinki, 29 August–1 September.
DfWP (Department for Work and Pensions), (2001), *Jobseeker's Allowance Statistics: May 2001 Quarterly Statistical Enquiry*, Analytical Services Division, Information Centre, Newcastle.
Dickens, R., Gregg, P. and Wadsworth, J. (2000), 'New Labour and the labour market', *Oxford Review of Economic Policy*, 16, 1: 95–113.
European Commission (1998), *Social Protection in Europe 1997*, Office for Official Publications of the European Communities, DG Employment and Social Affairs, Luxembourg.
European Commission (2001), *Employment in Europe 2001*, Office for Official Publications of the European Communities, DG Employment and Social Affairs, Luxembourg.
Eurostat (2001), *Eurostat Yearbook 2001. The statistical guide to Europe. Data 1989–99*, Eurostat, Luxembourg.
Finn, D. (1998), 'Labour's "New Deal" for the unemployed and the stricter benefit regime', in E. Brunsdon, H. Dean and R. Woods (eds), *Social Policy Review 10*, Social Policy Association, London, pp. 105–122.
Gallie, D. and Paugam, S. (2000), 'Replacement rates in Europe', in D. Gallie and S. Paugam (eds), *Welfare Regimes and the Experience of Unemployment in Europe*, Oxford University Press, Oxford.
Gallie, D., Paugam, S. and Jacobs, S. (2001), 'Unemployment, poverty and social isolation: is there a vicious circle of social exclusion?' paper presented at Euresco conference on Labour Market Change, Unemployment and Citizenship in Europe, Helsinki.
Gregg, P. and Wadsworth, J. (1999), 'Economic inactivity', in P. Gregg and J. Wadsworth (eds), *The State of Working Britain*, Manchester University Press, Manchester, pp.47–57.
Gregg, P., Hansen, K. and Wadsworth, J. (2000a), 'Poles apart: labour market performance and the distribution of work across households', *World Economics*, 1, 2: 55–72.
Gregg, P., Knight, G. and Wadsworth, J. (2000b), 'Heaven knows I'm miserable now: job insecurity in the British labour market', in E. Heery and J. Salmon (eds), *The Insecure Workforce*, Routledge, London.
Grover, C. and Stewart, J. (2000), 'Modernizing social security? Labour and its welfare-to-work strategy', *Social Policy and Administration*, 34, 3: 235–52.
Hauser, R., Nolan, B., with Mörsdorf, K. and Strengmann-Kuhn, M. (2000), 'Unemployment and poverty: change over time', in D. Gallie and S. Paugam (eds), *Welfare Regimes and the Experience of Unemployment in Europe*, Oxford University Press, Oxford.
Jackman, R. and Savouri, S. (1999), 'Has Britain solved the "regional problem"?' in P. Gregg and J. Wadsworth (eds), *The State of Working Britain*, Manchester University Press, Manchester, pp.47–57.
King, D. (1995), *Actively Seeking Work? The Politics of Unemployment and Welfare Policy in the United States and Great Britain*, University of Chicago Press, London.

Meager, N. (1997), United Kingdom. 'Active and passive labour market policies in the United Kingdom, Employment Observatory', *SYSDEM Trends*, no. 28, European Commission, DG Employment and Social Affairs, Berlin: IAS, pp. 69–75.

Millar, J. (2000), *Keeping Track of Welfare Reform: The New Deal Programmes*, Joseph Rowntree Foundation, York Publishing Services, York.

OECD (1994), *The OECD Jobs Study: Evidence and Explanations*. Part 1: *Labour Market Trends and Underlying Forces of Change*. Part 2: *The Adjustment Potential of the Labour Market*, OECD, Paris.

OECD (1997), 'Is job insecurity on the increase in OECD countries?' In *OECD Employment Outlook*, OECD, Paris.

OECD (1998), 'What works among active labour market policies: evidence from OECD countries' experiences', *Labour Market and Social Policy Occasional Papers* no. 35, OECD Working Papers, vol. VI, OECD, Paris.

OECD (1999), *Benefit Systems and Work Incentives*, OECD, Paris.

Ogus, A. and Wikeley, N. (eds) (1995), *The Law of Social Security*, Butterworth, London.

Peck, J. and Theodore, N. (2000), 'Beyond "employability"', *Cambridge Journal of Economics*, 24: 729–49.

Peck, J. and Theodore, N. (2001), 'Exporting workfare / importing welfare-to-work: exploring the politics of Third Way policy transfer', *Political Geography*, 20: 427–60.

Philpott, J. (1999), *Behind the Buzzword: 'Employability'*, Employment Policy Institute, London.

Robinson, P. (2000), 'Active labour-market policies: a case of evidence-based policy making?' *Oxford Review of Economic Policy*, 16, 1: 13–26.

Rowthorn, R. (2000), Kalecki Centenary Lecture: 'The political economy of full employment in modern Britain', *Oxford Bulletin of Economics and Statistics*, 62, 2: 139–73.

Spencer, P. (1996), 'Reactions to a flexible labour market', in R. Jowell et al. (eds), *British Social Attitudes: the 13th Report*, Dartmouth, Aldershot.

Stafford, B. (2002), 'Beyond lone parents: extending welfare-to-work to disabled people and the young unemployed,' *Journal of Policy Analysis and Management* (forthcoming).

Trickey, H. and Walker, R. (2001), 'Steps to compulsion within British labour market policies', in I. Lødemel and H. Trickey (eds), *An Offer You Can't Refuse: Workfare in International Perspective*, Policy Press, Bristol, pp. 181–214.

Turok, I. and Edge, N. (1999), *The Jobs Gap in Britain's Cities: Employment Loss and Labour Market Consequences*. Policy Press, Bristol.

Walker, R. (1999), 'The Americanization of British welfare: a case study of policy transfer', *International Journal of Health Services*, 29, 4: 679–97.

Wood, S. (2001), 'Labour market regimes under threat? Sources of continuity in Germany, Britain, and Sweden', in P. Pierson (ed.), *The New Politics of the Welfare State*, Oxford University Press, Oxford.

Chapter 10

Pension Reform in China

Nelson Chow and Yuebin Xu

Introduction

China's economic reforms from the early 1980s have helped give rise to a wide array of social problems. Among others, one immediate and urgent need has been to provide pensions for the increasing numbers of retirees emanating from economically constrained state-owned enterprises (SOEs), because these threaten social stability and impede the shift from a centrally planned to a socialist market economy. Under the former centrally planned economy, SOEs provided full and life-long employment for their employees with various employment-related benefits, such as pensions and health care, to cover their needs 'from cradle to grave'. Economic reform, however, has diversified the planned single public ownership economy into a mixed market economy, with various types of ownership and with the vigour of economic enterprise being shifted from the public to the non-public sector. As a result, China's traditional employment-centered social security system has been faced with with formidable challenges. To facilitate economic reform, yet to combat a rapidly ageing population as well, the government launched its reforms of the pension system with the purpose of creating a partially funded system, which has been widely held as the optimal measure for China to finance its ageing population. This chapter will focus on these recent reforms and discuss the viability of the partially funded pension system that China is currently attempting to establish.

The Goals of Pension Reform in China

Pension reform in China started and has since been carried on largely in response to the transition from a planned to a market economy and the need to deal with the security of a rapidly ageing population[1] (Chow and Xu 2001). The traditional pension system in China, which was first established in 1951 and subsequently underwent three major adjustments in 1955, 1958 and 1978 respectively,[2] was the product of a centrally planned economy. It was a largely urban-based, pay-as-you-go and defined benefit system, covering mainly the public sector in urban areas.[3] However, entering the 1980s and particularly since the start of economic reform, the traditional pension system proved a still-formidable obstacle to economic reform, and its viability was challenged. Among others, one urgent problem was that, by the mid-1980s, rapid increases in the number of retirees relative to that of employees in SOEs had resulted in huge pension burdens in the state sector,[4] leading to a 'pension crisis' for most SOEs. Another problem was that the traditional system's partial coverage not only impeded labour mobility – particularly from the state to the non-state sector, which has been the driving force for China's economic growth – but in the meantime, and worse, meant that a majority of China's currently becoming-old people would have no pensions on their retirement. This is because economic reform has turned the former single-public-ownership economy into a mixture of miscellaneous economic systems with various types of ownership;[5] with more and more of the labour force shifting as a result from the state to the non-state sector.[6]

Thus, pension reform in China was, at the beginning, intended to accomplish two immediate objectives: one was to relieve SOEs of the pension burdens inherited from the era of the planned economy, and the other was to facilitate the development of a labour market in the service of ongoing economic reform. Since the mid-1990s, however, the goal of pension reform has shifted to the transformation of the system from a pay-as-you-go to a partially funded scheme, attempting to resolve the problems of providing pensions for a rapidly ageing population.

The Implementation of Reform Policies in the Pension System

Local reforms in the pension system started as soon as the early 1980s, when individual localities began to explore possibilities for social pooling across enterprises, so as to solve the problems of uneven pension burdens between SOEs. Such locally based schemes were implemented on an experimental basis, thus differing widely in both their design and their administration. However, by the mid-1980s, a variety of locally administered pension schemes had been established,[7] geared to trying to convert the traditional pension system – financed and administered by individual enterprises – into a social-pooling system spread between enterprises sharing the same types of ownership.

National pension reform took place mainly during the 1990s. Between 1991 and 2000, the State Council issued four documents, which laid down the principles and direction of pension reform in China. Specifically, the State Council Document 33 of 1991 established social pooling across enterprises offering schemes based on individual contributions. Document 6 of 1995 laid down basic financing principles for social pooling and the management of individual accounts, with the purpose of establishing a partially funded pension system. Document 26 of 1997 stipulated the establishment of a provincially unified basic benefit system; and Document 42 of 2000 reaffirmed the partially funded approach; separated the management of individual accounts from that of the socially-pooled funds, and readjusted the size and structure of individual accounts. The following is a brief review of these four documents and the effects of their implementation.

State Council Document 33 of 1991

State Council Document 33 called for the establishment of a three-tier pension plan – a basic benefit, a supplementary benefit to be provided by individual enterprises, and a benefit based on individual savings – for all types of employees. Funding responsibility for the basic tier was to be shared between the government, enterprises and individual workers/employees were also required to make individual contributions. Its financing was geared to the actual pension expenditure and funds were to be raised according to the principle of 'financing according to expenditure plus small surpluses and partial accumulation'. Local governments were given discretion over the rates of contributions and accumulation. In particular, enterprises were required to contribute a certain percentage of the wage bill as set by local government, and employees to contribute a maximum of 3 per cent of the standard wage. The rate of individual contribution was to be gradually raised in accordance with economic growth and rates of increase in wages. Contributions by enterprises and employees were to be transferred to the 'pension fund account' established by local social insurance agencies in the bank and interest was to be credited to the funds. Part of the reserves could be invested in government bonds.

The second tier, supplementary benefit, was encouraged for enterprises with sound financial capacity. These enterprises were allowed to use funds hitherto reserved for the delivery of bonuses and employee welfare to fund a benefit pool for their own employees, and these funds were to be kept in the individual accounts of employees. The third tier benefit was a voluntary pension programme based on individual savings. Employees could participate in the saving programmes according to their own financial capacity. The design and management of these programmes could be linked to the enterprise supplementary benefit tier. These regulations applied mainly to SOEs, but collectively owned enterprises in the urban areas were allowed to design their own pension programmes with reference to the same regulations.

While outlining the new directions for pension reforms, that is, the establishment of a provincially unified system capable of covering all types of employees, Document 33 was basically a reaffirmation of the social pooling across enterprises which had been practised by some individual localities since 1984. It did not suggest changes in the methods of providing benefits, because its major objective was to raise revenues and spread the pension costs over a larger population. The provision of benefits continued to follow the regulations of the 1951 State Council Regulations on Labour Insurance, in that length of service and the standard wage[8] remained the bases for providing benefits for retirees. With social pooling generally established in the country by around 1992, both central government and the localities turned their attention to reforming the methods of providing benefits.

To make benefits more closely related to individual contributions, the Ministry of Labour issued Document 275 in October 1993, recommending local governments to reform their methods of pension provision. Specifically, the basic benefits consisted of a social pension and a premium pension. The wage base used for calculating the social pension was the average local wage, and benefits were provided based on the number of years of individual contribution, ranging from 15 to 25 per cent of the average local wage. The wage base used for calculating the premium pension was the worker's indexed monthly average wage during the contribution years, and benefits were provided based on both the indexed average wage and the number of years of individual contribution. A worker who had contributed for five years and above was to get 1 per cent of the indexed monthly average wage for each contribution year; whereas a worker who had contributed for less than five years received a lump-sum payment equivalent to three months' indexed average wage for each year of contribution.

State Council Document 6 of 1995

State Council Document 6 laid down the financial principle for the basic benefit tier: social pooling plus the individual account. Specifically, the document proposed two plans in which social pooling and individual accounts could be combined with different emphasis, and allowed local governments to choose between them or design their own plans according to their local situation.

Plan One placed more emphasis on individual accounts, made up by enterprises contributing 8 per cent of each worker's total wage and 5 per cent of the average local wage, and individuals contributing 3 per cent of their wages. Over time, the contribution from enterprises would decrease and individual contribution would increase, until individual employees would be responsible for half the total contributions to their individual accounts. Benefits would depend mainly on the individual account and the interest it had earned from the bank. When a worker reached retirement age, after contributing for at least 15 years, he/she would receive a monthly pension equal to 1/120 of the total funds accumulated in the individual account. However, individual accounts would apply only to new employees, joining work after the implementation of the plan. Those already retired, together with current employees not fully covered by individual accounts, would continue with the old arrangements. Their benefits were to be adjusted annually and paid out of the social pool.

Plan Two placed more emphasis on social pooling than on individual accounts. Individual accounts were to be established from part or the whole of the individual contribution, plus part of the enterprise contribution, the size of which last was allowed to vary depending on local circumstances. Benefits were to relate mainly to the local wage. For those who had contributed for more than 10 years, benefits were to consist of a social pension equivalent to 20-25 per cent of the average local wage, a premium pension equivalent to 1.0-1.4 per cent of the wage base for each year of contribution, and an individual account pension which could be drawn as a lump sum or as an annuity equivalent to the funds in the individual account.

The direction of pension reform according to Document 6 was to effect a transition from the current pay-as-you-go system to a partially funded system, based on social pooling and individual accounts. However, the implementation of Document 6 resulted in some unexpected consequences. First, due to the fact that Document 6 allowed local governments to choose between the two proposed plans or else to invent their own schemes according to their local situation, a variety of schemes – differing widely in design, administration and benefit levels – developed across the country. For instance, the size of individual accounts ranged between 3 per cent and 17 per cent of total contributions,[9] with benefits varying substantially depending on local ideologies about, or interpretations of, the principle of combining efficiency and social equity. Such a widely varying national pension system was not only difficult to administer by central government, it also posed problems of portability and gaps in benefits across and between localities.

Second, local governments tended to compete to provide a higher level of benefits by either reducing employee contributions or directly raising benefits. In 1995, the actual rates of employee contributions in most localities were around 2 per cent of wages, which was generally lower than the officially stipulated rates of 3-4 per cent by local governments; yet the pension replacement rates reached over 80 per cent.

Furthermore, replacement rates kept growing in the following years so that by 1998 the national average pension replacement rate amounted to 89 per cent[10] (China Labour and Social Security Ministry 1999: 178). Finally and most importantly, this divided pension system had become a new constraint on further economic reform.

State Council Document 26 of 1997

To correct the defects of the ongoing pension system and make it more conducive to economic reforms, in 1997 the State Council issued Document 26, which stipulated the establishment of a unified system for the basic benefit tier. Specifically, it first reiterated that a unified pension system should be established for enterprises and employees across all types of ownership. Second, contribution rates were to be unified. Previously, enterprise contributions had been based on the sum of pensions plus the wage bill. This time the base was to be the wage bill alone. A ceiling of 20 per cent of the wage bill was recommended for enterprise contributions, while a floor of 4 per cent of wages was set for individual contributions. In the years to come, individual contributions were to be raised 1 percent every two years until they reached 8 per cent of wages. Third, the size of the individual account was to be unified and set at 11 per cent of a worker's wage. Thus, with the individual contribution rate increasing to 8 per cent over time, enterprises were eventually to be contributing just 3 per cent. Finally, the method of providing benefits was to be unified. The basic benefit was to consist of a basic pension and an individual account pension, taking into consideration both the wage and the accumulated savings in the individual account. A worker who reached retirement age after contributing for at least 15 years was to get a monthly basic pension equivalent to 20 per cent of the average local wage in the year prior to his/her retirement, plus a monthly individual account pension equivalent to the funds in the individual account divided by 120. Thus, benefit replacement rates were to be reduced from over 80 per cent to below 60 per cent.

However, the implementation of this State Council Document 26 met with several problems. For instance, the compliance rate, that is, the percentage of employees and enterprises having actually made their contributions in the total number of those covered by the scheme, continued to decline. Between 1997 and 1998, the compliance rate declined from 90 per cent to 77 per cent, with 25 localities being unable to balance their pension funds and an increasing number of enterprises failing to deliver pensions for their retirees. Because of the increasing debts that enterprises owed their pensioners, and the continued declining compliance rates, the government's major efforts have since been directed at trying to force enterprises into providing for their retirees and laid-off employees.[11]

Two major factors accounted for the decline in compliance rates. One was the poor economic performance of SOEs. Since the mid-1990s an increasing number of enterprises had been running at a loss, and many of them even had difficulties in delivering wages to their employees, let alone in making social insurance contributions. The second factor related to administration. Due to the lack of social insurance law, contributions to the various social insurance programmes had in effect become optional choices for enterprises. Major efforts by fund management agencies to collect contributions amounted to campaigns, persuasion or personal relations. If an enterprise or an individual refused to pay contributions, there was virtually nothing that could be done about them.

To improve fundraising, the State Council issued *Temporary Regulations on Collecting Social Insurance Contributions,* in January 1999, which legalized the procedures and contributions for social insurance. The Regulations ordered all eligible enterprises to register with social insurance agencies and to pay their contributions. It also established penalties and legal procedures for dealing with enterprises or individuals who failed to perform in accordance to the regulations. Thus, social insurance became compulsory for both enterprises and individuals. Fund management agencies were able to place a penalty on managers and enterprises, or file a suit against them, if they refused to hand over their contributions.

Another problem, however, was that the system's coverage remained confined to enterprises under public ownership. By the end of 2000 the new pension system in China covered 91.24 million employees and 30.11 million retirees in enterprises, an increase of 5.4 and 5.3 per cent respectively over the previous year.[12] But compared with the total number of 212.74 million urban employees by the end of 2000, it covered only about 43 per cent of the urban active labour force. One major factor accounting for this situation was that, due to the continued shrinkage of the public sector economy,[13] the urban labour force has been shifting rapidly from the public into the non-public sector. In fact, since the economic reforms, increases in the number of urban employees have been mainly a non-state sector phenomenon. The number of urban employees in SOEs increased from 74.51 million in 1978 to 112.61 million in 1995, and then declined to 90.58 million by 1998. Similarly, the numbers of employees in collectively owned enterprises first increased from 20.48 million in 1978 to 36.28 million in 1991, but then decreased consistently to 19.63 million by 1998. By contrast, between 1985 and 1998 the number of urban employees in enterprises with non-public ownership rose steadily from 0.38 million to 48.97 million (*China Statistical Yearbook 1999*: 136). Yet the system is still mainly confined to the public sector. In 1999, among the covered employees, 68 per cent (64.55 million) were from SOEs; 16 per cent (14.79 million) from collectively owned enterprises; 9.7 per cent (9.26 million) come from enterprises with other types of ownership, private enterprises; and the self-employed; and the rest (6.43 million, 7 per cent) come from public institutions and government agencies (China Labour and Social Security Ministry 2000).

Although the establishment of a unified pension system capable of covering all types of urban employees and enterprises has been promoted by the central government since the early 1990s, it has proved difficult in practice for such a system to include non-public sector employees, particularly the employees of private enterprises and the self-employed.[14] The problem is that, in the course of the transition from a planned to market economy, enterprises or employees outside the public economy are also out of the effective control of the government. Specifically, first, the administration of these 'informal'[15] employees is difficult because they are widely scattered, frequently change or lose jobs, and usually do not have a stable or regular wage income. Thus the participation of labour forces outside the public sector depends effectively on the willingness of the employees.

Second, employees in the non-public sector generally lack the motivation to participate in the system in any case. In a time of drastic change, uncertainty prevails as to the social, economic and political future of China, and many people are suspicious about whether they will be paid the promised pension when they retire. To be sure, to expand the funding base, local governments have provided various favourable conditions to encourage the self-employed in particular to participate in the system (such as reducing the contribution rate and allowing them to choose between 60 and 300 per cent of the average local wage as their base for making a contribution), but the self-employed are still not motivated to participate. There is also a technical factor that has proved to be a disincentive for both the self-employed and non-public sector employees. The basic pension does not relate to the number of year of contribution, once one has contributed for more than 15 years. In other words, a worker's additional years of contribution are not counted in calculating his/her basic pension. Thus, even if compelled to enter the scheme, they would choose (or, in practice, delay) to contribute for only 15 years: just sufficient to qualify for the basic pension. This has also served to undermine the funding basis of the system.

Due to this partial coverage, the funding base of the system has also been shrinking relative to the increase in the number of pensioners. Thus pension burdens for the public sector have actually increased. Between 1996 and 2000, whilst the number of covered employees in enterprises increased from 87.58 million to 91.24 million, covered retirees increased from 23.58 million to 30.11 million (China Labour and Social Security Ministry 2001), which means that roughly three contributors are currently supporting one pensioner.[16] Over the years, pension burdens have kept on increasing, due to the limited coverage of contributors, continued increases in the number of pensioners and continued increases in the amount of pensions; leading to increasing deficits in the funds, with more and more provinces failing to balance their funds. In 1999, the total deficit stood at 17.94 billion yuan, with 30 provinces having pension expenditures in excess of their incomes.[17] In 2000 the deficit reached 35.7 billion yuan (China Labour and Social Security Ministry 2001) and it was estimated that the current pension system would have an accumulated deficit of 1,800 billion yuan over the next 25 years, averaging around 70 billion yuan each year (ibid).

Thus the new pension system was continuing to operate, in effect, on a pay-as-you-go basis. In other words, the efforts at pension reform had failed to accomplish the goal of establishing a partially funded system and, theoretically, they were going to fail to deliver pensions for China's rapidly ageing population. The new system had been designed mainly for the new labour force taking up work after its implementation. Their pension payments were supposed to consist of a pooled benefit and savings accumulated in individual accounts when they retired in around 30 years' time. In most localities, however, the savings in the individual accounts of new workers are notional. All contributions have been mixed and used to pay the pensions of the currently retired.

State Council Document 42 of 2000

In spite of the difficulties experienced in trying to move from a pay-as-you-go to a partially funded system, both researchers and policy makers in China widely believe a partially funded system to be the best choice for China to finance its ageing population; so the government is determined to achieve this transition. In December

2000, the State Council issued Document 42, which made some important changes in the social security system and decided to carry out a trial of the newly revised scheme in Liaoning Province.[18] This experiment started in July 2001, and its overall effects remain to be seen.

Within this new social security framework, three adjustments have been made to the pension system. First, the size of individual accounts was reduced from the previous 11 per cent of the wage down to 8 per cent and their establishment was to be based solely on individual contributions, which were also raised up to 8 per cent of the wage.[19] Second, individual accounts were to be managed separately from the social pooling funds, established based on enterprise contributions of 20 per cent of the wage. After this separation, individual accounts were to become fully funded funds, to be managed in the form of trust investment funds in the capital market. Thus, social pooling will no longer be able to borrow money from individual accounts. Third, to compensate for benefits reduced due to reduction of the size of individual accounts, the level of the basic pension was to be raised by relating it more closely to the years of contribution in excess of 15 years. A worker reaching retirement age after contributing for 15 years would get a monthly basic pension equivalent to 20 per cent of the average local wage. If the worker has contributed more than 15 years, he/she will get another benefit from the basic pension for each additional year of contribution until the total benefit reaches 30 per cent of the average wage.

In summary, pension reform in China has been moving along a winding road (Leung 1998), characterized by increment and experiment and slow in development. Reforms started in the 1980s with the immediate and rather urgent need to reduce and share pension burdens among SOEs. To increase revenues to deal with increasing pension burdens, Document 33 of 1991 established individual contribution with the goal of setting up a provincially unified system capable of covering all types of employees. Document 6 of 1995 stipulated the establishment of a partially funded pension system based on two sorts of benefit which have since remained the target for pension reforms in China: a pay-as-you-go social pooling and a fully funded individual account. But different provinces and cities then adopted different pension models with different proportions of pooled funds and individual accounts, resulting in a variety of locally fragmented systems that proved an obstacle to further reform in both the economic and social security sector. The implementation of Document 26 of 1997 reunified the basic benefit tier at the provincial level, but the new scheme continued to be on a pay-as-you-go basis, due to its partial coverage, declining compliance rates and the 'notionality' of its individual accounts. The most recent changes in the pension system, as contained in Document 42 of 2000, have separated the management of individual accounts from the social pooling funds, indicating the government's determination still to create a viable partially funded pension system.

The Viability of the Partially Funded System for China

Researchers and policy makers in China have varied widely in their opinions as to whether China should adopt a pay-as-you-go or a fully funded or a partially funded approach to pension reform (China Labour and Social Security Ministry 2000). Compared with a funded approach, in the current social, economic and political context of China the advantages of a pay-as-you-go system seem to be immediate and obvious: It would avoid the risks of inflation, the instability and vicissitudes of the capital market and the high management costs inherently involved with a funded approach. More importantly, a pay-as-you-go scheme is more practical and even seems the only valid option for China. The current system, although designed with the intention of accumulating some funds, has been running into difficulties even on a pay-as-you-go basis, and there is little prospect of the system accumulating meaningful funds either now or in the foreseeable future. Finally, some researchers consider the accumulation of funds to be only necessary when the population is ageing. After China's population ageing reaches its peak (around 2030), the dependency ratio should be declining, so there should be no further need to accumulate funds. Thus, instead of increasing pension burdens, a pay-as-you-go system would ensure reduced burdens for enterprises.

The disadvantages of a fully funded individual account, within the current context of China, are also obvious. Apart from the risks and high management costs already referred to, it is simply not affordable. China not only has to finance an ageing population, it also needs to provide for such mounting needs as laid-off employees and poverty-stricken households.[20] In addition, there are also technical problems attached to managing pension funds for such a huge population. In short, the funded approach would involve too many contingencies for China to be able to cope with – and increases in the value of the funds could not be guaranteed. It can only be an ideal, of theoretical appeal. At least, it is not what China should be attempting either currently or for the foreseeable future.

Nevertheless, one generally agreed advantage of a fully funded scheme is that it is more effective in combating population ageing, for which funds accumulation is required. Another advantage is that a fully funded system tends to be more equitable across the labour force irrespective of types of ownership, particularly across the state and the non-state sector. The traditional pay-as-you-go system was designed mainly to meet the needs of employees in the state sector. If employees in the non-state sector are included in such a system, however, inequity will result, as they would become net contributors. Finally, a funded approach is viewed as more efficient. It would not only reflect the market economy principle of self-reliance and individual enterprise that China has been encouraging since the economic reforms, but would also motivate or stimulate employees from outside the public sector to participate in the system, and thus invigorate it.

Although most researchers and policy makers in China regard the current partially funded approach to be the correct choice there remains, at least at the theoretical level, the possibility that the current partially funded pension system may eventually fall back into a pay as you go scheme, as is indeed currently the case. Indeed, along with population ageing and – in view of the current difficulties over funds accumulation – the probability of the accumulated funds being used up, it is likely that the system will evolve into a pay-as-you-go scheme, if alternative sources of funding are not made available. Although the ultimate viability of the partially funded system depends on factors in the macro environment such as continued economic growth and increases in the wages and contributions of covered employees in the future, it depends more immediately and crucially on how the transitional costs, that is, the current system's liabilities to both the old and new workers in its transition from a pay-as-you-go to a partially funded scheme,[21] are to be financed. If they are left to be covered by enterprises and employees alone, as is the case currently, it is inevitable that the new system will continue to run as a pay as you go scheme, with no possibility of transition to a partially funded system as is intended now.

The crucial point, therefore, is how alternative sources of funding are to be obtained or revenues to be increased. The general consensus amongst researchers in China is that the government has to take up responsibility for financing pension payments for the transitional cohorts who either do not have, or are not fully covered by, individual accounts. However, opinions vary as to how the government should actually finance these costs, including selling state-owned assets, issuing government bonds, levying a special consumption tax, financing through general revenues or investing funds in the capital market.[22] Second, action has to be taken to render the individual accounts gradually fully funded, and to ensure their management separately from the social pooling funds. Otherwise, a continuance of merely notional individual accounts will not only lead to further increases in the debts of the system, but will also have a negative effect on the confidence of people in the system, resulting in yet further declines in compliance rates. Finally, there have been also proposals that resort to rather traditional methods of tinkering with an ailing pension system: increasing contribution rates, lowering replacement rates, and raising the retirement age (China Labour and Social Security Ministry 2001).

Conclusion

The most important achievement of the pension system that China has been implementing since the early 1990s has been that it has, to some extent, resolved the problem of the previous enterprise-financed pension payments, so that 'workers are now ensured at least some form of payments when they retire, unrelated, as in the past, to the financial vicissitudes of their enterprises. At a time when the enterprises of China are going through a series of mergers and reorganizations, this guarantee of continued payment of old age pensions is particularly important' (Chow 2000: 123).

Indeed, the transition from a pay-as-you-go system to a partially funded system could not fail to be a challenging issue for all nations undertaking such a change, because it requires substantial increases in the amount of payroll taxes taken from the current labour force. This is even more challenging in the context of China, in that the transition from a pay-as-you-go to a funded approach is in the context of a transition from a planned to a market economy also. In addition to the rapidly increasing number of retirees demanding funds for retirement payments, the trend for labour and economic vigour to shift from the public to the non-public sector has resulted in increasing burdens for employees and enterprises remaining in the current system, given its considerable liabilities in respect of both old and new workers. Unless the government substantially increases its responsibility for covering such deficits, the continued financial viability of the system has to be in doubt. To be sure, the transition from a planned to a market economy has produced many other emergent needs[23] that the government has to meet immediately because they threaten stability. As such, China's pension reform has a long and winding road to travel before it can attain the goal of providing for its ageing population.

The ultimate financial viability of the new pension system in China is, after all, a matter of priorities. Most fundamental is the need to build confidence in the system among the general population, so that they believe that the promised benefits will be delivered. The frequent disturbances and drastic changes characteristic of modern China continue as vivid memories. With its coming entrance into the WTO, China looks set to face more challenges and uncertainties in both economic and political spheres. It is true that China's old people, both rural and urban, together with the many ordinary households falling into economic difficulties due to various factors, need some sort of protection. But pensions are only one of the options. Other social programmes, such as the ongoing Minimum Living Standards Guarantee Programme, should be designed to cater for the needs of the population as a whole.

Notes

1 By 2000, the elderly population in China reached 130 million, which is more than 10 percent of the national population, and in the large cities such as Shanghai and Beijing, the proportion was much higher (18.5 per cent and 14.6 per cent respectively). Demographic projections show that the elderly population will reach 11.4 per cent by the year 2020, and further to 20 per cent by the year 2050.
2 The 1951 State Council's Regulations on Labour Insurance established the first nation-wide social insurance system, which applied to state owned enterprises (SOEs), government units, public institutions and mass organizations all over China and covered all benefits for employees, including pensions, medical care, workers compensation, maternity benefits, and other temporary relief programs. In 1955, a separate system was established for employees in governmental organs and public institutions. In 1958, the two systems were combined into a single system; and in 1978 it was divided again into two systems, one for employees in enterprises and the other one for those in government organs and public institutions.
3 The public-ownership economy of China during the plan era consisted of two sub-economic systems: state-owned and collectively owned economy.
4 Between 1978 and 1985, the number of retirees increased fivefold, and overall pension costs rose from 2.8 percent of total wages for urban employees to 10.6 percent (World Bank, 1997).
5 According to the classification of the *China Statistical Yearbook 1999*, the current urban economic system in China consists of five types of sub-economic systems based on ownership: SOEs, collectively owned enterprises, individually owned enterprises, the self-employed and enterprises with other types of ownership (including joint ventures, shareholding corporations, foreign-funded enterprises, and enterprises funded by residents from Hong Kong, Macao and Taiwan).
6 In the past two decades, increases in the number of urban employees have been mainly a phenomenon in the non-state sector. For instance, between 1985 and 1998 the number of urban employees in enterprises with non-public ownership rose steadily from 0.38 million to 48.97 million *(China Statistical Yearbook 1999*, pp. 136-137).
7 These schemes were small pools across enterprises, often based on counties or districts or sectors.
8 The standard wage was the main financial compensation for employees during the plan era, which was designed by the central government and implemented with unified standards to

enterprises all over China. Based on positions held and length of service, it was related with neither the performance of individuals nor the economic efficiency of enterprises.
9   *China Social Security*, 1997 (11), p. 13.
10 The pensions of covered enterprise retirees averaged nationally 414 yuan, and the average wages of employees in enterprises were 466 yuan.
11 The laid-off employees are a special form of unemployment in China. Their number increased from 3 million in 1993 to 11 million in 1999. They are surplus employees laid off by their work units in the course of restructuring enterprises, but continue to receive basic living allowances from their enterprises in the reemployment service centers jointly financed by individual enterprises and the government. By the end of 2000, these centers covered 23 million laid-off employees, 95 percent of them received basic living allowances (Ministry of Labour and Social Security).
12 Ministry of Labour and Social Security.
13 Between 1980 and 1998, the percentage of GIOV made by SOEs and collectively owned enterprises decreased from 99.52 to 66.65. Whereas that of the non-public sector (including individually owned enterprises and enterprises with other types of ownership) rose from 0.49 to about 40 percent.
14 By 2000, the number of the self-employed in urban areas reached 20 million, occupying around 10 percent of the urban active labour force.
15 China's urban labour forces are divided into formal employees and employees. Formal employees are those who are registered in or recruited through labour departments, that is, through formal channels, and otherwise are employees or informal employees.
16 It was projected that by the year 2050 the support ratio will become 1.87 contributors supporting 1 retiree (Ministry of Labour and Social Security, 2001).
17 *China Social Insurance Yearbook*, 2000, pp. 237-238.
18 New changes in the social security system of China, according to the Document, include mainly adjustments in the pension system (see above), merging the laid-off employees into the unemployed, and emphasis on the establishment of the Minimum Living Standard Guarantee System, among others. The Liaoning province is one of China's old industrial bases, where pension debts were higher than elsewhere in China due to the existence of many old SOEs.
19 Nationally, the current individual contribution averages 5 percent.
20 Starting from 1993, the government re-structured its traditional social assistance program into the 'Minimum Living Standard Guarantee System', which was administered by the Ministry of Civil Affairs and financed through general revenues. A means-tested program, it was intended to provide a last-resort welfare safety net for urban households living below the 'poverty line' defined by local authorities. Using a variety of poverty measurements, the intended beneficiaries of the program covered urban residents with economic difficulties due to various social and economic factors. By 2001, the program covered over 15.89 million poverty stricken residents in the urban areas in China (Ministry of Civil Affairs, 2001: 1).
21 The current pension funds have incurred liabilities to three groups of participants: (1) old workers who retired before the implementation of the individual accounts and thus were out of the coverage; (2) those who were already employed when the new system was implemented and were thus not covered fully with the individual accounts; and (3) new workers who joined the labour force after the implementation of the reform policies, but their contributions in the individual accounts have been used to pay the pensions for the currently retired. The size of the debts was estimated to be between 2,000-4,000 billion yuan.
22 In early 2001, the Ministry of Labour and Social Security and a funds administration company jointly conducted a research on pension funds management. The resulting report recommended five measures for the government to apply to the pension system.

First, 10-15 per cent of the funds should be invested in domestic capital market. Previously, the government had been very conservative in funds management in that it allowed 80 percent of pension fund balances be invested in government bonds after a sufficient sum was retained for two months' retirement payments. Second, the government should each year allocate 5 per cent of revenues to subsidize the pension funds. In practice, government subsidies can take the form of selling a proportion of the state-owned shareholdings in the capital market. Third, the current statutory retirement age of 60 should be extended to 65 or 67. It was estimated that an increase of 1 year for the retirement age is able to reduce 20 billion yuan of the deficit. Fourth, individual accounts should be separated from the social pooling funds and managed through trust investment in the capital market. Finally, the wage base used for calculating contributions should be adjusted and managed to reflect real wage increases so as to increase revenues. Based on the above recommendations, the government enacted the decision to subsidize the system through general revenues and allowed a portion of the funds to be invested in the capital market.

23 For instance, one premise for the experiment of the revised pension scheme in Liaoning province is that laid-off employees and the currently retired have to be provided.

References

China Labour and Social Security Ministry (1999), *Social Security Administration Lectures*, China Labour and Social Security Ministry Press, Beijing (in Chinese).
China Labour and Social Security Ministry (2000), *A Survey Report on the Opinions of Experts on China's Social Security System*, unpublished pamphlets (in Chinese).
China Labour and Social Security Ministry (2001), unpublished papers (in Chinese).
China Statistical Yearbook (1999), China Statistical Publishing House, Beijing.
Chow, N. (2000), *Socialist Welfare with Chinese Characteristics*, Centre of Asian Studies, University of Hong Kong.
Chow, N. and Xu, Yuebin (2001), *Socialist Welfare in a Market Economy: Social Security Reforms in Guangzhou, China*, Ashgate, Aldershot.
Leung, J. (1998), 'Social security reforms: a long and winding road', in *China Review 1998*, ed. J. Cheng, Chinese University Press, Hong Kong pp. 480–99.
Ministry of Civil Affairs (2001), *China Civil Affairs, 2001(8)*, China Civil Affairs Ministry Policy Research Centre, Beijing.
World Bank (1997), *China 2020: Old Age Security*, World Bank, Washington, DC.

Chapter 11
Reforming Pensions

Alan Walker

Introduction

This response to Chow and Xu's chapter begins by congratulating them on their clear account of the pension reforms undertaken in China in recent years. They demonstrate the winding road of pension reform over two decades. The problem of scale has been compounded by the transformation of China from a planned to a market economy which has led, among other things, to a drastic decline in employment in state-owned enterprises (SOEs). In addition there is the problem of counting the self-employed (20 million in urban areas, representing 10 per cent of the employed). Since only two-fifths of the urban labour force are covered by the pension reforms there is a major issue of funding. These are huge challenges, but Chinese pragmatism appears to have concluded that root-and-branch pension reform is unwise while the economic system is in massive transition. Thus the policy of responding to urgent needs is a sensible one. As in Europe, pension reform in China has focused primarily on tomorrow's pensioners. Hence there is poverty and deprivation among *today's* pensioners that should be tackled as a priority. In particular there is the dire situation of many rural older people whose needs, as Chow and Xu acknowledge, are not being addressed by the recent reforms.

My response focuses on four main areas. First a brief review of the pension reform process in the European Union (EU) emphasizing the unusual case of the UK. Second, a commentary on the global drive towards individualizing pensions and the pros and cons of pay-as-you-go and funded pensions. Third, some observations on lessons from the EU, particularly on the need to 'join-up' the various policies that influence the demand for and funding of pensions. Finally, looking beyond the EU, I will emphasize key points arising from the forthcoming UN strategy on ageing, such as the need for a social safety net.

Pensions Reform in the EU

When discussing pensions reform we must beware constantly of the 'public burden' model of welfare masquerading as a technical response to population ageing. Longevity, after all, is a triumph of development. For example, crude age dependency ratios would suggest increasing tax burdens on the working population. However that pessimistic scenario rests on the classic economic assumption, *ceteris paribus,* which freezes present trends regardless of how far into the future the projections are being made, plus an assumption that taxes to pay for pensions are a 'burden'.

In fact the main issue for pension funding in Western countries is not population ageing *per se* but its combination with changes in birth rates, the structure of employment and the practice of retirement. In a very short space of time there has been a major restructuring of the life cycle in most EU countries, resulting from the truncation of employment prior to pension ages (Kohli et al. 1991; Walker 1997, 1999). In some EU countries this was a trend openly encouraged by public policy. Thus, paradoxically, as longevity has increased, the age at which people exit from economic activity has fallen. Since the 1950s there has been an average increase in longevity in the EU of around 10 years and a parallel decline in the age of final labour force exit of the same magnitude. As Esping-Andersen (1996) has put it, Europe has 'doubled pension benefit years and cut contribution years by around 25 per cent'. The realization that early exit created problems within employment as well as social protection (and that its benefits in terms of reducing youth unemployment were, at best, only partial), has led most EU governments to abandon or curtail its encouragement.

Unlike China, which is building a pension system, pension systems in the EU are long established. These pension systems should be regarded as major achievements of European civilization, and the EU's record in reducing poverty among older people is indeed remarkable. However, pressure for pension reform has built up over the last decade, chiefly from the macro-policy level rather than the grassroots. The main issue, of almost universal concern to policy makers and the media, is the growth of pension costs and, in particular, its fiscal implications. In some extreme cases this concern has been expressed in highly pessimistic rhetorical references to the so-called 'burden' of population ageing. There is not space here to consider the very flimsy construction of the 'demographic timebomb' arguments (which anyway appears to be a largely Anglo-Saxon notion) and the flawed nature of the dependency ratio calculations which are usually invoked to lend them scientific legitimacy. One comment must suffice. International economic agencies, such as the IMF and the World Bank have taken a prominent role in promoting pessimism about population ageing and in amplifying the prospects of inter-generational friction (Walker 1990). This is despite the fact that the OECD's analysis shows that demography has played a relatively small role in the growth of pension costs (OECD 1988) and the complete absence of evidence of any weakening of the generational contract – even in the USA, where the most concerted attempts have been made to undermine it.

Despite some of the alarmist rhetoric surrounding population ageing and the near universal nature of pension reform in the EU, the measures taken so far to reduce future pension costs are, for the most part, rather modest adaptations to existing systems. There are six main kinds of reform, all of which are top-down responses to the budgetary pressures of EMU, and designed to pre-empt the costs associated with population ageing.

1 Seven Member States are raising the legal age of retirement – Austria, Germany, Greece, Italy, France (by raising the number of contribution years), Portugal and the UK. In three cases this reform consists of raising the retirement age of women to bring it in line with that of men.
2 All countries, except Greece, Ireland, the Netherlands, Portugal and the UK, are introducing greater flexibility in the age of retirement and are promoting

gradual or partial retirement. With the exception of Spain, all EU Member States now allow the combination of a pension and income from work.
3   There are measures to restrict the pension formula. The most common reform is the extension of the contribution period for pensions, by tying the amount of the pension to the length of contribution (mainly Italy and Sweden, but to some extent Austria, France, Finland, Denmark, Germany, Portugal, Spain and the UK). In some northern countries (Denmark and Finland) new forms of income testing have been introduced, in respect of the cumulative total of income from the different pillars of pension provision. Several countries have altered their methods of financing pensions – chiefly to reduce the role of contributions, while increasing that of taxes (Portugal and Spain) and, most significantly, by adding a funded element (Finland, Sweden and, most recently, Italy).
4   There are measures to curtail pre- or early retirement policies (Austria, Belgium, Finland, France, Germany, Italy, the Netherlands and Spain).
5   There have been reductions in the levels of pensions, usually by means of changes in the methods of calculation, by price-indexation instead of wage-indexation. Wage indexation has been abolished, or substantially reduced, virtually everywhere.
6   There have been efforts to encourage a more mixed pension system. Especially in southern Europe, governments are trying to reduce reliance on the first pillar (compulsory public schemes) by stimulating supplementary ones, both occupational and private, as a way of introducing elements of funded financing, in parallel with pay-as-you-go (PAYG).

On the basis of these institutional reforms – remarkable for their concentration and universal nature – there is no doubt that pension expenditure has been stabilized. However the mood for reform is nowhere near being assuaged. There is a new conventional wisdom in Europe that further change is required – not only to ensure financial sustainability, but also to recognize that Europe's pension systems were created in a very different context with regard to work and family patterns and gender and inter-generational relations. Increased longevity and workforce ageing also cast doubt on the idea of retirement as a functionally separate and non-productive phase of the life-cycle. Certainly there are still strong pressures for pension reform, coming from international economic agencies as well as from vested interests in the private pension world.

In all this clamour for reform the voices of *current* pensioners do not seem to be audible. However, regardless of which direction is being chosen by the EU Member States, there are current generations of pensioners living in poverty in all countries. Somewhere in the pension reform agenda their needs have to be addressed.

The Unusual Case of the UK

Before concluding this section let me narrate a short cautionary tale concerning pension reforms in the UK. What is manifestly not apparent from the preceding review of recent pension reforms, is just how odd the UK looks in a Western European context. The UK's first pension reforms pre-dated those of most other EU countries by a decade. In global policy terms the UK was more in tune with the USA and Japan: countries that started pension reform in 1988 and 1986, respectively. But, in comparison with Italy for example, the UK's first and second tier pensions were already relatively low by EU standards and there was no suggestion of an impending pension crisis. In fact, the OECD specifically told the UK, in the 1980s, that there was no need to take any action on its pension system until 2010 at the earliest – partly because of the relatively low cost of pensions and partly because the UK's population had aged earlier than the populations of most other EU countries.

What actually happened in the UK, in the 1980s, is an extraordinary chapter in the annals of pension reform. In its desire to reduce public expenditure and shift future pension funding from the state to the private sector, the Thatcher government de-indexed the first tier pension from wages (in 1980), halved the State Earnings Related Pension Scheme (in 1986) and encouraged (via tax reliefs) the substitution of private, defined *contribution* schemes for the state's guaranteed or defined *benefit* scheme. What ensued was a remarkable episode in pension policy, by any standards – and one resonant with warnings. The major scandal of the mis-selling of pensions by over-zealous agents and insurance companies resulted from the responsibility for pensions being passed from the public to a poorly regulated private sector, without proper safeguards. It is estimated that over three million people were sold private pensions when they would have been better off staying in the state scheme.

Individualizing Pensions

In comparison with the measured and incremental pensions reforms for the most part being conducted in most EU member states, the example of the UK may appear too odd or extreme to offer any useful lessons for other countries. However the centre-piece of the Conservative (and now Labour) pension policy – the individualization of pensions and, with it an increase in the funding component – is precisely the course being encouraged by international economic agencies, and being considered by some Western European governments, and already being implemented in some Eastern European ones. So what lessons might be learnt from recent pension reforms in the UK? There are two main ones.

First, there is the danger of an ideologically-driven policy which stifles public debate. Thus, in the UK, there has been virtually no open discussion about the advantages of PAYG as a method of financing pensions, nor of the disadvantages of privately funded schemes, even in the wake of the mis-selling scandal. What usually occurs are simple top-down assertions that PAYG is unsustainable and that private is best.

But, for the record, let us rehearse some of the advantages of PAYG. First, under PAYG pensioners' incomes can rise along with general living standards, so long as a political decision is taken to peg pensions increases accordingly. (Though of course even governments may default on promises.) Second, PAYG schemes are superior with regard to the alleviation of poverty and the provision of insurance against inflation and investment risks, i.e. they tend to be socially inclusive, because they can cover everyone, provide protection for gaps in earnings and also job-changes. Nevertheless they are vulnerable to demographic change and a decline in employment. Third PAYG represents a contract between the generations and, therefore, an expression of social solidarity and a potential force for social cohesion. Those arguing for Chilean-style personal savings plans, fail to acknowledge either the importance of intergenerational solidarity or that the state-sponsored selfishness represented by such schemes may have an impact on the willingness of younger generations to contribute to other collectively provided services. Moreover why *should* younger generations fund the pensions of those in retirement when the deal they can expect in return will be worth so little? In any case, finally, PAYG schemes are usually simple to understand and relatively easy to administer.

Funded schemes are said to produce lower distortionary effects in the labour market and contribute to the development of financial markets. On the other hand they have several disadvantages:

- Low potential coverage (e.g. in Chile only 52 per cent of those in the labour force are contributors).
- Lack of democratic accountability in private schemes.
- Double taxation during the transition phase.
- High level of risk in private schemes (fraud, uncertainty of money markets, corporate mergers etc.).
- Inefficiency of private schemes i.e. high start-up costs falling mainly on the low paid and women.
- Poor insurance coverage of individuals for major risks, such as chronic sickness, disability, premature retirement and long term unemployment.
- Penalization of carers (because of their limited employment opportunities), which is exacerbated by the high administrative costs of private schemes.
- High public cost of private schemes in terms of tax reliefs and other incentives.
- High costs of administration.

Some of these disadvantages could be minimized, in theory, by making private funded schemes compulsory and by regulating them strictly. But there are no international precedents of 'compulsory' private schemes covering, in practice, more than two-thirds of a population. Also there is of course no guarantee that compulsory savings will yield sufficient income in retirement for large groups of workers (as in Singapore).

The absence of public debate in the UK on the future of pensions, has meant that these advantages and disadvantages were never considered, outside of expert committees. By contrast, these same issues were discussed in the run-up to the 1997 referendum on pensions in New Zealand. The outcome in this case was that 92.4 per cent voted against the government's proposal to replace the state PAYG universal superannuation scheme with compulsory private funded schemes, with only 7.6 per cent of voters in favour.

The second lesson concerns the failure to adapt the British pension system to changing times. What is remarkable about the 1980s is that the UK government was able to undermine the national insurance system without any discernible public outcry or political backlash. A leading British economic and social commentator has called the destruction of SERPS one of the greatest frauds perpetrated by a democratic government against its people in modern times (Hutton 1996). Of course this speaks volumes about the nature of the Beveridge welfare state but also, I think, it reflects a failure to modernize social protection. The irony is that the UK pension system may have been more secure from political interference – or more keenly defended – if its rights had been more individualized from the start.

There is no doubt that pension reform is high on the policy agenda of both the EU Member States and the countries of Central and Eastern Europe. So far, in the EU, the reform programme has been relatively modest, with one exception. Nevertheless several EU governments are promoting the growth of funded or capitalization-based private pensions (they are already compulsory in the Netherlands). However the UK experience provides warning signs against the dangers of an unbalanced approach to pension provision. Of course private funded schemes have a role to play, but the dangers arise when they are given a *central* role, where they can act as an engine of social exclusion. These problems are likely to increase rather than decrease as the 'post-modern' working life is characterized by economic insecurity for a majority – and gross insecurity for up to 40 per cent of the working population. Many women, in particular, will be unable to accrue adequate pension rights through private funded schemes. In fact, the principle of risk-pooling under social insurance – modernized to minimize exclusions and to maximize the sense of individual ownership – seems even better suited to today's labour market than it was when such schemes were first introduced in Europe.

In contrast to the UK experience, the new Swedish pension system seems to offer a more promising compromise between PAYG and individually funded pension entitlements. Sweden (like Italy) has developed the notional defined contribution PAYG system to deal directly with demographic and labour participation changes. In the NDC PAYG system wage earners pay contributions based on a fixed contribution rate and the value of these is credited to their notional accounts. Thus 2.5 per cent of the total 18.5 per cent pension contribution will be saved in a separate premium reserve system. This new 'defined contribution' (and partially funded) formula will co-exist with basic protection for those unable to build up sufficient contributions, and supplements will also be paid to those who are entitled to low contributory pensions (Palmer 1998).

Pensions and the Labour Market

Pensions reform should not be contemplated in isolation from other related policy areas. In particular we must consider the demand side of the pensions equation. It is remarkable how rarely the labour market features in discussion about the future of pensions and the implications of population ageing. Yet the age barrier between economic activity and inactivity has been changing rapidly in all EU countries, with the number of years worked being truncated, especially for men. As I have noted already, the trend towards early exit was encouraged by public policy. It has had two important consequences. On the one hand it has removed pension systems from their position as the key regulators of labour force exit. For example, in the UK and Germany, only roughly one-third of men enter the public pensions arena from full-time employment. In no country in the EU are more than half of men aged 60 to 64 still in employment and in every country, apart from Sweden, fewer than 30 per cent of women in this age group are still working. In the age range 55-64 only 47 per cent are in employment in the EU. This has contributed substantially to the pressure on social protection systems – from both the demand and supply sides. On the other hand it has reinforced the devaluation of older workers left in the labour market. As we have seen, EU countries have already removed public subsidies for early exit, but very few have tackled the widespread age discrimination in their labour markets which results in premature exclusion from employment (and the payment of taxes and pension contributions), and thence in recourse to social protection. The potential role of the fourth pillar of retirement income in reducing the pressure on the EU's pension systems has only recently come onto the policy agenda, chiefly via the 1994 Essen Council and the subsequent Luxembourg and Cardiff summits (Walker 1997).

So far, the policy responses of the EU Member States have been concentrated mainly on two fronts: closing down early exit options and trying to stem the flow out of the labour market by encouraging part-time employment instead of full retirement. Such measures have been taken in Austria, Belgium, Denmark, Finland, France, Germany, Italy and the Netherlands. There has been a widespread growth in part-time working among both male and female older workers in recent years (for men aged 55-59, from 4 per cent in 1991 to 5.5 per cent in 1996; for men aged 60-64, from 8 to 10.5 per cent; for women aged 55-59, from 36-40 per cent), though this is also true for younger age groups as well and, therefore, it is not possible to attribute this to the partial retirement policies themselves (European Commission 1998).

A third policy option – combating age barriers in the labour market and encouraging employers to recruit or retain older workers – has only just come on to the scene. It is the case that Europe's labour markets are characterized by age discrimination and, irrespective of the shift in policy emphasis, employers forced to reduce employment concentrate redundancies on older workers (often in agreement with trade unions) so that, in turn, long-term unemployment affects older workers more than younger ones. This denies older workers opportunities but also, of course, population-ageing means workforce-ageing and, therefore, this prejudice is both unfair and inappropriate.

Yet there are signs of change towards more positive attitudes on the part of employers. Thus, in recently completed research for the European Foundation, we collected more than 160 examples of good practice in combating age barriers, particularly with regard to job recruitment, retention and retraining (Walker 1997; Walker and Taylor 1998). This research involved seven Member States: Belgium, France, Germany, Greece, Italy, the Netherlands and the UK, with additional examples from Finland and Sweden. It was the first European research to focus on examples of good practice in the employment of older workers, and it has attracted a great deal of attention. I believe that it provides the basis for a new policy to revive employment among older people.

This issue has been slowly moving up the European policy agenda over the course of the 1990s, and has become more prominent following the ratification of the Amsterdam Treaty (Article 13 empowers the Commission to propose actions against discrimination). For example, the 1998 European Council Summit in Cardiff emphasized the need to pay special attention to older workers, as part of the priority actions to develop a skilled and adaptable workforce, and in recognition of the importance of tackling discrimination in the labour market. The annual National Employment Plans are providing opportunities to focus on the issue of employment among older workers. A project sponsored by the European Commission, involving eight Member States (including Spain), has designed a code of good practice to help employers to adjust to their ageing workforces and to avoid discrimination (Walker and Naegele 2000). The European Commission has issued a directive instructing Member States to legislate against age discrimination in employment by 2006.

A Strategy for Active Ageing

All of the elements are in place for a new approach to the later life course in Europe, one which would replace exclusion and decrescence with inclusion and activity – in short, active ageing. What would this new approach consist of and what might be its relevance for China?

First of all, Europe must *reverse* the trend towards early retirement. To reverse early exit will require active policy measures to a) preserve and strengthen the employability of older workers and b) to minimize, and possibly eradicate, age barriers in the labour market. In a future of portfolio and discontinuous employment, security of employability is likely to replace security of employment. This implies responsibilities on the part of *all* actors in the labour market to promote employability.

However, at the same time, there must be concerted action to combat age discrimination in employment. To raise pension ages while leaving ageism unchecked is simply to consign older workers to exclusion, low incomes and, eventually, to an inadequate pensions. Age discrimination is the antithesis of active or productive ageing. The Age Barriers Project showed that it is possible to reverse discriminatory practices and revealed a continuum of good practice, stretching from very limited and narrowly focused measures to comprehensive ones. We concluded that, rather than the present reactive approach adopted by most employers and policy makers, an integrated age management strategy would be most effective. This would encompass both *preventative* measures (such as life-long education and training) and *remedial* ones (such as training for older workers lacking specific skills, for example in new technology (Walker 1999). Education and exhortation are not likely to be sufficient to overcome age discrimination; so, therefore, legislation has a role to play in Europe. The logical extension of a policy against age discrimination would be the abolition of mandatory retirement ages and the institution, instead, of minimum pension ages. Then incentives could be introduced to encourage people to work beyond the minimum. Sweden currently allows the postponement of pensions to the age of 70, and the new Italian pension system allows postponement until 68.

Second, if measures are taken to extend working life by raising pension ages *without* action being taken on the impact of employment on health, then the result will also be exclusion and an increase in the take-up of disability pensions. If this latter option was then also closed to older workers, the impact would be severe and unjust. Although there is a trend towards a reduction of the incidence of disability at older ages, and although we might expect the shift away from manual employment to diminish the significance of age-related health problems (OECD 1998: 136), nonetheless the onset of such problems still affects the timing of retirement for significant numbers of older workers. Poor health is significantly related to age and, in turn, is a cause of large productivity differences among older workers. To paraphrase the UK Black Report, 'in the collective effort of production some people's bodies wear out faster than others' (Townsend and Davidson 1982). Paradoxically, employment is both a major cause of ill-health and an important source of health gain, in terms of activity, self-esteem and social contact. But unless the ill-health-producing aspects of employment are negated, the productive ageing option will not be open to all on an equal basis. Put more positively: if the health of workers is maintained then they will be more willing and able to extend their working lives.

Again a preventative strategy is likely to be the only effective one, and there are plenty of examples of good practice in this respect, particularly among the Nordic countries. For example the Finnish Institute of Occupational Health has operated two relevant programmes. Finn Age aims to promote the health, employability and well-being of those over 45; while the Small Workplace programme aims at encouraging small firms to adopt relevant good practices in the interests of the welfare of all employees (as well as themselves). It goes without saying that a healthy workforce is likely to be a productive one and that, as the workforce ages, employers will not be in a position to rejuvenate their organizations as readily and wastefully as they did in the past.

Of course a strategy to break the link between employment and ill-health will necessitate improvements in the health status of successive cohorts of retired people. By the same token, however, one of the risks associated with a policy of active ageing is that it adds to the exclusion of those outside paid employment or who are already dependent. (Dependency is itself a source of pressure on social protection systems but beyond the scope of this paper.) Third, therefore, we should raise our sights from the workplace and focus on *preventing morbidity wherever it occurs*, thereby extending the quality of life of all of those who reach retirement. This would entail a broad public health approach in the Member States and at EU level, aimed at preventing ill-health and disability. The link between activity and health is well-known. Thus what is required in all Member States is a concerted effort to encourage healthy lifestyles and healthy ageing. As the WHO has put it: 'years have been added to life, now we must add life to years'. This would certainly enable people to remain productive for longer. For those outside the labour market, active ageing should mean active citizenship, including engagement in unpaid voluntary activity, but not excluding the provision of help and support *within* the family. Again, the European Commission should have an important role here, under Article 129 of the Amsterdam Treaty, which enables it to initiate actions to improve public health and prevent disease.

The relevance of this strategy to China is that, as the new pension system is constructed, attention must be paid to the funding base. The prevention of exclusion on age grounds is the key to both pension system financial viability and social justice.

The Global Context

Turning briefly to the global context, the striking feature of China's pension system is the division between urban and rural areas. The needs of rural dwellers have been neglected in the various pension reforms and there is a high level of poverty and deprivation among rural older people – and a heavy reliance on family support. This emphasizes the need for universal pension provision, covering both rural and urban areas – or, at least, for the provision of a social safety net. It is not necessary to create a new social assistance or social insurance system overnight. Something approximating a safety net could be built by a series of categorical non-contributory schemes. This is how the Greek Government, for instance, has constructed its social safety net, including a non-contributory old age pension for the rural sector.

The new UN International strategy on Ageing, launched in Madrid in April 2002, provides some guidelines for policy development. In particular the eradication of poverty is a key aim and the strategy places emphasis on the need to tackle poverty among older men. Under the broad objectives contained in the strategy there are numerous detailed policy proposals. For examples with regard to the eradication of poverty the draft strategy states:

> The eradication of poverty in old age is a fundamental aim of the International Strategy...
>
> Objective: Reduction of poverty among older persons by half by 2015.
>
> Objective: Promotion of programmes to enable all workers, including those engaged in the informal sector, to acquire basic social protection, including old-age pensions.
>
> Objective: Sufficient minimum income for older persons, paying particular attention to socially and economically disadvantaged groups.

Conclusion

It will take a long time for the story of China's pension reforms to end, and perhaps it will never end. Meanwhile there are pressing social problems to be solved now, including poverty and exclusion among large numbers of older people and an over-reliance on the family as a source of support, especially in rural areas.

In the longer term, Chinese policy makers must remember that pension systems are essentially risk-pooling mechanisms, not savings schemes. If individual accounts are introduced, there will have to be some back-up system of risk-pooling, based on intergenerational solidarity, to provide income for those unable to build up their own accounts (mainly women, self-employed, insecurely-employed). The most effective way forward is likely to be a universal first-tier pension, based on solidarity, with private schemes constituting the second-tier. In constructing a new pension system China has the opportunity to avoid the disadvantages built into most western pension systems – such as gender discrimination, and disincentives to continuing employment. But this will be more difficult if it chooses the funded route. If it does decide on the funded route, it should at least ensure a tight regulatory regime to reduce the risks inherent in this approach.

References

Esping-Andersen, G. (1996),'Welfare States at the End of the Century', OECD, Paris (mimeo).
European Commission (1998), *People in Europe*, DG5, Brussels.
European Commission (1998), *Social Protection in Europe 1997*, European Commission, Brussels.
Hutton, W. (1996) *The State We Are In*, Verso, London.
Kohli, M., Rein, M., Guillemard, A.M. and van Gunsteren, H. (1991), (eds), *Time for Retirement*, Cambridge University Press, Cambridge.
OECD (1988) *The Future of Public Pensions*, OECD, Paris.
OECD (1998) *Employment Outlook*, (June), OECD, Paris.
Palmer, E. (1998) 'Swedish Pension Reform and Work After 60', National Insurance Board, Stockholm.
Townsend, P. and Davidson, N. (1982), *Inequalities in Health*, Penguin, Harmondsworth.
Walker, A. (1990) 'The Economic "Burden" of Ageing and the Prospect of Intergenerational Conflict', *Ageing and Society*, Vol. 10, No. 4, 1990, pp. 377–396.
Walker, A. (1997), *Combating Age Barriers in Employment*, Office for the Official Publications of the European Communities, Luxembourg.
Walker, A. (1999), *Managing an Ageing Workforce – A Guide to Good Practice*, Office for the Official Publications of the European Communities, Luxembourg.
Walker, A. and Naegele, G. (2000), *Ageing in Employment*, Eurolink Age, London.
Walker, A. and Taylor, P. (1998), *Combating Age Barriers in Employment – A European Portfolio of Good Practice*, Office for the Official Publications of the European Communities, Luxembourg.

Chapter 12

Financing Health Care in China's Cities: Balancing Needs and Entitlements[1]

Gerald Bloom, Yuelai Lu and Jiaying Chen

Introduction

During the period of the command economy most urban residents were covered by work-based health insurance. The government paid almost the entire cost of medical care for its employees; state-owned enterprises also subsidized health care highly. Workplace and government clinics and hospitals provided these services. The government also financed and organized preventive programmes.

The system of urban health finance has changed considerably during the transition to a market economy. The government is now highly decentralized and the proportion of tax revenue subject to fiscal transfer is relatively small. City governments have considerable discretion over the use of their own resources. However, total public expenditure has declined substantially as a proportion of GDP. In the late 1990s the government divided responsibility for urban health services between the ministries of Health and Labour and Social Security.

There are three major sources of finance for urban health services: government health budgets, insurance and out-of-pocket payments. By the late 1990s a considerable proportion of urban residents were uninsured and paid for services in cash (Gao et al. 2001). City health departments financed and organized public health services and preventive programmes. They also provided modest subsidies to hospitals and health centres. Government grants typically covered around 10-15 per cent of facility budgets. The government and state-owned enterprises still provide medical benefits to their employees; however, there was increasing pressure for reform.

Since the mid-1990s the government has encouraged local governments to establish pilot insurance schemes. The preferred model is a combination of individual savings accounts and social pooling, influenced by the so-called 'Singapore model' (Barr 2001). Employers and employees contribute to individual accounts and the social pool. Beneficiaries claim reimbursement with a complex mix of co-payments, deductibles and ceilings. The design of benefits has changed over time; the current model allocates most of the social pooling funds to hospital care. Recent government documents call for the establishment of compulsory basic insurance for all urban employees and optional contributory work-related top-up schemes (State Council 1998, 2000). Most municipalities are just beginning to implement this policy.

This chapter situates urban health systems in the context of China's demographic and epidemiological transition, transition to a market economy and transition to an urban, industrial society (Hussain 1999). It argues that one can best understand the process of urban health finance as an effort to agree new rules of entitlement to benefits in a period of rapid and sustained change.

Changing Medical Needs

Williams (1991) defines medical need as the existence of ill health for which an effective treatment is available. Need is a measure of the physiological and psychological status of individuals, their expectations of what constitutes well-being, the availability of effective interventions and the social arrangements that determine the roles of households and health providers in caring for the sick. This section discusses how changes in urban China are affecting these determinants of need.

Demographic and Epidemiological Transition

The structure of China's population is changing rapidly. There are proportionately fewer children and more elderly. The share of the population over 65 years old doubled and the proportion over 75 years old increased from 0.8 to 2.1 per cent between 1964 and 1997. Some 8.0 per cent of registered urban residents were over 65 years and 2.3 per cent were over 75 years in 1997.

The ageing of the population is expected to continue. The China Population Information and Research Centre projects that the percentage over 65 years will rise to 8 per cent by 2010, 11 per cent in 2020 and 20 per cent in 2040. Around 30 per cent of people over 65 were over 75 years, in 1990; this proportion is projected to rise to 35 per cent in 2010 and around 50 per cent in 2050 (Sun 1998).

The demographic transition has been accompanied by an epidemiological transition. Improvements in the standard of living and specific public health measures have contributed to a substantial fall in the incidence of infectious diseases in urban areas. The ageing of the population and high rates of risky behaviour, such as smoking, have led to increases in the prevalence of non-communicable diseases. Recent studies among the elderly identify a number of problems with chronic disease (Deng et al. 2000; Ou and Zhu 2000; Zhou and Wang 1998).

Data from advanced market economies suggest that average medical care costs rise rapidly with age (Barer et al. 1987). People over 75 years have a particularly great need for expensive health care. The elderly account for a substantial share of medical expenditure in urban China. This is illustrated by an analysis of the disbursements of Nantong's government insurance scheme, which showed that pensioners claimed over twice as much as current employees, and veterans of the liberation war (many over 75 years old) claimed a great deal more than that (Shu et al. 2001). Pressure on the medical system is likely to grow as the numbers of old-old increase.

The high cost of care for the elderly reflects their complicated health problems and the cost of effective interventions. It also reflects changes to family structures, which have made people less able and willing to care for very dependent people at home (Xiong 1999). The lack of affordable medical support for the aged puts a heavy burden on family caregivers, particularly women.

Economic Development and Restructuring of the Labour Market

China's cities have experienced rapid economic growth for more than two decades. This has increased the availability of effective interventions and altered urban residents' expectations of medical care. It has also led to an influx of migrants and the emergence of a more segmented labour market.

New Interventions and Changing Expectations

Disposable income per urban resident more than trebled, in real terms, between 1978 and 1998 (China Statistical Yearbook 1999, Table 10.2). Health expenditure grew even faster (Zhao 1999). This was associated with a change in the kinds of health care people use.

Urban residents can afford increasingly sophisticated medical care. Their tastes have been strongly affected by changes in communications, which have increased their knowledge of lifestyles elsewhere. There has been a rise in the marketing of medical products to health facilities and the general population. These factors have combined to alter the expectations of both the providers and the users of health services.

The locus of care has largely shifted from clinics and simple inpatient facilities, to outpatient departments and wards of sophisticated hospitals. The consumption of drugs, particularly expensive branded products, has grown rapidly. In 1993, 52 per cent of total health expenditure in China was on pharmaceuticals (World Bank 1997). Expenditure on other inputs has also risen rapidly. The Ministry of Health (MOH 1998) recently reported that 50 per cent of 3640 county and higher-level hospitals had a CT scanner. This reflects the proliferation of diagnostic and treatment technologies.

The shift towards a more expensive style of medical care reflects increased access to modern technology. It also reflects inappropriate government policies. Government health budgets have risen less rapidly than have salaries. None the less, some local governments have encouraged health facilities to employ more staff. These facilities have had to generate revenue to meet the income expectations of their employees (Bloom et al. 2000). The government has controlled the price of a consultation with a health worker and a day in hospital, while allowing health facilities to earn a mark-up on drug sales and the use of sophisticated equipment. This has encouraged costly forms of practice. During the early 1980s there were few pensioners over 75 years of age and enterprises could afford sophisticated hospital care. By the 1990s, when there were more pensioners over 75 years of age, an expensive style of care had already become the norm.

Migration and Social Segmentation

The restructuring of the labour market has led to the emergence of vulnerable groups (Cook 2001). There are many laid-off workers and unemployed; but also there were around 80 million rural-urban migrants in the mid-1990s (Wong 1998).

Health-related problems seem to be linked to social segmentation in a number of countries (Wilkinson 1996). This is due to the direct effect of deprivation on health, higher levels of exposure to environmental and occupational hazards, and the tendency of socially disadvantaged groups to engage in behaviour that is risky for health. The experience of the former Soviet Union, where male mortality rose sharply during a period of economic crisis and social change, demonstrates that socioeconomic factors can have a major impact on health (Shkolnikov et al 2001). The HIV/AIDS epidemic also illustrates the link between ill health and social conditions that encourage drug abuse and the growth of the commercial sex industry.

There is little systematic information on the living conditions and health situation of vulnerable groups in urban China. A significant number of people live in poverty. There are indications that these groups have more health problems and less access to services than other city dwellers. Two recent national surveys show that the proportion of registered urban residents reporting no health insurance rose from 28 to 44 per cent (Gao et al. 2001). The percentage of urban residents, who did not consult a health worker during a sickness episode or seek hospital admission when advised to do so, grew between 1992 and 1997 and a larger number attributed this to financial difficulties. Some 20 per cent of people referred to hospital declined admission in 1992 and 40 per cent of them said it was due to cost. Five years later 32 per cent declined admission and 65 per cent said it was due to cost.

Migrants tend to be young and healthy. Studies of their health problems have mostly focused on infectious diseases. Chen (2000) associates the resurgence of tuberculosis and sexually transmitted diseases (STD) in the cities, with rapid urbanization. Wang et al. (2000) report that 60 per cent of STD cases were associated with migrants in Xiaoshan City, Zhejiang. Migrants tend to use health services less than registered residents do. This has been shown for reproductive health services in Shanghai and Chengdu (Zhan et al. 2000; Tian et al. 1999).

Urban public health services and preventive programmes have not expanded to cope with these additional needs. A recent study in Nantong reports that their share of the government health budget has fallen (Shu et al. 2001).

Changing Patterns of Entitlement to Social Benefits

This section discusses how economic changes are affecting entitlements to social benefits. Entitlements are legitimate claims by individuals on the state or other institutions. A government's ability to honour entitlements is an important source of legitimacy. Attempts to renegotiate entitlements involve political costs. China has hitherto assigned entitlements to social benefits mostly on the basis of a person's place of residence and the kind of work they do (Wong 1998; Solinger 1999; Bloom 2001).

One aspect of the transition to a market economy has been the transformation of entitlements from informal claims on employers and government into ownership of assets and rules-based rights to government assistance. One example is the sale of housing to employees at subsidized prices. These changes are institutionalizing new patterns of access to social benefits (Wang 2001).

A paper by the Chinese Academy of Social Sciences (CASS 1998) argues that China has reached the '*middle stage*' of its reforms. It argues that '*difficult questions of patterns of interest*' must be addressed and that successful reforms will depend on the management of the '*readjustment of basic interest relationships*'. It stresses the need to ensure that all social groups benefit from development and identifies the following interests to be reconciled during the establishment of a new social security system over the next 10–15 years:

- the very high financial burden of social benefits on state-owned enterprises compared to other categories of enterprise;
- the difference in social benefits between urban and rural residents and the rapid growth of employment in enterprises outside the cities;
- the differences in earnings and access to benefits between well-developed and under developed regions and the need for substantial investment to close the gap;
- the effort by governments of rich localities to limit the outflow of tax revenue and by national government to reduce inter-regional inequality.

The following section applies this perspective to the reform of urban social benefits.

Balancing Claims of Rural and Urban Residents

The household registration system, which limits the movement of people, underpins a sharp divide between rural and urban residents (Cook and White 1998; Chan and Zhang 1999). Rural residents have been entitled to little more than access to the means of agricultural production. The government makes modest fiscal transfers to poor areas and organizes national poverty reduction programmes. Local governments and collective bodies finance basic support for the poorest people. Urban residents, on the other hand, have been entitled to what Solinger (1999) calls 'the urban public goods regime'. But this demarcation between urban and rural entitlements is eroding.

There is an increasing divergence between the number of registered urban residents and the actual urban population. Hussain (1999) points out that 32.2 per cent of the population is classified as non-agricultural by household registration, but 53.4 per cent of the labour force actually works in services and industry. This is due to the rapid growth of township and village enterprises. Hussain estimates that 51 per cent of the population live in urban settlements, with high population density and a preponderant share of non-farming activities in the local economy. He points out that employees of enterprises in 'rural' localities are mostly entitled to fewer social benefits than urban residents.

Rural-urban migrants work in a variety of settings (Solinger 1999). Some are registered residents in the smaller centres; however, most retain their rural registration. Chan and Zhang (1999) point out that the urban workforce is stratified into categories of registration such as fully registered, newly registered, temporary residents and unregistered peasants. These categories have quite different entitlements to benefits.

Urban registration is still associated with much higher levels of entitlement to benefits. Thus, for example, only a small proportion of Shanghai's migrants has health insurance (Wang and Zuo 1999). The labour market is much more complex than it was. There is no longer a simple identity between urban registration and non-agricultural employment. So the challenge is to create a rules-based system of entitlements that reflects this complexity (CASS 1998).

Changing Patterns of Entitlement Amongst Urban Residents

Entitlements to most benefits are based on employment. The government- and state-owned enterprises provide comprehensive packages of benefits. Other employers provide less generous benefits. Local governments also finance benefits for specific social groups; health departments fund medical care for veterans of the liberation war and certain retired government officials, and departments of civil affairs provide a basic living allowance to people whose household income falls below a locally determined minimum living standard.

Urban residents have a strong sense of entitlement to social security and services. The report by the Chinese Academy of Social Sciences cited above highlights this: *'the elimination of workplace security in cities means the elimination of employees rights and benefits. Widespread resistance to this measure is therefore a matter of course'* (CASS 1998: 89). Croll (1999) and Howell (1997) cite recent outbreaks of civil disturbance and strikes in defence of jobs, pensions and health insurance as evidence of the strength of feeling on this issue. Government strategies for social sector reform have been strongly influenced by these attitudes.

The transition to a market economy has led to changes in the pattern of entitlements (Howell 1997; Selden and Lou 1997). There has been a shift from permanent employment to fixed-term contracts. Between 1986 and 1997 the proportion of employees of state enterprises on short-term contracts rose from 7 per cent to 51.6 per cent (Hussain 1999). Enterprises can lay off workers. Urban residents are no longer guaranteed a job. Government has acted to prevent large-scale unemployment (Wong 1999). It has encouraged people to retire; it has pressured government institutions, such as hospitals, to increase their workforce; it has subsidized loss-making enterprises; and it has established a system of unemployment benefits.

However, a growing number of urban residents work for neither government nor state-owned enterprises (see Table 12.1). Categories of enterprise vary considerably in the age and sex of their employees and the levels of pay and benefits they provide. Government institutions and state-owned enterprises tend to have older employees with well-established entitlements. Their new employees are more likely to be on short-term contracts with fewer benefits. Some new employees may not even have full urban registration.

Table 12.1 Number of employed persons by type of enterprises (million)

Year	Number of employees in different type of enterprises in urban areas							
	State owned	Collective owned	Joint owned	Share holding	Foreign funded	Other types of ownership	Private	Individuals
1980	80.2	24.3	–	–		–	–	0.1
1985	89.9	33.2	0.4	–	0.1	–	–	4.5
1990	103.5	35.5	1.0	–	0.1	–	0.6	6.1
1995	112.6	31.5	0.5	3.2	5.1	0.1	4.9	15.6
1996	112.4	30.2	0.5	3.6	5.4	0.1	6.2	17.1

Source: China Statistical Yearbook (1997).

Other categories of enterprise tend to be newer and to employ younger people. Successful companies pay high salaries but provide fewer benefits. The authors visited a joint venture, which employed mostly young female migrants from surrounding counties. The company provided excellent maternity benefits but was not building a fund for future health-care needs.

Older workers and those who have been in the same job for a long time are more likely to have health insurance. A survey of 22 cities by Hu et al. (1999) found that older workers are more likely to have health insurance than younger ones. A survey in Shanghai found that 47 per cent of those hired within the past ten years had health insurance, compared with 80 per cent of those hired before then (Wang and Zuo 1999).

State-owned enterprises are finding it increasingly difficult to finance health insurance. Over a third of some enterprises' workforce are retired. Their health benefits are costly. Many state-owned enterprises are losing money and cannot afford to pay these benefits. Late payment or non-payment of medical costs is common.

The government is establishing city-based social security institutions. It has to reconcile the interests of different age cohorts and categories of enterprise and people with varying registration status in defining contributions and benefits. Selden and Lou (1997) put this forward as an explanation of the difficulty it is having in establishing a uniform pension scheme. They suggest that compliance rates below 100 per cent reflect the unwillingness of new enterprises to contribute to a fund from which the main beneficiaries will be current pensioners. Yu and Ren (1998) make a similar point about health insurance, suggesting that a company's decision to join a local scheme is influenced by the size of contributions, the age of their workforce and whether they own a health facility. The most recent policy statements call for compulsory contributions to a rather basic insurance package.

Meeting Needs and Entitlements to Health Services

The government is managing two simultaneous processes in reforming urban health finance. It is attempting to establish a system of rules-based entitlements, which people trust. It is also endeavouring to fund current entitlements. Policy debates in China mostly concern the broad shape of future social security arrangements. They tend to reflect the views of national ministries and heads of provincial governments (Liu and Bloom 2001). Implementation, on the other hand, is strongly influenced by the immediate concerns of local government, social groups with political influence and enterprises. Young and old, men and women, and employees of different categories of enterprise have different interests. The following subsections present a framework for thinking about the reform of urban health services that takes these issues into account.

Health Needs and Entitlement Groups

Figure 12.1 maps entitlement groups based on employment, poverty/vulnerability and place of residence against three categories of medical need: treatment of chronic disease and major illnesses, prevention of non-communicable disease and prevention and treatment of infectious diseases including HIV/AIDS. The figure points to issues that policy makers need to address. It does not include all medical needs.

Several factors have led to a rapid rise in the cost of medical care for an ageing urban population. This rise is likely to continue as more people reach 75 years. A substantial proportion of the urban population has had the right to virtually free health care; they have come to expect an expensive, hospital-based style of medical care. There are strong pressures on employers and local governments to meet this expectation.

The government and long-established state-owned enterprises have a disproportionate number of pensioners and bear a large share of the cost of health insurance. Some companies can no longer afford this benefit. Others are heavily disadvantaged in competition with newer firms. This has led to pressure to spread the burden more evenly by translating fuzzy claims on enterprises into rules-based claims on an insurance scheme.

Categories of need			
Basis of Entitlement	Chronic disease / major illness	New health problems/ rise in non-communicable diseases	Infectious disease, including HIV/AIDS
a) Employment status (employee, family member of employee, unemployed, pensioner)	• depends on kind of employer • fewer health benefits for family member of employed • fewer health benefits for employees of rural enterprises • most farmers are not insured	• covers IP care, some OP care but no prevention or community support • weaknesses of preventive programmes • diseases related to occupational hazards and pollution • diseases related to behaviour influenced by social factors (drug/alcohol abuse, smoking, diet)	• population movements between rural and urban areas • sex industry • public health systems lagging behind rapid urbanization • possible need for AIDS-related services
b) Poor or vulnerable (poor, disabled)	• needs of disabled • illness and problems of access linked to poverty		
c) Registered residence (urban, rural, migrant)	• compulsory insurance linked to registration • lack of insurance for migrants		

Figure 12.1 Health needs and entitlement groups in urban areas

In creating health insurance schemes, the government has to reconcile the perspectives of insured people, who have a strong sense of entitlement to medical care and newer entrants to the labour market, many of whom are not insured. Large flows of migrants into the cities and also the emergence of vulnerable groups are additional sources of pressure on health services. These people have a number of health-related needs and most are not insured. Decision makers have to balance claims by those with insurance against pressures to meet the needs of the uninsured.

Thinking about Health Reform

The division of responsibility between the Ministries of Health and Labour and Social Security is encouraging an integrated approach to social security and poverty reduction. However, it has also fostered a split in policy discussions between demand- and supply-side issues and between insurance-funded curative care and government-funded health services. This section outlines a framework for looking at the health system as a whole. It identifies five objectives for health development that address the changing pattern of needs and entitlements and outlines directions for reform (Figure 12.2):

Effective public health programmes. City governments have to ensure that their public health and preventive programmes take into account a changing situation. They may need to shift their emphasis from maternal and child health and infectious disease to the needs of the elderly, migrants and poor and vulnerable groups, and also to AIDS prevention. They also need to monitor for emergent problems among vulnerable groups. Local governments will have to allocate sufficient funds to meet these needs.

Access to effective and affordable health services for the elderly. Many health insurance schemes have experienced financial problems associated with the high cost of benefits for the elderly. Some have collapsed and others have remained solvent only by raiding individual medical accounts. They all face rising costs as more beneficiaries reach 75 years.

It is difficult to convince the young and healthy to contribute to a scheme from which the major beneficiaries are the elderly, unless they believe they will eventually derive benefits themselves. It is difficult to foster such a belief in a period of rapid change. Local governments may need to supplement insurance contributions with funding from tax revenue, borrowing and the transfer of assets (in cash or shares) to a health insurance fund.

International experience suggests that referral hospitals do not provide the most cost-effective health care for the elderly. Existing insurance schemes encourage people to seek care from these facilities. A major effort is needed to identify an appropriate mix of community support, basic preventive and curative services, and care in hospitals and nursing homes. The government could encourage some cities to experiment with an integrated benefit for the elderly, rather than the present insurance provisions. The benefit could be financed in the same way as existing schemes. However, the benefit fund would pay for services in different ways, such as capitation payments adjusted for age, or contracts with specified facilities to provide services on demand. The purpose would be to test alternative approaches for addressing the needs of the elderly.

Health insurance phased in. The government has enunciated principles for health insurance reform. Questions remain about the breadth of coverage and sources of finance. Present proposals suggest that all urban residents should be entitled to a basic benefit (State Council 2000). Government will have to subsidize membership by low-income earners. Or, other beneficiaries will have to contribute an extra amount. There is a trade-off between the size of the basic benefit package and the feasibility of extending coverage to all. The proposals are not clear about the degree to which contributory insurance schemes should cover family members. This is important, if significant numbers of working-age people will not be employed.

Objectives for reform	Implications for demand side	Implications for supply side
a) Effective public health and preventive programmes	• Fund local government public health services adequately • Define the responsibilities of these services more clearly • Coordinate health activities funded from different sources with the ultimate aim of integration	• Reform public health services to address new needs • Monitor emerging needs linked to social change
b) Access to effective and affordable health services for the elderly	• Define basic health entitlement and redefine benefit packages to remove incentives for hospital-based care • Establish sources of finance (contributions, tax, transfer of assets) • Define relative responsibilities of local government- and insurance-funded services	• Restructure health system (facilities and service delivery) to give greater emphasis to primary care services • Strengthen facility management and improve efficiency • Introduce new payment mechanisms to reduce incentives for cost increases
c) Health insurance scheme phased	• Establish compulsory scheme and convince beneficiaries that it is sustainable • Define geographic base of scheme • Define family members to be covered in contributory schemes	• Define roles of local government services in terms of prevention and community support systems
d) Health safety net for the poor and vulnerable	• Decide whether to include all urban residents in basic insurance • Define criteria for eligibility for government support • Growth of charitable foundations	• Strengthen programmes to meet needs of vulnerable groups • Make low-cost services more available
e) Reduce urban-rural imbalances in public health	• Ensure adequate funding of urban local government health services • Fund basic rural public health • Begin discussions about insurance for migrants and rural workers	• Expand public health system and preventive programmes in cities • Low-cost services for migrants • Strengthen rural public health services

Figure 12.2 Agenda for urban health development and reform

There are questions about the geographic basis for pooling. A scheme that covers all cities in a province would put a heavy strain on poorer localities unless there were fiscal transfers between cities. This in turn would reduce inequalities between cities, but might increase rural-urban segmentation. The larger the commitments of city governments to finance benefits for urban dwellers, the greater the likelihood they will resist fiscal transfers to poor rural localities. This kind of trade-off becomes particularly important as coverage is extended to workers in rural-based enterprises and to rural-urban migrants. There are also questions about the kinds of health services to which the insured population should be entitled. This involves the balance between ambulatory care, hospitals, prevention and community support. It also involves choices between more or less cost-effective interventions.

The most important challenge is to convince young people that they will eventually benefit from the newly established schemes. One reason for the introduction of individual accounts was that they provided assurance to account holders that they had a firm claim on these resources. The fact that insurance schemes have had to draw down the balances in these accounts means that they have to find an alternative strategy to win the trust of potential contributors.

Health safety net for the poor and vulnerable. There are only minimal arrangements to finance health care for the urban poor. Municipal health departments need to take the problems associated with poverty into account in planning their preventive programmes. They also need to devise strategies to make effective basic services available at an affordable cost where people live.

Local departments of civil affairs finance little more than *ad hoc* arrangements to write off the bad debts of hospitals. There is a growing recognition that poor health and the high cost of medical care are important contributors to household impoverishment. This suggests the need for a safety net. The design of a targeted health benefit will not be easy. Government will have to address issues such as the identification of beneficiaries, the definition of a package of appropriate health services and the design of payment mechanisms which encourage facilities to provide services of a reasonable quality and price. In establishing this kind of benefit, policy-makers should be aware of the ultimate aim of providing universal coverage to urban residents. Nonetheless measures will be needed to protect the poor and vulnerable during the period of transition.

The government is encouraging the establishment of charitable foundations to address the health needs of the indigent. This development raises difficult questions about the relative responsibility of government and private charities for raising money from profitable enterprise and people with substantial incomes, and for supporting those in need.

Urban-rural imbalances in public health to be reduced. The health of urban and rural populations is interlinked. The reduction of structural barriers in the labour market will make it increasingly difficult to maintain large differences in entitlement to health insurance between urban and peri-urban residents. The high burden on urban enterprises of health insurance gives an advantage to those operating outside the city boundary. New enterprises may well take this into account in deciding where to locate. This could ultimately erode urban social benefits. The presence of many rural-urban migrants can also serve to push the social wage down. Such pressures can only be addressed by controlling the cost of urban health insurance and gradually extending coverage to rural-based workers.

There is a constant threat that infectious diseases will spread to the cities. One way to address this problem is by ensuring that local public health services keep up with urbanization. Another approach is to improve rural public health. This is one reason for cities to agree to an increase in fiscal transfers from themselves to poor rural areas. Also, migrant workers and their employers could be required to contribute to a health insurance fund. The contributions would accrue to individual medical accounts and/or be transferred to a health fund in the migrants' registered places of residence.

Conclusions

This period of rapid change has created both a need for health reform and an opportunity for achieving it. It should be possible to win support for quite new arrangements among young workers. However, the entitlements of older workers will have to be renegotiated. The outcome will reflect the influence of different stakeholders.

Policy makers face the challenge of establishing a health insurance system appropriate to the emerging patterns of labour market segmentation. They need to avoid a race to the bottom in which the social benefits in rural areas become the norm for cities. This will ultimately require the establishment of compulsory basic health insurance schemes that can be extended to all employees. Measures are needed to protect the governments of poor localities from an excessive burden in financing this benefit. Health insurance reforms will thus have to be linked to system-wide changes to government financial management.

Discussions about future insurance arrangements have paradoxically been dominated by negotiations about how to finance *existing* medical benefits. Once explicit agreements have been reached on this latter issue, it may become easier to agree on longer-term reforms of urban health finance.

International experience suggests that it is very difficult to change expectations of entitlement to care, once they have been created by a health insurance scheme. An inappropriate scheme can preserve unequal access to benefits and become an impediment to labour market development (Mackintosh 1997). The outcome of the present efforts to negotiate new rules of entitlement to urban health services will influence China's health system for a long time.

Notes

1   The authors would like to acknowledge helpful comments by Cai Renhua, Sarah Cook, Hilary Standing, Thomas Uhlemann, Xiong Xianjun and participants at workshops on Social Policy in China at Shanghai in July 2000 and Oxford in October 2001. The preparation of this paper was jointly funded by an ESCOR grant to the IDS programme on Social Policy and an ESCOR grant for a study of urban health reform in China. The opinions expressed are the sole responsibility of the authors.

References

Barer, M., et al. (1987), 'Ageing and health care utilization: new evidence on old fallacies', *Social Science and Medicine*, 24,10: 851–62.
Barr, M. (2001), 'Medical savings accounts in Singapore: a critical inquiry', *Journal of Health Politics, Policy and Law*, 26, 4: 709–26.
Bloom, G. (2001), 'Equity in health in unequal societies: meeting health needs in contexts of social change', *Health Policy*, 57: 205–24.
Bloom, G., Han, L. and Li, X. (2000), *How health workers earn a living in China*, IDS Working Paper no. 108, Institute of Development Studies, Brighton.
Chan, Wingchan and Zhang, Li (1999), 'The Hukou system and rural-urban migration', *China Quarterly,* 618–53.
Chen, X. (2000), 'Health problems and countermeasures during urbanization', *Medicine and Society*, 13, 3: 1–3.
China Health Statistical Abstract, (1998), National Health Statistical Centre, Beijing.
China Statistical Yearbook (1997), China Statistical Publishing House, Beijing.
China Statistical Yearbook (1998), China Statistical Publishing House, Beijing.
Chinese Academy of Social Sciences (CASS) (1998), 'Project Group on Social Development in China, Institutional reforms and challenges at the middle stage of China's reform', *Social Sciences in China, English Language Edition*, 19, 2: 83–93.
Chinese Academy of Social Sciences (CASS) (2000), 'Research Group on China's Social Security System, A study of China's social security system', *Social Sciences in China*, 21, 4: 50–9.
Cook, S. (2001), *After the Iron Rice Bowl: extending the safety net in China,* IDS discussion Paper 377, Institute of Development Studies, Brighton.
Cook, S. and White, G. (1998), *Changing Pattern of Poverty in China: Issues for Research and Policy*, IDS Working Paper No. 67, Institute of Development Studies, Brighton.
Croll, E. (1999), 'Social welfare reforms: trends and tensions', *China Quarterly*, 684–99.
Deng P., Mi, G.M., Wang Y.C. et al., (2000), 'Study of health services demand of elderly people in an urban community', *Chinese General Practice*, 3, 5: 373–4.
Gao, J., Tang, S., Tolhurst, R. and Rao, K. (2001), 'Changing access to health services in urban China: what implications for equity?', *Health Policy and Planning*; 16, 3: 302–12.
Howell, J. (1997), 'The Chinese economic miracle and urban workers', *European Journal of Development Research*, 9, 2: 148–75.
Hu, X. (1996), 'Reducing state-owned enterprises' social burdens and establishing a social insurance system', in H.G. Broadman (ed.), *Policy Options for Reform of Chinese State-Owned Enterprises*, World Bank discussion paper no 335, World Bank, Washington DC, pp. 125–48.
Hu Tehwei, Ong, M., Lin, Zihua and Li, E. (1999), 'The effects of economic reform on health insurance and the financial burden for urban workers in China', *Health Economics*, 8: 309–21.
Hussain, A. (1999), 'Social welfare in China in the context of three transitions'. Unpublished paper, Asia Research Centre, London School of Economics.
Liu, Yunguo and Bloom, G. (2001), *Designing a rural health reform project: the negotiation of change in China*, IDS Working Paper no. 150, Institute of Development Studies, Brighton.
Ma, Q. (2000), 'How to strengthen the administration of epidemic prevention of the floating population', *Chinese Health Economics*, 19, 6: 52.
Mackintosh, M. (1997), *Managing Public Sector Reform: The Case of Health Care*. Development Policy and Practice Research Group Working Paper no. 37, Open University, Milton Keynes.
MoH (1998), *Health Resources and Utilization since the 1980s,* Statistics and Information Centre, Ministry of Health, Beijing.

Ou A.H., and Zhu, Y., (2000), 'Analysis of condition of elderly people and their health service utilization in Guiyang City,' *Chinese Primary Health Care* 14, 3: 47–8.
Selden, M. and Lou, L. (1997), 'The reform of social welfare in China', *World Development*, 25, 10: 1657–68.
Shkolnikov, V., Field, M. and Andreev, E. (2001), 'Russia: socioeconomic dimensions of the gender gap in mortality', in T. Evans et al. (eds), *Challenging Inequities in Health*, Oxford University Press, Oxford.
Shu, B. et al. (2001), 'Health finance and expenditure in Nantong City'. Presented to workshop on urban health reform, Beijing, December.
Solinger, D. (1999), *Contesting Citizenship in Urban China: Peasant Migrants, the State and the Logic of the Market*, University of California Press, Berkeley.
State Council (1998), *The Decision on Establishing Basic Health Insurance System for Urban Employees*, Beijing.
State Council (2000), *Guidelines for Urban Health and Medicine System Reform*, Beijing.
Sun, F. (1998), 'Ageing of the population in China: trends and implications', *Asia-Pacific Population Journal*, 13, 4: 75–92.
Tian, A.P., Lu, S.F. and Qu, L. (1999) 'The situation of reproductive health care need and provision for the floating population in Chengdu City', *Journal of Chinese Family Planning*, 7, 5: 211–13.
Wang, F. and Zuo, X. (1999), 'Inside China's cities: institutional barriers and opportunities for urban migrants', *American Economic Review*, 89, 2: 276–80.
Wang, Y.L., Ma, D.G. and Fang, J. (2000), 'The immunization issues caused by immigrating population and the corresponding solution strategy in Xiaoshan', *Chinese Rural Health Services Administration*, 20, 3: 41–2.
Wang, Y.P. (2001), 'Prospects and problems of urban housing reform'. Presented to workshop on Social Policy Reform in Socialist Market China, Oxford, October.
Wilkinson, R. (1996), *Unhealthy Societies*, Routledge, London.
Williams, A. (1991), '"Need" – an economic exegesis', in A. Culyer (ed.), *The Economics of Health*, Vol. I, Elgar, Aldershot.
Wong, Chack-kie (1999), 'Reforming China's state socialist workfare system: a cautionary and incremental approach', *Issues and Studies*, 35, 5: 169–94.
Wong, L. (1994), 'China's urban migrants – the public policy challenge', *Pacific Affairs*, 67, 3: 334–55.
Wong, L. (1998), *Marginalization and Social Welfare in China*, Routledge, London.
World Bank (1997), *China 2020 Issues and Options: Financing Health Care*, World Bank, Washington, DC.
Xiong, Y. (1999), 'Social policy for the elderly in the context of aging in China: issues and challenges of social work education', *International Journal of Welfare for the Aged*, 1: 107–22.
Xu, F. (1998), 'Expenditure under labour insurance medical service scheme', *China Social Insurance*, 10: 19–20.
Yu, W. and Ren, M. (1998), 'The conflicts of social ideals and actual interests – the contradictions and problems existed in the reform of social medical insurance in the towns of China', *Chinese Health Economics*, 17, 9: 5–8.
Zhan Shaokang et al. (2000), 'Maternal care for internal migrants in Shanghai', presented to the conference on Rural Health Reform and Development in Beijing, China November.
Zhao, Y. (1999), 'Estimation and analysis of the nation's total health spending in 1996', *Chinese Health Economics*, 18, 1: 29–31.
Zhou, L.P. and Wang, R.Z. (1998), 'Analysis of health need and utilization of elderly population in Hangzhou City', *Journal of Zhejiang Medical University*, 27, 2: 84–7.

Chapter 13

China's Health Policy: A Comparative Footnote

Rudolf Klein

Introduction

In attempting to put China's health care performance, policies and prospects into a comparative context, one question demands an immediate answer right at the start. Does such an exercise make any kind of sense? The reason for asking this question is that no country matches China for size and diversity. There is the sharp division between urban and rural populations. There are great regional differences in per capita incomes and in the rate at which they are changing. In many respects, moreover, Chinese society straddles different historical epochs. While there are tracts of China scarcely touched by the industrial revolution of the nineteenth century, there are others which are rapidly moving towards the post-industrial economy of the twenty-first century. In terms of health problems and policy, China is therefore at one and the same time building on the public health tradition of Chadwick and Simon, designed to deal with the casualties of the industrial revolution, while at the same time coping with the diseases of affluence, an ageing population and the costs of high technology medicine. In the former respect, China shares its challenge with developing nations. In the latter respect, it shares an agenda with the rich countries of the Organisation for Economic Cooperation and Development (OECD).

As if this were not enough to deter an outside analyst (especially one without any qualifications whatsoever in Sinology), there is a further difficulty. This is that viewing China as being simply lower in the evolutionary cycle of health policy – on the same path as the OECD countries with comprehensive health care systems, but with a long way to go – would be misleading. Economic determinism – i.e. the assumption that economic growth inevitably leads to convergence in the kind of health care system adopted – is bad theory and poor as a guide: witness the case of the United States, the odd-man-out among the wealthy nations in its incapacity to create a comprehensive health care system. Further, investment in health care can be seen either as creating the conditions for economic development or as the dividend of successful growth (Sen 1999). In any case, it cannot be assumed that the policy goals will – or necessarily should – be the same: for example, in the case of China the evidence appears to be that economic efficiency trumps distributional equity (Lin 2001).

With these reservations in mind, I adopt two strategies in what follows. First, I look at China's health care performance in the context of countries at roughly the same stage of economic development (while recognizing that national averages and ignoring variations around them may hide as much as they reveal, and not only in the case of China). Second, I look at the historical experience of Western Europe. Here my assumption is that 'Europe' was (and is) as varied, if not as large, an entity as China with large geographical variations in per capita income and the level of industrial development. Analysing the evolutionary history of Europe's component states – and their patterns of policy change over time – may therefore provide some clues about China's future. Lastly I discuss some general issues which are likely to prove as relevant to China as they are to other health care systems.

Comparing Performance

In trying to 'place' China in an international comparative context, there is a paradox. If performance is to be judged by outcomes, then China is a reasonable success story. In terms of the population's level of health, China ranks 61st among the 191 countries in the league table produced by the World Health Organisation (WHO 2000). Disability-adjusted life expectancy at birth is 61.2 for men and 63.3 years for women. This puts it ahead of countries such as the Russian Federation (56.1 and 66.4), Brazil (55.2 and 62.9), Pakistan (55 and 56.8), India (52.8 and 53.5) and South Africa (38.6 and 41), among the 100-plus nations below it in the league table. If, however, performance is to be judged by the overall organization and effectiveness of the health care system, according to the criteria used by WHO, then China is a conspicuous laggard. It is ranked 144th by WHO for its 'overall health systems performance'. In this respect China ranks lower than the Russian Federation (130th), Brazil (125th), Pakistan (122nd) and India (112th) – but higher than South Africa (175th).

This paradoxical picture may simply be an artefact of the WHO's curious and much-criticized methodology in compiling its league table, using a composite score compiled from a variety of indicators. However, it also suggests that China may have been more successful in implementing traditional nineteenth.century public health policies than in building a modern health care system. Given that the determinants of health are largely social and economic – that a combination of clean water, good drains, a decent diet and education can produce great gains in life expectancy – China's respectable performance in terms of outcomes probably reflects its success in developing the relevant infrastructure and other non-health-care policies. Whether progress in this respect will continue – under the pressure of rapid urbanization and industrialization – is another matter. Here the case of the Russian Federation is a warning: recidivism is possible.

The WHO exercise is perhaps more revealing if we unpackage the various indicators used in composite score to explore just why China ranks so low for overall systems performance. First, China is – if the WHO figures are to be trusted – an extremely low spender on health care: 2.7 per cent of GDP. This compares with 7.1 per cent for South Africa, 6.5 per cent for Brazil, 5.4 per cent for the Russian Federation 5.2 per cent for India and 4.0 per cent for Pakistan, to stick with the same group of comparator countries in order to underline that there appears to be very little relationship between health outcomes and the level of health care spending. Second, parsimony apart, the financing of Chinese health care is remarkable in another respect as well – the balance between public and private spending. In China, this is 25:75. This is not out of line with India and Pakistan where the role of public funding is smaller still. But it is out of line with South Africa and Brazil, where the split is nearer 50:50, let alone the Russian Federation where public spending approaches 80 per cent of the total – roughly the norm for European countries. Given that public spending tends to be redistributive while private out of pocket payments tends to be regressive, it is therefore not surprising that the WHO exercise ranked China 188th in the world for 'fairness in financial contributions'.

To an extent these figures may exaggerate China's poor performance in this respect. There may be definitional problems. The WHO data equates private spending with out-of-pocket expenditure: i.e. payments by users of the health care system. But it may be that this category also includes spending by firms providing health care for their workers: if so, the picture of a highly regressive system of funding would have to be modified somewhat. However, as is clear from chapter 12 in this volume, the trend in urban areas has been away from work-based insurance towards a geographically based model of social insurance – with a large, and rising, proportion of the population lacking any kind of coverage. Add the fact that the new model of geographically based social insurance has been implemented only very partially, even in those cities which have piloted the new policy (Duckett 2001), and it is clear that the funding of China's health care system is indeed regressive, and that access to the system is related to the patient's ability to pay. Interestingly, differentiating China's policies from those of the wealthy countries of the West, the policy aim appears to be to emphasize the role of personal contributions to health care costs, rather than seeking to minimize these through a system of collective insurance. Furthermore, the aim appears to be to have a three-tier model of funding health care: a basic health care benefits package, collectively funded, plus personal health care accounts, on the Singapore model, and some private insurance.

Paths to Health Care Provision

In this, as in other respects, the evidence suggests that China is not just at a different stage in the evolution of its health care system compared to wealthy countries (a fairly trite observation), but is deliberately following a different evolutionary strategy. Despite China's history of extreme collectivism, there is more than a hint of individualism in the health care policies being pursued: i.e. emphasizing the responsibility of the individual, and his or her family, for meeting at least part of their own health care costs. In short, China appears to be following the example of the 'Confucian welfare states' (Jones 1993) rather than adopting the standard Western-type model. Given that China has the ambition of emulating the economic performance of the 'tiger economies' – Singapore, Taiwan and Hong Kong – it is not surprising that it is also tempted to follow their social policies. For example, Singapore's personal medical savings accounts seem, despite their deficiencies, to have influenced China's policies (Barr 2001).

However, before embracing that conclusion unreservedly, it is worth looking at how the European model evolved over time and stressing that, even now, important differences remain between the systems of the wealthy countries. Here the key point is that countries marched at different speeds, and sometimes to a different tune, towards the goal of providing comprehensive health care coverage. If for Europe we read China (treating it as not one unitary actor but as a collection of different entities at different stages of development), history suggests that we can predict with some confidence that economic and social diversity will be mirrored by diversity in health care provision. Whether that diversity will represent variations on the Confucian or the Western theme remains to be seen, but variations there will certainly be.

Only consider the pattern of European development. As late as 1960 there were considerable variations both in the public/private ratio of funding and in the extent of coverage (OECD 1985). So, for example, Greece and Portugal – both relatively poor countries – relied much more on private, out-of-pocket funding than other West European countries. Public expenditure on health care was respectively 1.7 per cent and 0.9 per cent of GDP in these two countries, as against an average of 2.5 per cent for the OECD countries as a whole. Social insurance coverage for specific services also varied considerably – in the case of hospital care, the range was from 18 per cent of the population in Portugal and 30 per cent in Greece to 100 per cent in Sweden and the United Kingdom. It is also worth noting, as being of particular relevance to China, that the process of building up a system of entitlements began almost everywhere with industrial workers – often excluding their dependants in the first instance – and that the rural population were usually the last to come under the shield of protection. Although universalism is now the hallmark of the European (though not the US) model of health care, this was slow to come and was achieved only incrementally, over a half century or more. Thus China's halting, piecemeal approach is very much in line with what might be expected, on the basis of the European experience.

The collective European experience suggests a further tentative conclusion: i.e. that diversity is enduring. Although there has been some convergence among the European countries as living standards have levelled up, there is no uniformity. There has indeed been a general move towards universality and comprehensiveness in coverage. But differences in the types of funding, and in the organization of providers, remain. Path dependency (Tuohy 1999) tends to be the rule: the best – though not infallible – predictor of where nations are today, is where they were when they started to build up their systems, almost a century ago. Public finance and public provision is the dominant (if not exclusive) norm in the Scandinavian countries and the UK. Social insurance funding and a plurality of providers is the norm in most other West European countries. Institutions, once created, change the political landscape – and create constituencies for their own survival.

Two highly speculative conclusions about China might be drawn from this deliberately over-simplified comparative analysis. First, the decisions being taken now are mapping out the path to the future and will be difficult to reverse: policy creates interests and these interests will, in turn, constrain future policy options. Second, variations in the funding and organization of health care within China will persist. Only a highly flexible system – with a tolerance for a large degree of diversity – is likely to be able to take the strain of adapting to socioeconomic geographical differences and to widening inequalities in incomes. To move towards uniformity in access and level of provision would require a geographical redistribution of resources on an unprecedented scale, and there is little evidence that China's political institutions and leaders would have the capacity to carry out such an exercise, even if there were a will to do so. In the circumstances WHO's use of the distributional equity criterion for assessing China's health care system seems irrelevant, if not misguided.

Whether by design or not, China's emergent three-tier system of health care seems calculated to accommodate diversity. If a basic package of collectively funded benefits were to become standard across the country, then the top-up schemes – individual accounts and private insurance arrangements – could reflect variations in individual income and economic geography. There would indeed be inequalities, but there would be a medical safety net for all (ironically the kind of system associated with the liberal, minimal welfare state of unmodified capitalism in the West). Much would, however, depend on how the basic benefits package was defined and funded.

Defining such a basic package is not easy. International experience suggests that such packages tend to be elastic, with a habit of expanding in line with changing technology. In turn, this suggests – because entitlements are likely to expand over time and become more expensive – it is over-optimistic to hope that it will be possible to devise a funded system. Here the comparative message is that pay-as-you-go systems (whether tax- or social insurance-based) are the norm, for the very good reason that health care funding is very different from pension funding: demography is much more predictable than the future pattern and incidence of illness and disability – or, more important still, than the cost implications of technological change.

Organising the Supply Side of Health Care

Technological change is, however, no more a 'determinant' of expenditure on health care – whether private or public – than is demography or a country's position in the economic league table. Again, the simple comparative message is that countries vary in their capacity to cope with the cost consequences of both demography and technological change. They are all on the same escalator, but there is considerable scope for controlling the speed at which the escalator moves. The characteristics of the system for funding and delivering health care are crucial variables when it comes to using resources effectively and controlling cost escalation. And while China may not at present be worried about a cost explosion – given its low starting point – it seems safe to predict that concern will soon surface, as it does sooner or later in all countries.

As far as funding is concerned, the evidence suggests that 'single-payer' countries are better able to control spending than those where the money comes from a variety of sources: i.e. countries where there is a single budget for health care, set by central government – for example, Sweden and the UK – have generally been more successful in moderating the year by year rise in expenditure, than have more diverse systems. They also tend to have the advantage of being monopsonies: i.e. as the main (if not exclusive) employers of doctors and nurses, they are better able to restrain the rise of labour costs – the main element in the health care budget. So while pluralistic systems of finance have their advantages – relieving the demands on central government as well as providing more scope for promoting competition and consumer choice – there is a price to be paid. Short-term political expediency – diffusing the payment burden – can spell long-term problems.

Yet there is another policy concern for all health care systems, at least as important as the overall bill and how best to meet it. This is how to ensure that resources, at whatever level, are well spent: i.e. that more money buys more *effective* health care. Here, as Chapter 12 in this volume suggests, China faces a major challenge. The present system of remuneration for providers appears to encourage them to maximize their use of expensive technology, such as CT scanners, and to promote the consumption of pharmaceuticals. If the government controls the per diem price of hospital stays, or the charge per consultation, then there is a clear incentive to multiply the number of days and consultations, as well as to make a profit by prescribing as many drugs as possible. And all the evidence is that such perverse incentives will maximize cost inflation but minimize the effectiveness of medical practice – promoting waste and the incomes of providers, but not health.

One possible reaction to this kind of challenge is to argue for a command-and control system: i.e. a bureaucratic-managerial system whereby the government can exercise more direct control over what health care providers actually do. For example, hospitals and doctors can be required to work according to centrally determined guidelines, which specify what drugs will be prescribed for whom. Similarly, governments can exercise direct control over the number of posts in hospitals and over the extent of investment in expensive equipment. However, the general trend – with the possible exception of the UK – has been away from such central control strategies. Certainly, such a strategy would seem particularly inappropriate for China, given the scale of the bureaucratic-managerial task that would be involved in a country of such size and diversity. Some tasks will inevitably fall on central government: for example, the assessment of new technologies. But any attempt to micro-manage the system as a whole would clearly be to court disaster.

This suggests that policy effort should be invested, not in developing stronger bureaucratic regulation, but in devising incentives which will push the health care system in desired directions: towards providing appropriate, effective medical care in the most parsimonious way possible. But what incentives can be provided for patients to seek (and professionals to provide) low cost as distinct from high-tech treatment? How can the incentives be changed, so that providers will deliver appropriate as distinct from remunerative treatment, that they will be as concerned with preventive as with repair medicine? Can incentives be devised which will improve the distribution of health care and encourage doctors to move into primary care?

In summary, then, the future of health care in China may depend as much on the small print of reward structures as on the methods of funding. And a crucial criterion for judging the methods of funding should be whether they encourage or inhibit appropriate incentives. Even with better incentives, health care expenditure will continue to increase: there is no reason to expect that China will buck international trends in this respect. Even with better incentives and higher expenditure, great inequalities in access will remain: given China's diversity, and the values driving policy, it would be foolish to expect any other outcome. However, a minimal but sensible hope would be that China manages to create a system whose dynamics drive it to promote effective medicine, rather than to inflate costs.

References

Barr, Michael (2001), 'Medical Savings Accounts in Singapore: A Critical Inquiry' *Journal of Health Politics, Policy and Law* Vol.26 No.4 709–726.

Duckett, Jane (2001), 'Political Interests and the Implementation of China's Urban Health Insurance Reform' *Social Policy & Administration* Vol.35 No.3 290–273.

Jones, Catherine (1993), 'The Pacific Challenge: Confucian welfare states' chapter in Catherine Jones (ed.), *New Perspectives on the Welfare State in Europe* Routledge, London.

Lin, Ka (2001), 'Chinese Perceptions of the Scandinavian Social Policy Model, *Social Policy and Administration* Vol.35 No.3 321–340.

OECD (1985), *Measuring Health Care, 1960–1983* OECD, Paris.

Sen, Amatya, (1999), *Development as Freedom* Oxford University Press, Oxford.

Tuohy, Carolyn (1999), *Accidental Logics* Oxford University Press, New York.

World Health Organisation (2000), *World Health Report, 2000* WHO, Geneva.

Chapter 14

Progress and Problems of Urban Housing Reform

Ya Ping Wang[1]

Introduction

Housing in China has been organized differently in rural and urban areas since the Communists came to power in 1949. In rural areas, private home ownership has been largely preserved, although the style and quality of housing in villages has changed over time. In urban areas, housing provision has gone through several major changes over the last 50 years. This chapter reviews these latter changes and focuses on the outcomes of urban housing reform during the 1990s. Major problems of the current housing system and recent policy development will be discussed. Housing policies in China cover a huge area, and there are also important variations in practice and implementation peculiar to each city. It will be impossible to provide a detailed review in respect of every area, within the limited space available here. Relevant references have been included at various places, which readers may find useful.

The Urban Housing System and its Reform

Housing in Chinese cities was mainly in private ownership and controlled by landlords before 1949. In the late 1950s and early 1960s, most private rental housing was nationalized through a socialist transformation movement. At the same time, public housing was built and distributed free to employees by government owned enterprises and institutions (the work units). By the late 1970s, a public sector-dominated welfare housing provision system had been established in urban areas (Wang 1992). This system resembled many features of the East European housing model (see Chapter 15, this volume). During the 1980s, there was large-scale investment were made in housing construction by the government and other public sector organizations, which increased the public housing stock further (Wang 1995).

However, not every urban household in Chinese cities has access to public housing. In the late 1950s, Chinese government introduced a residence registration (*hukou*) system. This system not only created a division between urban and rural areas, it also divided the urban population, according to employment sectors and status, into several categories. The state sector included cadres and workers. The cadre category itself included government and party leaders, professionals and academics employed by various government and public organizations. Meanwhile the worker category included all skilled and unskilled employees engaged in industrial factories or other organizations. Apart from the state sector, there was a collective enterprise sector as well. Only senior managers in the collective sector have a similar status to the state sector employees; general workers in the collective sector have a lower social status in the cities. Housing provision differs in important ways between these population groups (Logan and Bian 1993). Public housing was distributed according to the employment status rather than family housing need. Best-quality housing was given to those residents of highest political and social status in their employment. Politicians, administrators, and professionals thus had better access to public housing than did workers. State sector workers had to wait longer in the housing queue than did their leaders. Meanwhile, most non-state sector workers did not have direct access to public housing and relied either on traditional family homes or on family members who were employed in the state sector (Wang and Murie 1999a).

One of the main features of this form of urban housing provision was the role played by work units in the state sector. Housing production, distribution, maintenance and management was decentralized to each public institution or enterprise, rather than being managed by a unitary housing authority (Wang 1995; Wu 1996; Zhang 1997). In 1981, over half (54 per cent) of urban housing was managed directly by work units and 28 per cent by housing authorities run by the municipal governments (Editors Committee of Almanac of China's Economy 1983). Private housing was reduced to less than 20 per cent. Most large state enterprises and institutions had residential quarters adjacent to their workshop and office areas. Housing was also regarded as a part of state welfare provision rather than as a commodity. Rents were extremely low because the provision of housing had been taken into account in determining wage levels.

This housing system had generated many problems, such as shortage and overcrowding, inequality of distribution, corruption, inefficient management and mal-maintenance (Logan and Bian 1993). Of this list, the problem of shortage was the most prominent. Statistics showed that average housing floor space per person in most Chinese cities had actually declined in 1978, by comparison with 1949 when the communists came to power. This was a result of many years of underinvestment in housing, combined with the increase in urban population.

From the early 1980s, the Chinese government put forward new policies designed to reform the urban housing system. A series of reform experiments were carried out in various locations from 1979 to 1988. This led to the publication of a central government policy document, *Implementation Plan for a Gradual Housing System Reform in Cities and Towns*, in 1988 (State Council 1988; World Bank 1992). This year thus marked an effective turning point in housing reform, from pilot tests and experiments in selected cities to overall implementation in urban areas. The objective of this plan was to 'realise housing commercialisation according to the principles of socialist planned market economy'. This plan was interrupted briefly in 1989 by economic and political problems. However housing reform gained pace again in 1991, with the publication of another central government resolution, *On Comprehensive Reform of the Urban Housing System* (General Office of the State Council 1991). This document reinforced the 1988 policies, and required all urban authorities to carry out housing reform. This resolution led to the large-scale sale of existing public housing at very low prices, particularly to current occupiers. But, in the middle of 1993, concerned about such low-price sales of public housing, the government suspended its housing reform programme.

However, in 1994, a new set of reform policies was introduced (Housing Reform Steering Group of the State Council 1994). They included:

- *A new housing savings system*: this involved the establishment of a housing provident fund through which every employer and employee made a contribution to the employee's housing saving account. The saving could only be used for housing purposes or as an addition to a personal pension when the employee retired. The rates of saving varied from place to place. In most cities, it started from 5 per cent of the employee's monthly salary and gradually increased to 10 per cent by 2000.
- *Sale of public housing*: the sale of public housing to sitting tenants was a major area of housing reform. Steady progress has been made in this area. By 2000, about 60 per cent of public housing had been sold.
- *Rent reform (increase)*: it was originally planned that, by the year 2000, rents should cover the costs of building, repair, management, interest on loans and property tax and would total about 15 per cent of a couple's salary.
- *Reform of housing maintenance and management*: this involved the setting up of a real estate management system in new or existing housing schemes, to replace the functions performed by work unit or municipal government in the past.
- *Affordable Housing (Economic and Comfortable Housing – jingji shiyong fang and anju projects)*: subsidized commercial housing for low- and middle-income families was introduced in 1994 and special central government loans and free land allocations were used as the main mechanism for the development of this type of housing (Wang and Murie 2000).

To speed up the process of housing commercialization in urban areas, a major decision was made by central government in July 1998, which put a stop to the practice of housing distribution by public sector employers to their employees. According to this policy, public sector employees should acquire housing directly via the market rather than from their employers. Employers are still allowed to issue a housing subsidy to their employees, but not to be directly involved in housing construction, distribution and management. Higher-income households were encouraged to obtain high-standard housing through the market. Affordable housing, built with government support, was seen as the main source of new housing for low- and middle-income groups. Poor families were entitled to apply to their employer or to the government for subsidized rental housing (State Council 1998). (For details on housing reform, please see Wang and Murie 1996, 1999b, 2000; Wang 2001; Bian and Logan 1996; Chen 1996; Chiu 2001a, 2001b; Lau 1993; Lee 2000; Li 2000a, 2000b; Wu 1996, 2001; Zhou and Logan 1996).

Urban housing reform has brought many changes to the housing provision and consumption system in China. There have been obvious improvements in general living conditions in Chinese cities. New housing estates of various styles can be found in every city and they form a large part of the new urban landscape. The scale of improvement can also be seen from the improvement in the average floor space of housing per person. Before housing reform in 1978, the urban population had a per capita average of 3 square metres of housing floor space. By the end of 2000, according to official reports, this had increased to 20 square metres of construction floor space (Xie 2001). A substantial proportion of urban residents enjoys better housing now than at any time in history. There has also been diversification of housing investment with more and more housing costs being met by urban residents themselves. This has increased the total volume of investment for housing. Government statistics show that by the end of 2000, about 77.1 per cent of official urban residents owned their homes (State Statistics Bureau 2001). This is a dramatic increase from the very low proportion of home ownership (less than 20 per cent in most cities) characteristic of the pre-reform period.

Major Outstanding Problems

Despite these successes, housing reform has not solved all the problems of the old system. At the same time, problems associated with the new urban economy and housing market have also emerged (Lee 2000). This final section discusses some of these problems.

The Continuation of Inequality

The pre-reform housing system, particularly in its management of distribution, was criticised as unfair. It was hoped that housing privatization and commercialization would solve this problem and that urban households would acquire housing from the market according to their ability to pay. However, inequalities in housing distribution and consumption have continued. The old distribution ideas were not entirely abandoned. Housing has not been distributed to employees as material any more, but cash subsidies for housing have been calculated according to the official housing entitlement standards. In other words, the reform has not addressed the question of inequality in housing consumption. Senior government officials, academics, professionals and enterprise managers have been the main population groups to benefit from housing privatisation. The continuation of this inequality in housing distribution is demonstrated by the allocation/entitlement standards (Table 14.1). There were also many households that had never been entitled to public housing. For such people, housing privatisation policies had very limited direct impact. They had to rely on the housing market to improve their living conditions, and they had to pay a very high price for this (Wang 2000).

Emerging Problems of Poverty

Before 1980, most households lived under very poor conditions in Chinese cities. But over the last 20 years, a large number of urban residents have experienced some improvement in housing. However, because of the inequalities of distribution and access mentioned above, housing conditions now vary from area to area and from household to household. Some of the old housing areas have become focal places for the newly emerged urban poor. Recent fieldwork in two large industrial cities revealed that the housing situation for industrial workers remains poor. The following findings

Table 14.1 Housing entitlement in different periods

Cadres' employment status	Workers' grade or year of services (1999)	1955 (m²)	1981 (m²)	1999 (m²)
Minister		60–95		220
Deputy minister				190
Bureau director		46–68	80–90	120
Deputy bureau director				105
Department head		36–55	60–70	90
Deputy department head	Senior technician			80
Section head/deputy head	Middle to high grade worker, or over 25 years of services	14	45–50	70
Ordinary cadre and workers	Below middle grade workers.	3.6		60

Notes: (a) Entitlement was based on employment status only and no consideration was given to family size.
(b) Workers' entitlements seem reasonable, but workers who started employment after 1984 were on short contracts and were not entitled to housing allocation.
Sources: Shaanxi Province People's Committee (1955); State Urban Construction Bureau (1981); General Office of The Central Committee of Chinese Communist Party and General Office of State Council (1999).

from a household survey carried out in Chongqing and Shenyang (October/November 2000) highlight the general housing conditions of poor urban areas:

- Poor residents live in old traditional houses. In the survey, 86 per cent of residents live in houses built before 1980 and 30 per cent in houses built before 1949.
- Most poor residents have experienced no major change in their housing condition since the reform began.
- The size of houses in poor areas was very small, with 60 per cent of them less than 30 square metres in floor space and 12 per cent less than 15 square metres. Some 30 per cent of households had less then 6 square meters of floor space per person. In Shenyang, over 50 per cent of the households surveyed lived either in only one room or were sharing a room with another family.
- Only about 20 per cent of households had exclusive access to a toilet; and more than 30 per cent of households had no kitchen. Some 10 per cent of households in Shenyang, and 5 per cent in Chongqing, had to share water taps with other families (Wang et al. 2001).[2]

The study also found that the impact of housing reform in these poor areas was very limited. In terms of sale of public housing, only 11.6 per cent of households (mainly in the enterprise housing estates) had bought their house through privatization. The one housing reform policy which claimed to have had the widest impact in social terms, was the housing provident fund system. Yet among the heads of households and their spouses surveyed, only 16 per cent had participated in this provident fund. For the majority of urban poor families, housing privatization and subsidy were seemingly irrelevant.

Urban poverty can also be related to changes made in the rent system. Rent increases in the last several years have not reached the planned targets for most cities. This has been because better-off residents have bought their housing through privatization, so that the remaining tenants in the public sector are mainly low status workers, who either occupy a house unsuitable for sale or could or would not afford the purchase price for the house they rented. The income of these remaining tenants has been affected by restructuring in the state enterprises. A large proportion of them have become unemployed. Further rent increases could affect their life living standards in general and thus cause social instability, which the government has been most anxious to avoid.

Social and Spatial Segregation and Exclusion

Housing construction has been the most important building activity over the last ten years, but new housing estates built at very different standards have raised important questions about spatial and social segregation in Chinese cities (Wang and Murie 2000). Old housing areas were physically and socially related to workplaces and there was no clear division of housing areas by social and economic status. New housing estates, by contrast, have been planned and developed for different social groups. Access to such housing depends on family income or support from employers. These new housing estates are very different from the old housing areas, not only in respect of their physical structure and supporting facilities, but also because of the higher social and economic status of the residents. In each city, there are special housing estates for the very rich – such as cottage houses in the suburban areas and centrally located luxury apartments. There are housing estates for the ordinary urban residents, which are themselves of varying standard and facilities. There is also relocation housing for the poor residents, whose homes have been demolished in the urban redevelopment process. The peripheral estates built for such relocated population in the suburban areas do not offer many employment opportunities. They also lack the old-established social and kinship networks. These peripheral estates of poor residents could become deprived housing schemes, which in turn will require regeneration in the near future. In short, this pattern of development could lead to serious social problems.

Housing Policies Driven by Economic Considerations

As in many other countries, urban housing has a close relationship with economic development in China. In the past, housing investments were made along with other industrial development investment. Housing as a social welfare service was linked with employment and organized by the employers directly. Early urban economic reform was aimed at improving efficiency in production. The main concern of government was economic growth, rather than establishing a Western-style welfare housing system. Indeed, housing reform and policy development has continuously been influenced by economic concerns. For example, the subsidized sale of public housing in 1985 and 1986 was aimed at changing the national industrial structure through the adjustment of urban household consumption style, thus paving the way for property-led development. Large-scale sales of public housing in 1991 were aimed at controlling inflation and reducing the amount of money in circulation. The development of *anju* (subsidized housing) projects in 1995 was geared in part to solving the oversupply of steel. The introduction of cash subsidies to public sector employees in 1998 was aimed at stimulating housing consumption by the middle class to push forward the property market and sustain urban economic growth.

Urban housing reform is a very important part of the economic reform process rather than a carefully designed attempt at social restructuring. As long as the housing system contributes to the urban economy, the increasing disparity between rich and poor can be tolerated. The urban economy is now property led. Commercial housing construction has been seen as an important contribution to national economic growth. Although new commercial housing had been in oversupply since 1995 in many large cities, the government could not afford to slow down the property development process, because it has important implications for a series of related industrial sectors. Attempts to develop affordable housing in the recent years have revealed some new problems. The objective of this policy has been to provide low-cost housing for the low- and middle-income groups; but many developers have actually sold these houses simply to anyone who has enough money. Not many poor urban households can afford these new houses anyway.

The High Price of New Housing, by Comparison with Low Household Income

The price for new commercial housing in most Chinese cities is very high – far beyond the reach of the majority of urban residents. In Shanghai, for example, prices in the central area were around 6000 *yuan* per square metre for ordinary standard housing and 10,000 *yuan* for a high-standard apartment in 1998. In suburban areas, the price for ordinary commercial housing was 2-3000 *yuan* per square metre. An unfurnished apartment of 80 square metres of construction floor space in the central area would cost over half million *yuan*. (Data collected during fieldwork in 1998) Further housing price increases have been reported in the city in the last two years. The average annual salary in the city in 1999 was only 16,641 *yuan*. So it would cost a working couple 15 years' total salary to purchase a standard flat on the open market. Given such a big difference between incomes and housing prices, it is not surprising to find there to be a huge stock of unsold commercial housing in the city. At the end of 1999, official statistics show that, in Shanghai alone, unsold commercial residential housing floor space had reached 9.2 million square metres, or about 100,000 units (Shanghai Municipal Statistics Bureau 2000).

The so-called 'ordinary commercial housing' is actually not for urban residents with an ordinary salary at all. It was built for those who have made a substantial amount of money from business, or had some other source of income: i.e. the high demand for good quality commercial housing over the years has actually come from people possessed of extra-ordinary income or employer support. It is not difficult to discover that some urban families have changed housing several times or have bought several properties as investment over the last ten years, while others have experienced no change in their housing condition at all. Property development has followed this pattern of demand over the last few years. The standard of new housing has increased substantially. In the 1980s, a flat of 80 square metres was a very big house but, by the late 1990s, not many new flats were so small. Most new houses now being built are over 100 square metres in floor space. Since only the rich have been very active in the new housing market, the developers have found bigger houses easier to sell than smaller ones.

Sustainability of the High-Rise Housing Estates

Many Western housing specialists visiting Chinese cities believe that China is making the same mistake Western countries made during the 1960s and 1970s. They think that tower-block housing is not sustainable. The most common explanation given by Chinese housing policy makers has been the shortage of agricultural land. Chinese cities *cannot* be built at the low density same as that found in Western cities. However, although this may be an important reason, there are many other factors also contributing to the preponderance of high-density and high-rise housing:

- Property developers hope to maximize their profits, so as to build as many housing units as possible on whatever piece of land they have acquired; thus many housing areas have been built to a higher density than that approved by the urban planners.
- Poor design skills have resulted in development companies copying from each other's design.
- Wrong perceptions about modernity and the acceptance of high-rise living as a long term new fashion.
- There has also been influence from developers in Hong Kong and other Asian cities.

A relatively higher density in some large cities (e.g. Beijing and Shanghai) in China is necessary, but the spread of high-rise and high-density housing toward the suburban areas in many other smaller cities is questionable. High-rise flats built under a less-well regulated building boom have usually proved dangerous and not sustainable. Fast-changing perceptions about housing quality among the urban population over the last few years do not suggest a good prospect for poorly designed high-rise housing. These could simply become the poor and problematic residential areas of the future.

Separation of Urban and Rural Housing

Housing reform in China did not aim to eliminate the differences between urban and rural areas. Rural housing continues with the traditional tenure of owner-occupation; while urban housing has been moving towards private market provision system. There was no policy attempt to bring these two different systems together, though there are much stronger economic links between urban and surrounding rural areas now, than ever before. There has also been no encouragement of urban residents to move to suburban villages and to integrate with rural populations. All urban housing requirements have been met from the formal large-scale housing construction system. Large areas of rural land have indeed been taken over for house building and consumption by urban residents. But with such a large proportion of the Chinese people still living in the countryside, such a closed urban housing market does not look sustainable either, particularly given the rapid urbanization process. An integration of the urban and suburban housing markets should be explored as a long-term solution to the problem. Improvements in rural housing conditions over the last few years have indeed made urban and rural integration possible. Many rural households built new housing, though some of this has been underused, as a result of residents moving to the city for employment. The integration of urban and rural housing markets should allow urban residents to utilize rural resources and land and also to contribute to the development of the rural economy.

Urban housing has been referred to as a closed system, with reference to the manner in which rural-urban migrants have been treated. They have been excluded from both the formal housing provision system and from the commercial housing market (which most of them could not afford in any case). The only housing units available to them have been poor-quality private houses owned by low-income urban families or suburban farmers. Thus poor rural migrants have tended to join the urban poor and to fill the vacancies in poor housing areas.

Recent Policy Development

Some of these problems discussed above may be unavoidable during a period of economic transition, certainly they demand further research and new policy responses. Yet policies developed in the last few years have begun to address some of these problems. Since 1998, apart from continuation in sale of public housing, major government policies have concentrated on encouraging more urban residents to purchase new commercial housing in cities. A series of measures have been introduced to this end:

- to reduce the price of new housing by cutting government charges and controlling development profit;
- to increase income in the public sector;
- to encourage urban household spending on housing by cutting interest rates and the introduction of income tax on saving;
- to support mortgage lending by all state and commercial banks;
- to develop new housing legislation to protect private home ownership; etc.

Policies have also been introduced to support the secondary urban housing market and encourage previous public sector tenants who had bought their houses under privatization regulations to move on. Apart from Shanghai, this secondary market is still at a very early stage of development. Most owners of privatized flats have already spent their savings on the previous purchase and on refurbishment (which was often very expensive as well). Industrial restructuring made many urban residents feel insecure about their financial situation. There have also been large-scale increase in other costs such as education and health. In short, not many urban households can afford the price of new commercial housing.

To deal with the emerging urban poverty problem, a new social housing allocation policy based on household income was introduced by central government in 1998. Local housing authorities and work units were instructed to use old or difficult-to-sell public housing to provide shelter for these families also. Rents for such properties are all either subsidized or waived. This is meant as a positive approach to bring urban poverty under control, but the future depends on the general condition of the urban economy. Many cities are still at the policy development stage. Not many such houses have so far been offered to families in difficulty. Indeed, the continuous increase in the numbers of urban poor – and in rural-urban migrants – could overload this system almost before it has begun. The effects of these recent policies on the problems identified above are summarized in Table 14.2.

Conclusion

Over the past 20 years, urban housing reform in China has gone through several stages, from commercialization of construction, privatization of public housing and development of an urban housing market. Policy development has drawn on the experiences of many other countries. Initial reform ideas benefited from housing changes in the former socialist countries of Eastern Europe. During the late 1980s and the 1990s, however, privatization in West European countries, particularly Britain, provided another example. Numerous housing delegations from both central and local governments were sent to Western countries to study their different urban housing systems. These visits covered a wide range of areas, including privatization, finance, legislation, insurance, mortgage lending, property rights, planning etc. Several international workshops and conferences related to housing were held in China, which provided policy makers with useful information. International organisations, such as the World Bank, carried out several special housing projects in Chinese cities and produced implementation strategies to help policy development (World Bank 1992). The World Bank also provided funds to local government to carry out enterprise housing reform as demonstration projects. The current housing market, particularly the expensive, commercially developed house sub-market operates more or less in the way it should operate in a market economy.

Apart from experiences from Western countries, housing policy development in China has benefited from experiences in other Asian economies. The high-rise and high-density housing design is similar to that found in all major Asian cities. In fact, many property developers and designers operate across the boundaries between China, Hong Kong, Taiwan, Singapore, Japan and Korea. Several major current housing policies in China have been based on models developed elsewhere in Asia. For example, the idea of housing provident funds – one of China's main housing reform policies – was based on the Singapore model; whereas the municipal housing committee set up by Shanghai followed the Hong Kong model.

Table 14.2 Housing problems and policy responses

Problems	Policy responses
Inequality	No intention to eliminate urban housing inequality, but more emphasis has been given to enterprise housing reform, which may help some of low-income state enterprise workers.
Urban poverty	Subsidized social housing was introduced for the urban poor in 1998, but the scale is far from enough to solve the problem. Urban redevelopment was seen as the main mechanism to upgrade poor and old housing areas, but the property developer led approach was only successful in central locations where land value was high and failed to deliver in the marginal areas where large number of urban poor families could be found. Government led redevelopment approach was tested in some cities (e.g. Beijing), which could improve some poor residential areas.
Social and spatial segregation	No formal policy to reduce or monitor social and spatial segregation. Social segregation is indirectly promoted by the different standards of new housing. The new style of estate management has created many closed urban communities.
Housing as economic consideration	Urban economy development and growth is still the key government consideration. Housing and property development is an important part of the urban economy and a major contribution to national economic growth.
High price and affordability	Various policies have been introduced in the last a few years to reduce the price and increase affordability: • Increase income in the public sector, • Provide housing subsidies according to employment status and year of services, • Increase the contributions of provident fund, • Encourage consumption rather than saving, • Encourage mortgage lending, • Reduce barriers in the housing exchange market such as tax or fees, • Promotion of the secondary (re-sale of privatised houses) housing market, and • Development of affordable housing for the low and middle income groups.
High-rise	No fundamental change in policy, but some sign of limiting the number of tower blocks in large coastal cities such as Shanghai.
Urban/rural integration	Some relaxation of labour movement control, but no specific policies to bring the rural and urban housing market together.

After more than 20 years' reform, an urban housing market, similar to that in other market economies, is gradually emerging. The current system, however, is still not a perfect one as discussed in this chapter. It would be easy to relate these problems to the transitional nature of Chinese society. However, there are also deep-rooted reasons for these problems. In contrast to the fast changes introduced in East European countries, China has adopted a pragmatic approach to urban housing reform. Experiments have been carried out sector by sector in the area of housing construction, distribution and management over a relatively long period. This is the strength of the Chinese approach, which has effectively avoided social shocks and instabilities. But this approach also has its problems. Housing reform practice has often been piecemeal. The general trend towards commercialization and privatization has not always been supported by a clear vision of what kind of urban housing system the reform was aiming for. Policies were often based on new ideas imported from other economies. The social and economic consequences of implementation in Chinese cities were not always carefully studied. The promotion of home ownership, for example, was taken to the extreme. Western housing researchers believe there is a relationship between the level of home ownership and the level of economic development. But recently reported figures show that home ownership in Chinese cities has reached 77.1 per cent. Since all rural housing can be classified as owner-occupiers as well, this means that home ownership in the country as a whole has reached a very high level. The scope for further privatization has thus become questionable. The over-emphasis on home ownership has also undervalued the urban rental housing market; current rental housing being mainly for the urban poor.

The housing system relies very heavily on the formal construction, marketing and distribution model. There is also a tendency to replace all other forms of housing in cities and towns with products of the commercial property developers. The price-income ratio and affordability, discussed before, is only part of the problem. The practice reduces housing choices, particularly for low-income groups, the urban poor and rural-urban migrants. More importantly, the property boom has resulted in a total destruction of the traditional Chinese urban landscape in some cities. It has substantially altered the traditional way of living in cities as well. The social and psychological effects of these changes will have a profound impact on the Chinese society.

Improving housing and living conditions in cities will become an attraction to rural residents and speed up the urbanization process in China. Housing reform has been practised within a narrowly defined area and aimed to solve urban housing problems. No attempts were made to put housing policy inside a wider social and economic framework and no attempts were made to assess the demand and supply of housing at the regional level. This could be a major problem for future urban development. It is important to bring rural housing into this market system. Better rural and urban integration would pave the way, not only for a sustainable housing provision system, but also for sustainable social development. Such an approach should provide an important opportunity for preserving some of China's traditional way of living and traditional style of built environment. In these respects, China can learn from the Western experience by seeing housing development not only as an economic function but also as an important area of social service, particularly in relation to low-income people and the poor. It would be a mistake to move straight from one extreme – total welfare provision – to another – free-market housing for everyone. More in-depth comparative analysis is required, with regard to different housing systems and the relationship between housing provision and national political and economic systems.

Notes

1 This chapter has benefited from a research project 'Social Implications of Urban Reform in China', supported by The UK Department for International Development (DFID, 2000–2001). DFID supports policies, programmes and projects to promote international development. DFID provided funds for this study as part of that objective but the views and opinions expressed are those of the author alone.
2 Fieldwork in the two cities was carried out in October and November 2000 and involves questionnaire surveys of 802 households from 7 different poor residential areas.

References

Bian, Y.J. and Logan, L.J. (1996), 'Market transformation and the persistence of power: the changing stratification system in urban China', *American Sociological Review*, 61, 5: 739–58.
Chen, A. (1996), 'China's urban housing reform: price–rent ratio and market equilibrium', *Urban Studies*, 33, 7: 1077–92.
Chiu, R.H. (2001a), 'Commodification of housing with Chinese characteristics', *Policy Studies Review*, 18, 1: 75–95.
Chiu, R.H. (2001b), 'Housing reform in a marketized socialist economy: the case of Shanghai', *Urban Policy and Research*, 18, 4: 455–68.
Editors Committee of Almanac of China's Economy (1983), *Almanac of China's Economy 1983*, Beijing Economic Management Publishing House, Beijing.
General Office of the Central Committee of Chinese Communist Party and General Office of State Council (1999), 'Plan for Further Housing Reform in Central Government and Party Organizations in Beijing', [Document (1999) no. 10] in Central Party and Government Organization Housing Reform Office (ed.) (2000), *Document Collection on Housing System Reform in Central Committee of CCP and State Organization*, (unpublished documents).
General Office of the State Council (1991), *On Comprehensive Reform of the Urban Housing System*, Document no. 73 (unpublished documents).
Housing Reform Steering Group of the State Council (1994), 'The decision on deepening urban housing reform', in Housing Reform Steering Group of the State Council (ed.), *Urban Housing System Reform*, Reform Press, Beijing.
Lau, K.Y. (1993), 'Urban housing reform in China, amidst property boom year' in J. Cheng and M. Brosseau (eds), *China Review*, Hong Kong University Press, Hong Kong pp. 24.1–24.35.
Lee, J. (2000), 'From welfare housing to home ownership: the dilemma of China's housing reform', *Housing Studies*, 15, 1: 61–7.
Li, S.M. (2000a), 'Housing consumption in urban China: a comparative study of Beijing and Guangzhou', *Environment and Planning A*, 32: 1115–34.
Li, S.M. (2000b), 'The housing market and tenure decisions in Chinese cities: a multivariate analysis of the case of Guangzhou', *Housing Studies*, 15, 2: 213–36.
Logan, J. and Bian, Y. (1993), 'Inequalities in access to community resources in a Chinese city', *Social Forces*, 72, 3: 555–76.

Shaanxi Province People's Committee (1955), 'Provisional regulations of housing distribution standards in the state organizations', in Housing and Property Management Department of Xian (ed.) (1960), *Collection of Documents on Housing and Property Management in Xian*, 1, pp. 126–8 (unpublished documents).

Shanghai Municipal Statistics Bureau (2000), *Statistical Yearbook of Shanghai 2000*, China Statistics Press, Beijing.

State Council (1988), *Implementation Plan for a Gradual Housing System Reform in Cities and Towns*, Document no. 11 (unpublished documents).

State Council (1998), *The Notice on Further Reform of Urban Housing System and Speeding up Housing Development*, Document no. 23, 3 July (unpublished documents).

State Statistics Bureau (2001), *Urban Residents' Living Standard Has Reached the Comfortable Level (xiao kang shui ping)*, Series reports for the Ninth Five Year Economic and Social Development Plan Period, no. 18 (unpublished documents).

State Urban Construction Bureau (1981), Supplementary Regulations for Housing Design Standards (Document no. 22 [1981]). In S.H. Tang and W.D. Xie (eds), (1992), *China Housing and Real Estate Industry Guide (Zhongguo fangdichan shiwu quanshu)*, New Age Press, Beijing.

Wang Y.P. (1992), 'Private sector housing in urban china since 1949: the case of Xian', *Housing Studies*, 7, 2: 119–37.

Wang Y.P. (1995), 'Public sector housing in urban China since 1949: the case of Xian', *Housing Studies*, 10, 1: 57–82.

Wang Y.P. (2000), 'Housing reform and its impacts on the urban poor', *Housing Studies*, 15, 6: 845–64.

Wang Y.P. (2001), 'Urban housing reform and finance in China: a case study of Beijing', *Urban Affairs Review*, 36, 5: 620–45.

Wang, Y.P., Dai, Y.Z. and Long, H. (2001), *Social Implications of Urban Reform in China: A Case study of Housing for the Poor*, unpublished final project report.

Wang Y.P. and Murie A. (1996), 'The process of commercialization of urban housing in China', *Urban Studies*, 33, 6: 971–89.

Wang Y.P. and Murie A. (1999a), *Housing Policy and Practice in China*, Macmillan, Basingstoke; and St Martin's Press, New York.

Wang Y.P. and Murie A. (1999b), 'Commercial housing development in urban China', *Urban Studies*, 36, 9: 1475–94.

Wang Y.P. and Murie A. (2000), 'Social and spatial implications of housing reform in China', *International Journal of Urban and Regional Research*, 24, 2: 397–417.

World Bank (1992), *China Implementation Options for Urban Housing Reform*, World Bank, Washington, DC.

Wu, F.L. (1996), 'Changes in the structure of public housing provision in urban China', *Urban Studies*, 33, 9: 1601–27.

Wu, F.L. (2001), 'Housing provision under globalization: a case study of Shanghai', *Environment and Planning A*, 33: 1741–64.

Xie, J.J. (2001), *The achievement and future of housing system reform in China*, paper presented at the International Conference on Managing Housing and Social Change: Building social cohesion, accommodating diversity, held at University of Hong Kong, 16–18 April.

Zhang, X.Q. (1997), 'Chinese housing policy 1949–1978: the development of a welfare system', *Planning Perspectives*, 12, 4: 433–55.

Zhou, M. and Logan, J.R. (1996), 'Market transition and the commodification of housing in urban China', *International Journal of Urban and Regional Research*, 20, 3: 400–21.

Chapter 15

Housing in China: A View from the West

John Doling

The lesson seems clear: if you have socialist housing systems you will get socialist-type gains as well as socialist-type problems; if you have market capitalist housing systems you will get market capitalist gains and problems. But, it is not as simple as that, not least because *socialist* and *market capitalist* do not each represent a uniform concept. Witness the tradition, greatly reinvigorated in the 1990s, of identifying welfare regime types each with different characteristic outcomes.

Learning lessons from the study of different types of market capitalism, at a scale sufficiently macro to apply to the sort of system-wide changes being undertaken in China, however, is, for other reasons also, far from straightforward. Their size, centrality and complexity make it difficult to know where housing systems and their consequences start and the wider system stops. Typically in the richer Western countries, around a fifth of total private consumption is expended on housing, and housing accounts for a quarter of total investment. In economic terms – and in political and social ones also – housing systems are vast and complex. Disentangling housing from its society-wide system is difficult enough; identifying what works and what doesn't, or even what the first- and second-order effects are, is no mean task.

But First a View from the Old East (or New West)

The characteristics and developments of the housing system in urban China bear comparison with those of the countries of Eastern Europe. Notwithstanding differences in detail, the Marxist ideology that formed the basis of their politico-economic system structured a common approach to housing that has been labelled by Hegedus and Tosics (1992) the 'East European housing model' (EEHM), the principal characteristics of which may be summarized in terms of characteristic approaches to the housing tenures:

- Private renting was not sanctioned. The demanding of rent by a private landlord was seen as a form of exploitation, and housing that was privately rented in 1945 was commonly taken over by the state.
- Owner occupation, widespread in 1945, particularly in rural areas, was tolerated; frequently it was starved of materials necessary for maintenance and upgrading, and exchange made difficult.
- State housing, whether provided directly through the state, an employer or some form of cooperative, was promoted. Housing was viewed as a social right for which the state should take responsibility, and provided as a social overhead:

publicly or cooperatively provided and owned, and consumed by citizens paying minimal rents.

As in China, there were characteristic limitations of these arrangements. These were brought to the attention of Western researchers by Ivan Szelenyi (1983) who presented a convincing argument that the limitations were inherent in the very nature of the socialist approach. First, the viewing of housing as a social overhead meant that it was seen as consumption, which, in the long run, tended to be given lower priority than economic investment. Not only did this mean that in the EEHM shortages of housing were perpetuated, indeed generally exacerbated, but the minimal rents did not ensure even sufficient funds properly to maintain the physical fabric of the buildings. The result was increasingly long waiting lists for accommodation that was small and in deteriorating condition.

Second, notwithstanding the principle of consumption according to need, in practice the allocation of increasingly scarce state housing favoured those who held senior positions in the sphere of production. In Szelenyi's view this was inevitable once the principles of reward for working had been established:

> If wages are set officially to exclude the cost of housing and other public goods and services, then housing and the other goods and services must obviously be allocated to all comers, including those with high incomes. If any of the services happens to be scarce – as new housing must always be, since only a small fraction of the housing stock can be new each year – those scarce goods are always likely to be allocated to the most meritorious citizens in the most essential jobs, who tend to be those with the highest incomes. It could scarcely be otherwise. How could the state say to its rising managers and bureaucrats, 'If you get promoted you will *reduce* your housing chances?' (Szelenyi 1983: 10; emphasis in the original).

Szelenyi (1983), at the time a recent émigré from Hungary, recognized that a solution lay in the introduction of market elements, though he was eager to stress that the intention was not to displace the socialist housing system, simply to modify some of its processes. This he encapsulated in a neat aphorism:

> while under capitalism the market creates the basic inequalities and the administrative allocation of welfare modifies and moderates them slightly, under socialism the major inequalities are created by administrative allocation, and the market can be used to reduce inequalities (Szelenyi 1983: 11).

In fact his was not the only reforming voice. Albeit starting at different times in different countries, and proceeding along different routes at different speeds, during the 1970s and 1980s dissatisfaction with the outcomes of the EEHM came to be accompanied by reform. Broadly, the changes can be described as 'tendencies towards a market solution' (Turner 1993: 1), so that by the time of the collapse of the Soviet Union and independence for the Eastern European countries, some of the groundwork for the creation of housing systems more closely resembling those of Western countries had already been laid.

One of the dimensions of these reforms has been the transfer of ownership of rental housing from the state and various forms of cooperative institution, including enterprises, to private individuals. For this, the British policy of council house sales as established by the Housing Act 1980, provided those guiding the reforms with a strong precedent. Not only was this probably the most internationally known housing policy of its decade (Doling 1993) – that had influenced housing policy developments in the USA, for example (see Silver 1990) – but it was known certainly to East European housing researchers, who had, for some years, had direct exposure to Western research findings, partly through attendance at international conferences sponsored by the European Network for Housing Researchers. In addition, some of those researchers, such as Hegedus and Tosics in Hungary, were to become centrally involved in the policy-making processes in their own countries.

But, as in the case of China, housing sector reform involved much more than the sale of state housing, not least because of the pervasive influence in all of these countries of free-market economists. This was not the remedial insertion of market mechanisms supported by Szelenyi, but widespread restructuring of the housing system to replace socialist with capitalist dynamics. Central to these reforms were the re-establishment of systems of property rights that recognized private ownership, the increasing of rents at least to the point that they covered management and maintenance costs and beyond to converge on the supply-demand determined level, and the establishment of sources of financial support for housing market actors.

It quickly became apparent that the reforms were leading to new patterns of housing consumption that incorporated new forms of inequality. As early as 1992, Hegedus and Tosics had noted evidence of 'increasing polarization' (Hegedus and Tosics 1992: 325). By mid decade, the development of processes of gentrification and of ghettoization had been firmly established (Andreusz et al. 1996: Sykora 1996). It had not taken long, therefore, for the EEHM and its characteristic outcomes to begin to resemble the characteristic of some Western, market-oriented models. In particular there was a sifting of people according to their socioeconomic status into different geographical areas.

Any conclusion, drawn from the evidence of both urban China and Eastern Europe, that the replacement of a socialist housing system with a market one necessarily replaces a socialist inequality with a market one, however, is too simplistic. There are at least two reasons for this that are dealt with in turn: the first that housing systems are multi-dimensional, the second that socialist and market systems are in any case ideal types.

The Housing Provision Chain

It is now widely recognized in the Western housing literature that analyses of national housing systems cannot be adequately pursued by examination of housing tenure alone, since tenures themselves constitute a taxonomy only of forms of housing consumption. Thus a policy of, say, the sale of state housing to private owners, tells us nothing in itself about how the state housing got there in the first place nor how future housing will get there. It is important, analytically, to recognize that, for each unit in the housing stock of a country, there is a process of provision that predates the process of consumption, and that, in order to 'clarify the policy issues' it is necessary, in Peter Ambrose's words, to 'unpack the provision processes into the relatively discrete stages through which all housing units pass' (1992: 173).

The provision process (Figure 15.1) begins with the act of development which involves an individual or agency initiating the conditions which can support the construction stage: ensuring legal title to land, the obtaining of any appropriate planning permission, and the availability of sufficient capital, either from own resources or from an external source, to finance the next stage. The availability of land, labour and materials is, then, a prerequisite for the construction stage, which involves the bringing together of the factors of production in the building process in order that physical structures are produced. This is followed, in turn, by a consumption stage at which decisions are made about the persons who are to occupy the dwelling and under what terms. The terms will include the user price of the dwelling in the form of the amount of capital required to purchase it, of loan repayments or of rent. Sometimes the allocation stage will occur only once in the lifetime of the dwelling, but, more frequently, there will be periodic reallocations, because a tenant leaves or the owner decides to sell the property, for example. Running in parallel with these stages is a requirement for finance – in advance of realizing a return on production and in advance of consumption – and land.

All the stages in the housing provision process are of course located within a wider framework or context. The behaviour of actors and the range of possibilities with which they are faced are influenced by events in the wider economy such as developments in wages, in interest rates, in family structures, in patterns of retirement and so on. Whereas identification of the stages is useful for allowing the exploration of the terrain on which the main parts of housing policy are located, it is important also to appreciate that there are many non-housing policies which may have significant impacts upon housing systems.

Notwithstanding this wider framework, it is possible to use the three main stages in the housing provision chain to construct a typology of housing policy regimes (Doling 1999). At each stage of the chain there may be different actors operating. In some stages they may be predominantly state actors – civil servants, local officials, politicians – making decisions based on bureaucratic and political criteria. Sometimes they may be predominantly private individuals and businesses operating within private market frameworks. The distinction is a crude one, of course (how, precisely, are 'bureaucratic', 'political', 'market' and so on operationalized?), but it is possible to propose two ideal types: the market liberal and the socialist regime types (see Figures 15.2a and 15.2b). In the former ideal type, markets, largely unfettered by state intervention, dominate all three stages: housing is seen as a private good, decisions to provide new housing are taken by private developers working without the constraints of strong planning legislation, houses are built by private construction companies and sold or leased to individuals on the basis of willingness and ability to pay. In terms of consumption outcomes it is to be expected that this regime type will result in high levels of inequity reflecting the distribution of household income. The USA is the archetypal case.

In the latter ideal type, decisions are made by the state on politically driven criteria. The state decides what, how and when to develop, is directly responsible for construction with the completed housing allocated according to notions of need. As noted above, inequality in consumption based on employment status can be expected. Pre-housing-reform China is archetypal.

There are at least two other ideal types to which archetypal cases can be ascribed (see Figures 15.2c and 15.2d). The Western, mainland European model – archetypally Sweden – is characterized by a development stage that is strongly directed by the state. Local municipalities are charged with identifying the need for additional housing of different sizes, tenures, qualities and locations. They acquire land at a price that does not reflect its future, residential, use and they contract private builders to construct to specified designs at a competitive price. State control of the development process has enabled the Swedes to provide an adequate supply of high-quality housing at relatively low prices. Further influence over prices – for example through rent regulation – and over household budgets – through subsidies – ensured a consumption stage in which principles of need are significant in allocation (Dickens et al. 1985).

In the Little Tigers model – Hong Kong, Taiwan, Korea and Singapore, of which the latter is archetypal – there is also state control at the development stage. With strong government control of the economy and highly directive five-year plans, governments have been able to determine much of the speed, location and nature of development. In all these countries, the construction stage is undertaken by private companies often building to contract. The major divergence from the Swedish case is that there is little attempt to ensure consumption according to need; the relative size and quality of housing consumed by different households is not greatly influenced by state subsidies or other arrangements but rather largely reflects each household's income (Chua 1997; Doling 1999).

A Market is a Market is a Market is a . . .

Analyses of the retrenchment of welfare states – particularly in recent decades and particularly with a comparative dimension – using ideas such as public provision, privatization, commodification, marketization, commercialization and so on, have made it clear that these terms can be both analytical devices and ideological tools. Although it has become commonplace to talk of public and private sectors and of public or state provision and private or market provision as if they were distinct and mutually exclusive categories, this is not so; state or bureaucratic systems incorporate market relationships and markets incorporate state relationships. Consequently, the nature of a specific market will depend in part on the nature of the involvement of the state, for example, in the nature of regulation, of the legislative framework, the influence of the state on the distribution of the income of consumers, the provision of subsidies to producers and consumers and so on. A private rental sector in which the state provides subsidies to suppliers enabling them to offer accommodation at low rents, for example, is likely to be quite different to one in which the state provides subsidies on a means-tested basis to consumers. Important to an understanding of the outcome of a specific market, therefore, will be the understanding of the nature of the relationships between the state and the market, not so much generally but in relation to that specific market.

If one key to understanding the consequences of the commercialization of housing in urban China is the specification of the new relationships between the state and the market, another lies in the recognition that even leaving aside the role of the state, markets will differ one from another. Different markets have different actors who have different, and changing, relationships one with the other, and each operates within different frameworks of institutional contingencies. Avoiding analyses founded on what Barry Hindess (1987) referred to as the 'essentialism' of the market, requires a recognition and identification of market diversity.

Equally, we must recognize the ideological device of the 'essentialism' of the state. What the role of the state is in different stages of the housing provision chain, who the state actors are, what their objectives are, and so on, will vary not only between those different stages but also over time and place. Thus the nature and consequences of the state provision of housing in 1950s Britain – high-quality housing, aimed at all groups, much sought after – was very different from that of the 1990s – a sector in decline, low-quality, mainly occupied by those without paid incomes.

It also follows from this that terms such as 'home ownership', 'public housing', 'private building companies', 'financial institutions' and indeed 'market' do not necessarily have meanings that translate one-to-one from one country to another (Doling 1997; Kennett 2001). In fact, the language of comparative housing analysis (indeed more general comparative social policy) being largely founded in English and emanating particularly from North America and Britain has often imposed (implicitly or not) meanings on these concepts that have less relevance in other countries. One result, presented with respect to the use of tenure as a concept, has been a tendency towards an 'elision between taxonomic and substantive collectives' (Barlow and Duncan 1988: 219). The point has also been made by Michael Ball and his colleagues:

> there are no universal forms of provision whose efficacy can be analysed through international comparison of their operations. Cross-country comparison of tenure, one of the bread-and-butter subjects of comparative research, must be aware that distinct structures of provision are being examined even though they exist within apparently common tenure forms (Ball et al. 1988: 30).

Consideration by British observers of the housing reforms in China, therefore, needs to be sensitive to the ethnocentricity problem.

And so, which Housing Model is Best?

Of the thousands upon thousands of studies of housing policy in Western countries published over the last few decades, very few indeed have systematically explored questions of which policy systems provide the best outcomes. This has not been for the want of an ideological position, but, whether the reluctance to examine systems in this way has been a consequence of the difficulty of deciding appropriate criteria, getting relevant data, simply the enormity of the task or some other reason, the predominant approach has been to explore one tenure, one set of administrative arrangements, a single policy change and so on. Of the system-wide, normative studies, some have predominantly considered issues of equity, others of efficiency.

Equity

An early attempt to consider the relationship between the type of housing system and equity in the consumption of housing was undertaken by Bruce Headey (1978). On the basis of the assembled evidence, he concluded that of the three countries he studied – the United Kingdom, the United States and Sweden – the first two had housing systems that had not achieved – even if that were the intention – high levels of horizontal or vertical equity. Of Sweden, however, he concluded that the state had

> succeeded in greatly improving working-class housing and neighbourhoods both absolutely and relative to those of middle-class people. They have brought about a situation ... in which wage earners pay lower proportions of their income for housing than middle-class salary earners (Headey 1978: 16).

Further, he concluded that such an outcome was the consequence of the creation of a 'socialist market', that being 'socialist' because the system has been moulded by the state to operate in accordance with its social and economic objectives and a 'market' because of the space created for competition between suppliers and between consumers. The policy instruments were those that enabled the state to closely control development and prices and to redistribute income among households through housing subsidies.

Efficiency

Various operational definitions of efficiency have been adopted, but – at the risk of overgeneralizing or being under-technical – they have broadly taken as the objective that of ensuring an adequate supply of housing available at qualities and prices that are appropriate to the income of the population. On such matters there is a body of research in relation to developing countries, emanating from both academic researchers and international bodies such as the World Bank and the United Nations. (e.g. Mayo et al. 1986; UNCHS 1996). Their aim has been to specify through what policy goals and instruments countries with low levels of GDP per capita should develop their housing sectors. Again at the risk of overgeneralizing, the prescribed approach is through the encouragement of markets – reducing state intervention, easing regulations, and encouraging competition and private investment – within a framework that addresses the weaknesses of entirely unregulated markets. The latter requirement – the 'market-friendly' approach – is focused in particular at the development stage and concerns inefficiencies arising from the unavailability of appropriate infrastructure and monopolies over the supply of land.

Studies of the efficiency of housing systems in the economically advanced countries have placed even less emphasis on free markets and more on government regulation. On the basis of a three-country study – of Britain, France and Sweden (again) – Barlow and Duncan (1994) concluded that Sweden had been the most successful in providing appropriate amounts of high-quality housing at lowest cost. They identify two main factors contributing to this: first, the strong control by the Swedish state over the development process; second, the extent to which regulation has encouraged tenure diversity, particularly encouraging the development of non-profit provision.

The lesson from Singapore supports the first conclusion but not the second. Whereas the state's intervention in the land market, in the financial system and in planning residential development has been crucial in achieving a long-term improvement in the standard of housing while controlling prices, almost 90 per cent of the stock is in a single tenure: home ownership (Chua 1997).

Constituting ideal types, the diagrams of Figure 15.2 do not, of course, describe actual housing systems. Nevertheless, they assist the identification of some of the possible consequences of different sets of policies. Based on the above studies, the highly reduced picture, with an all-other-things-being-equal proviso, is that housing systems are likely to be efficient where state intervention in development is significant but there is a competition in construction (Figures 15.2c and 15.2d), and are likely to be equitable when states intervene to regulate prices and allocation (Figure 15.2c).

The Wider System

One limitation of these types of study is their focus on the *housing* system and its characteristics. We noted earlier that the housing provision chain is located within a wider framework or system in which interest rates are determined, unemployment trends developed, household structures changed and so on. Just as these impinge on and influence housing system structure and actor behaviour, the housing system itself impinges upon the wider framework. Just over 20 years ago Bernard Kilroy estimated that the value of residential dwellings in Britain exceeded the value of all the assets of British industry (Kilroy 1979). In the succeeding two decades, house prices have continued their cyclical increase while British industry has, to the say the very least, withered. Little wonder, then, that many millions of home owners, though acting individually, may, in their decisions about releasing housing equity to spend on consumer goods or not, throw the economy into recession or drag it into expansion (Maclennan et al. 1993).

Some of the linkages between the housing system and the wider economy and society are not well understood, however. For example, no one has adequately explained the meaning (if any) of the significant, negative, statistical relationship between a country's GDP per capita and its rate of home ownership; in other words, rich countries tend to accommodate their populations in rental housing (Kemeny 1981). More recently, Oswald has shown a significant, positive, relationship between home ownership and unemployment: home-owning countries tend to have higher rates of unemployment (Oswald 1999). It would seem possible on the basis of such findings, therefore, that what results in 'good' housing outcomes, results in 'bad' economic and social outcomes.

Concluding Remarks

In the economically advanced countries, the housing system constitutes a large part of national economies and contributes directly to the well-being of all citizens. Much of the western literature, including that of and about the old Eastern European countries, however, has dealt, rarely with the entire system and its relationships with wider society, and more frequently with individual elements in their systems: trends in home ownership, the construction industry, the regeneration of social housing estates, the effects of rent control, and so on. The overall complexity of housing systems themselves and their location within wider, national, economic and social systems, in any case, perhaps mean that the whole is different from the sum of the parts. In other words, what seems in one country to work as housing – what is 'good' housing policy – may have less than good consequences for that country's wider society; it may also not work at all in another country with a different housing system and different wider society. This does not necessarily mean that there are not and cannot be policy lessons and successful policy transfer, but certainly they may be difficult to disentangle. One consequence, of pertinence to the restructuring of the housing system in China, is that while the limitations of the old system are clear, what will be gained and lost from the new one – indeed, what in all aspects the new one entails – is not yet completely clear.

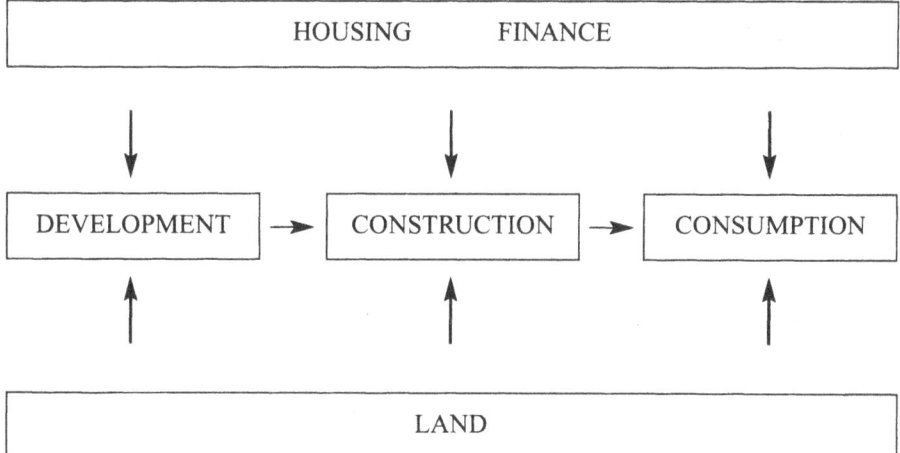

Figure 15.1 The housing provision chain

(a) Liberal

	Market	State
Development	X	
Construction	X	
Consumption	X	

(b) Socialist

	Market	State
Development		X
Construction		X
Consumption		X

(c) European

	Market	State
Development		X
Construction	X	
Consumption		X

(d) Little Tigers

	Market	State
Development		X
Construction	X	
Consumption	X	

Figure 15.2 Housing regimes

References

Ambrose, P. (1992), 'The performance of national housing systems: a three nations comparison', *Housing Studies*, 7, 3: 163–76.
Andreusz, G., Harloe, M. and Szelenyi, I. (eds), (1996) *Cities after Socialism: Urban and Regional Change and Conflict in Post Socialist Cities*, Blackwell, Oxford.
Ball, M., Harloe, M. and Martens, M. (1988), *Housing and Social Change in Europe and the USA*, Methuen, London.
Barlow, J. and Duncan, S. (1988), 'The use and abuse of tenure', *Housing Studies*, 7, 4: 255–67.
Barlow, J. and Duncan, S. (1994), *Success and Failure in Housing Provision: European Systems Compared*, Pergamon, Oxford.
Chua, B.H. (1997), *Political Legitimacy and Housing: Stakeholding in Singapore*, Routledge, London.
Dickens, P., Duncan, S., Goodwin, M. and Gray, F. (1985), *Housing, States and Localities*, Methuen, London.
Doling, J. (1993) 'Encouraging home ownership: trends and prospects', 'in C. Jones (ed.), *New Perspectives on the Welfare State in Europe*, Routledge, London.
Doling, J. (1997), *Comparative Housing Policy: Government and Housing in Advanced Industrialized Countries*, Macmillan, London.
Doling, J. (1999), 'Housing policies and the Little Tigers: how do they compare with other industrialised countries?' *Housing Studies*, 14, 2: 229–50.
Headey, B. (1978), *Housing Policy in the Developed Economy: The United Kingdom, Sweden, the United States*, Croom Helm, London.
Hegedus, J. and Tosics, I. (1992), 'Conclusions: past tendencies and recent problems of the East European housing model', in B. Turner, J. Hegedus and I. Tosics (eds), *The Reform of Housing in Eastern Europe and the Soviet Union*, Routledge, London.
Hindes, B. (1987), *Freedom, Equality and Markets*, Tavistock, London.
Kemeny, J. (1981), *The Myth of Home Ownership*, Routledge and Kegan Paul, London.
Kennett, P. (2001), *Comparative Social Policy*, Open University Press, Buckingham.
Kilroy, B. (1979), 'Housing finance – why so privileged?' *Lloyds Bank Review*, 133: 37–52.
Maclennan, D., Gibb, K. and More, A. (1993), 'Housing finance, subsidies and the economy: agenda for the nineties', in D. Maclennan and K. Gibb (eds), *Housing Finance and Subsidies*, Avebury, Aldershot.
Mayo, S., Malpezzi, S. and Gross, D. (1986), 'Shelter strategies for the urban poor in developing countries', *World Bank Research Observer*, July: 193–203.
Oswald, A. (1999), 'Buy your home and kill a job', *New Statesman*, 28 June: 10–11.
Silver, H. (1990), 'Privatization, self-help, and public housing home ownership in the United States', in W. van Vliet and J. van Weesep (eds), *Government and Housing: Developments in Seven Countries*, vol. 36, Urban Affairs Annual Reviews, Sage, Newbury Park.
Sykora, L. (1996), 'The Czech Republic', in P. Balchin (ed.), *Housing Policy in Europe*, Routledge, London.
Szelenyi, I. (1983), *Urban Inequalities Under State Socialism*, Oxford University Press, Oxford.
Turner, B. (1993), 'Housing reforms in Eastern Europe: an introduction', in B. Turner, J. Hegedus and I. Tosics (eds), *The Reform of Housing in Eastern Europe and the Soviet Union*, Routledge, London.
UNCHS (1996), *An Urbanizing World: Global Report on Human Settlement*, Oxford University Press, Oxford.

Chapter 16
Women's Rights and Protection Policy in China: Achievements and Problems

Peiqun He

It is a fact that women have played a very important role in creating human civilization and promoting social development and progress in both material and cultural terms in the history of mankind. Women can be said to have propped up 'half the sky' in human society. However, there has been prejudice against women, and they have not been treated as equals with men over the long history of the development of human society.

Nowadays, the issue of women has become one of the major social issues of common concern in the international community, and women's cause has become a lofty undertaking for the whole of mankind. China as a member of the international community has also attached great importance to the issue of women in recent years. Madame Peng Peiyun, State Councillor of China, stated – as Deputy Head of the Chinese Delegation at the Fourth World Conference on Women – 'The Chinese Government has always regarded gender equality as an important measurement of civility' (Peng 1995). The Chinese government has made gender equality a basic state policy, and has taken many concrete steps to protect the rights and interests of women, e.g. increasing the participation of women in political affairs, enhancing women's human rights, ensuring women's full participation in economic development, developing women's education, improving women's institutions, etc. The Chinese approach to government includes respect for women, protection of their fundamental human rights and the provision of conditions that give full play to their talent and potential in the legal framework and ethics of society as a whole (Peng 1995).

In one word, social progress, the liberation of women, and gender equality have become irresistible trends of history. China has scored great achievements in the protection of women's rights, especially viewed from the perspective of policy making. However, many problems remain unsolved in different aspects of social life.

The Changing Status of Chinese Women: A Brief History

It is true that 'the development of women's cause is always closely linked with the progress of the whole society . . . The progress of the whole society, on the other hand, cannot be achieved without the development and advancement of women' (Peng 1995).

The traditional Chinese society was patriarchal. From the Zhou Dynasty in the eleventh century BC to the Qing Dynasty in the nineteenth century, the patriarchal social system, the domination of men over women, the unequal relationship between male and female, remained largely unchanged (more or less the same) over about 3,000 years. Women were subordinate to men in almost every aspect of life in such a society, and had very few, if any, right(s), let alone institutional protections. Women were regarded as appendages/accessories of men, and were strictly restrained in almost every field, e.g. political participation, education, family. The 'Qing Dynasty Law' (*Daqing Lü*) issued by the Qing government, for instance, explicitly restricted women's rights of inheritance to the husbands' property as wives and to the fathers' property as daughters.

A profound change with regard to Chinese women's ideas and social position took place in the mid-nineteenth century, and this change came along with China's involvement in the world modernization trend, regardless of whether such an involvement was active or passive on the part of China. The change eventually brought up the issue of Chinese women's rights, which, to some extent, became an organic part of China's early modernization. After 1840, Western missionaries came into China and gradually exerted their influence in many ways. They proposed that churches should establish schools for girls/women, and maintained that foot-binding[1] of little girls and the killing of baby girls should be regarded as corrupt customs or vile practices, and thus be abolished. In 1875, some missionaries established the first 'Natural Foot Association' (*Tian Zu Hui*) in Xiameng (Zheng and Du 2000: 67), and then Shanghai and other places followed suit. Acquired from western countries, the ideas of equality between men and women, and of women's independence and self-reliance, started to spread and were gradually accepted by the Chinese people. On 1 June 1898, some Chinese people founded the first girls' school named 'Jingzheng Girls' School' (*Jingzheng Nüxue*) in Shanghai. Twenty girls in the first year, and seventy girls in the second year were enrolled. In 1897, the first Chinese women's society/world, 'Chinese Women's Association' (*Zhongguo Nü Xuehui*), was formed in Shanghai. On 24 July, 1898, the first Chinese women's newspaper entitled *Women Education Newspaper* (*Nü Xue Bao*) was published by 'Chinese Women's Association' (Zheng and Du 2000: 69-70). Statistics show that from 1901 to 1904, four girls' schools were founded every year in the whole country, and in 1906, three girls' schools were founded. From that point on, all the big cities in China had at least one girls' school. From 1901 to 1911, there emerged over 50 women's associations in the whole country. Among the newspapers published by women in 1910 and 1911, about 40 kinds of newspapers can still be found now (Wei 2000: 211).

Through the founding of girls' schools, the formation of women's associations and the publication of women's newspapers, Chinese women, for the first time in Chinese history, collectively expressed their strong wish to pursue and subsequently to protect women's rights; and they eventually succeeded in influencing the policy making of the then Chinese government concerning the issue of women through their unremitting efforts. In 1907, the government of the Qing Dynasty issued the first regulation for girls' schools called 'Regulation of Girls' Schools Made by the Ministry of Education' *(Xuebu Zouding Nüzi Xiaoxuetang Zhangcheng)*. Women's education, therefore, was legitimized by governmental regulation for the first time in Chinese history, which resulted in a quick growth in the number of girls/women attending schools in China, and in an increase in the numbers of women going abroad to study.

The year 1911 saw the founding of the Republic of China, and the publication of the 'Provisional Constitution'. This temporary Constitution specifically defined the rights of the citizens of the Republic under the framework of the legal system of Western countries. As citizens, women, for the first time in Chinese history, were entitled to the same rights as men, and were allowed to vote and to participate in political life. They were also entitled to enjoy the rights and freedoms of inhabitancy, of speech, of press, of assembly, of correspondence, of religious belief, etc. This temporary Constitution, however, failed to address the issue of inequality between men and women which had existed throughout the history of China over 3,000 years. As a result, the Constitution could hardly guarantee women's rights in reality. Thus women, to a certain degree, were still 'second-class citizens', and their entitled rights were incomplete. For example, with regard to the right of inhabitancy, the inequality between men and women remained unchanged until 1929, when 'The General Principle of Republic of China's Civil Law' was issued and put into effect. This document prohibited sexual prejudices between men and women as a form of legal principle. The general principle stipulated that all the restraints on women and their activities be banned; women, including married women, should be entitled to a complete right of disposal of personal property. It also stated that the relations between rights and duties should not differ according to gender (Yang 1990: 907-8).

During the Chinese Liberation War (or Civil War, 1945-1949), the Central Committee of the Communist Party issued 'Policy and Task for the Rural Women's work in the Liberated Areas'. In 1949, the first plenary meeting of the Chinese People's Political Consultative Conference passed 'The Common Guiding Principle', a provisional Constitution, entitling women to equal rights with men in every aspect of social life, such as in politics, economics, culture, education, etc., thus relieving women from the yoke of the feudal ethical code and old ideas.

The first law issued by the People's Republic of China was the Marriage Law. The Constitution of the People's Republic of China was promulgated in 1954, stipulating that 'women enjoy equal rights with men in all spheres of life, e.g. political, economic, cultural, social, and family life'. The Marriage Law, and later the Inheritance Act, the Electoral Law, the Criminal Law and the Compulsory Education Law have all stipulated in detail women's rights in relevant areas and thence worked out measures for the protection of these women's rights. In 1992, China's National People's Congress passed the Law on the Safeguarding of Women's Rights and Interests. This law ensures that women's rights should not be infringed upon under any circumstances. Many other laws, regulations and even social or economic measures have been made to protect women's rights in the light of gender equality since 1949.

By the end of 2000, the total number of women leaders at all levels of government and in the state-owned enterprises in the whole country was 14,894,500 – 36.2 per cent of the total number of leaders. In professional occupations, there are 11,707,000 women professionals – 40.6 per cent of the total. Among women professionals, 436,000 have high academic or technical titles, and 3,263,000 have intermediate titles.[2]

According to Madame Peng Peiyun, 'Women's workforce has increased by 114 million, up 25 per cent on that of 1985. Tens of millions of women have shaken off poverty and become prosperous. The number of illiterate women has gone down by over 30 million, and over 96 per cent of girls of school-age are in school ... the average life expectancy of women has reached 72. In short, Chinese women are now enjoying the equal rights which were denied to them for thousands of years in old China and which took the present-day developed countries hundreds of years to recognize' (Peng 1995).

The arduous course for Chinese women seeking their own rights, to some extent, reflects the wide spread of Western thought in China and the great influence of Western thought upon Chinese society. The change in the policies concerning the protection of Chinese women's rights meanwhile also reflects China's recognition and acceptance of the values of the West and its legal principle of policy making.

UN World Conferences on Women and the Global Context of the Chinese Government's Policies for the Protection of Women

By the end of the 1970s and the beginning of the 1980s, tremendous changes were taking place in the political and economic fields, as well as in social life in China. The long period of China's great economic development began at this moment. So did the period of China's opening up to the world and the period of international capital continuously pouring into China, as well as China's process towards globalization. Hence, the Chinese government's policies for the protection of women's rights, in a certain sense, were also made in the context of a global discourse. The four, particularly the later three, UN World Conferences on Women and their resolutions played a very important role in incorporating China's policy making (related to women or women's rights) into the international framework.

The First UN World Conference on Women was held in Mexico in 1975, and the UN Ten Year Plan of World's Action for Women from 1976 to 1985 was made at this conference. Unfortunately, China had not opened her door to the world at that time, and no Chinese women attended this conference.

The Second UN World Conference on Women was held in Copenhagen in 1980, in which the 'Pact of Elimination of All Kinds of Prejudices Against Women' was passed. A Chinese delegation attended this conference and signed the pact. This pact clearly defined not only all kinds of women's rights, but also the duties and responsibilities for carrying out the pact on the part of all the signatory states, and required in unequivocal terms that every signatory 'make laws to ensure/guarantee women's full development and progress, and take measures and establish institutes to practically protect women against prejudices in every field' (Peng 1995). In the same year, the pact was ratified by the Standing Committee of the National People's Congress of China, and it became effective in China in September 1981.

The Third UN World Conference on Women was held in Nairobi in 1985, in which the 'Strategy of Enhancing Women's Status by 2000' (Nairobi Strategy) was agreed. This strategy was a guiding principle for enhancing women's status, and was composed of three themes, i.e. equality, development and peace, plus three sub-themes, namely employment, health care and education. It defined the goals to be attained and the measures to be taken by 2000 concerning the three themes and the three sub-themes. In President Jiang Zemin's view, the theme of this women's conference – Action for Equality, Development and Peace – has undoubtedly instilled fresh vitality into the global women's cause (Jiang 1995). 'After the Third

World Conference on Women, the Chinese Government has continued to attach great importance to women's cause in earnest implementation of the Nairobi Strategy' (Peng 1995).

On 4 September 1995, the Fourth World Conference on Women was held in Beijing, which was a precious chance for China to formulate her policy for women in accordance with the international trend. At the welcoming ceremony, President Jiang Zemin stated clearly the views of the Chinese government on the issue of women, proclaiming that 'we attach great importance to the women's development and progress, and regard the equality of men and women as a basic national policy of promoting development of our country' (Jiang 1995). This conference formulated and ratified the 'Beijing Declaration' and 'Platform for Action' for the carrying out of the Nairobi Strategy, and also put forward strategic goals for resolving the world's women issues, and specified actions for attaining those goals.

In July 1995, in order to comply with the convocation of the Fourth World Conference on Women, the Chinese government, based on the above-mentioned 'Platform for Action' and the specific situations of China, had formulated 'The Development Programme for Chinese Women (1995-2000)', specifying 11 goals to be attained by 2000 concerning Chinese women's participation in politics, employment, work protection, education, family, human rights, shaking off poverty, etc. and the measures to be taken to attain the goals. The Chinese government has thus brought women's development into line with the general state plan for national economic and social development. All this shows the Chinese government's efforts and actions in the planning and implementation of women's policies, as prescribed by the UN World Conferences on Women.

China has gradually established a legal system to protect women's rights. Within the Constitution, and with the Law on the Safeguard of Women's Rights and Interests as its base, this system also consists of some other laws, regulations and policies. The functional departments of government and local government at every level have all made pertinent regulations and policies for the purpose of protecting women. The Department of Work and Social Security is doing its best to increase the chances for women to be employed. In its training programme for young people waiting for jobs, women account for over 50 per cent every year. The Agriculture Department has taken measures to link women's development to the comprehensive development of agriculture. The Ministry of Education has made some favourable policy provisions for promoting the education of women.

The World Conferences on Women are closely related to the promotion of Chinese women's rights. From the Chinese government's signing of the legal document at the Second World Conference on Women, to her hosting the Fourth Conference and initiating the Platform for Action, China has also moved from the recognition and study of Western policy-making systems to the active promotion of global values and policy development; thus not only making China's policies of protecting women's rights suitable for the Chinese reality, but at the same time making China herself a well-qualified member of the international community. This process has been completely in accordance with the trend of China being incorporated into the global system over the last 20 years.

Women's Participation in Politics

History shows us clearly that the fate of women is definitely linked with that of the whole of mankind, and that full and equal participation by women is indispensable to the fulfilment of all the major tasks facing the present-day world.

In 1906, Finnish women obtained the right to vote and to stand for election, which was the first time that women had had such rights. The year 1906 also saw a Finnish woman becoming a member of a legislative assembly for the first time, and thus ushering in a new epoch of women entering legislative assemblies/parliaments.

By 1999, in the legislative assemblies of over 180 countries in the whole world, there are about 4,500 women members, accounting for 12.9 per cent of the total members, 2 percentage points higher than the number of women members in the early 1990s, 1.6 percentage points higher than the 11.3 per cent at the time of the UN Fourth World Conference on Women in 1995. Northeern Europe, nevertheless, has the highest proportion of women members, i.e. 40 per cent in Sweden, 39 per cent in Norway, 37 per cent in Finland, one-third in Iceland. Up till now, however, there has been no woman member in about ten countries' legislative assemblies, and some countries have had women members only in recent years (He 2001).

The functions and powers of the National People's Congress (NPC) of China, namely the making of law, the monitoring of the government's administration, etc. are the collective embodiment of popular participation in government and political affairs, or to make it simpler, the embodiment of political participation. In 1954, there were 147 women deputies to the First National People's Congress, amounting to 12 per cent of the total deputies; by 1993, there were 626 women deputies to the Eighth NPC, accounting for 21.03 per cent of the total. In the Ninth NPC in 1998, there were 650 women deputies, amounting to 21.81 per cent of the total, being 0.78 percentage points higher than for the Eighth NPC.

The standing committee of the National People's Congress of China is a permanent organization of the NPC. There were only four women members in the standing committee of the First NPC in 1954, amounting to 5 per cent of the total. Up until the Eighth NPC in 1993, there were 19 women members, amounting to 12.3 per cent.[3] The proportion of women deputies and members increased for every NPC. From 1978 to 1993, the proportion of women deputies held steady at about 21 per cent, but increased in 1998 to 21.81 per cent (Li 2000). This increase resulted from a particular policy decision of the Chinese government in 1997, namely ... 'The Resolution on the Issue of Election and the Number of Deputies to the Ninth NPC Made in the Fifth Meeting of the Eighth NPC' in July 1997. It stipulated that 'the proportion of women deputies to the Ninth National People's Congress should be higher than that of the Eighth National People's Congress'.

According to statistics prepared by the Federation of Parliaments, the proportion of women deputies to the NPC in China has increased steadily every year in percentage terms, yet when compared with the proportion of women members of parliaments in other countries, China's position in the rank ordering has lowered gradually. In 1994, China's proportion of women deputies was ranked twelfth, but ranked sixteenth in 1997, and then twentieth in 2000. This indicates that the level of women's political participation has been quickly and greatly raised in parts of the rest of the world, while the steady increase in the percentage of women's political participation in China has none the less failed to keep pace with expanding Western countries (Li 2000).

Since the Fourth World Conference on Women in 1995, the Chinese government has been committed to promoting women's political participation, especially in the fields of decision-making and the management of state and social affairs. However, compared with many other countries and considering the size of China's population, the proportion of Chinese women active in politics or holding top government positions remains relatively low. Women's involvement and leadership are comparatively high at the lower level, but rapidly decline the further one moves up the scale of political or administrative hierarchy. The proportion of women leaders is relatively low compared to the total number of leaders in China (Tan and Peng 2000: 152-3).

Women's Rights and the Debate over the Revision of the Marriage Law

In April 1950, the Seventh Meeting of the Committee of the Central (People's) Government passed the 'Marriage Law of the People's Republic of China', which was promulgated and put into effect on 1 May 1950. The Marriage Law was the first law made by the government of the People's Republic of China to promote equality between man and woman and freedom of marriage, thus marking a revolutionary change in China's marriage system. The core of this law was to abolish the feudal marriage and family system. It banned arranged and compulsory marriages, made it illegal to regard men as superior to women and prohibited gender differentiation with regard to offsprings' rights of inheritance to family properties. Meanwhile, it also implemented the marriage and family system which guaranteed freedom of marriage, monogamy, gender equality, protection of the rights and interests of women and children, etc. This was an event of great historic significance and of profound influence in Chinese social life. It established a new form of relations for marriage and the family, saved women from the oppression of men, and enhanced women's status in society.

In 1980, the Fifth Session of the Third Meeting of the National People's Congress ratified the revised 'Marriage Law of the People's Republic of China' which was put into effect on 1 January 1981. This revision of the law marked the end of the period when family relations were politicized. Two basic principles were added: the protection of the rights and interests of the old, and the implementation of family planning. The age of getting married prescribed by law was raised from 20 to 22 for men and from 18 to 20 for women. A provision of divorce was added and the legal adjustment of family relations was emphasized in order to make an end of the politicization of family relations (Xu 2001).

On 11 January 2001, the proposed draft of the revised Marriage Law made by the Legal Committee of the Standing Committee of the National People's Congress was published in major newspapers and magazines, and soon the committee received over 4,000 letters from all walks of life, and thousands of messages through newspapers, magazines and the internet. This proposed draft was meant to involve as many people as possible. It received an array of wide-ranging opinions, and aroused many heated debates as well. These debates, to a great extent, reflected negotiations going on with regard to policy making and policy differences concerning the efficacy of the protection of women's rights in the process of revising some aspects of the law. The debates involved such issues as civil compensation for extramarital affairs, childbearing rights, spouse's rights, the punishment of the 'third party',[4] etc.

Some experts maintained enthusiastically that the so-called spouse's right (*pei'ou quan*)[5] should be added into the Marriage Law in order to punish the 'third party', i.e. to give the innocent party the right to demand compensation because of the third party's infringement upon his/her spouse's right. But other experts insisted that to add the 'spouse's right' into the law was unnecessary, and could even have negative effects, such as the legitimization of marital rape. This was not only because divorce proceedings usually did not involve the third party, and so were without any legal basis to demand the third party to make compensation, but also because – if the spouse's right was added into the law and became a legal right – the male party, who had hitherto occupied a favourable position in terms of physical strength and social resources, could lawfully have intercourse with his wife, totally neglecting his wife's need or even against his wife's will, based on the fact that the law would give him the right to satisfy himself/his desire. So the spouse's right finally was not added into the revised Marriage Law, which also suggests the denial of the legal punishment/sanction of the third party (including mistresses). The principle of compensation from the party who did something unfaithful or wrong, however, was added into the law. Article 46 of the newly revised law stipulates that the innocent party should have the right to demand compensation from the guilty party in the divorce proceedings, resulting from his/her committing bigamy, domestic violence, having extramarital affairs, maltreating or deserting family member(s), etc. Adding this article into the law has its social background, i.e. more and more men have mistresses. Women's status is rapidly deteriorating and their rights are being infringed upon day by day. Such victimized women, through the government's administrative legislation, should be able to get some economic and spiritual compensation both in the divorce proceedings and after divorce.

There remain different opinions about compulsory compensation in divorce proceedings in respect of the party who brings harm to the family. Some experts who are against it maintain that it lacks feasibility since it is very difficult to obtain evidence. One part of a married couple living together with someone other than the spouse, not in the name of man and wife, does not necessarily mean that he/she is wrong. This is something that belongs to the private sphere and should not be interfered with in the public sphere. The practice of compulsory compensation could entail many negative effects in society, such as the infringement upon one's privacy and human rights, the intensification of a couple's conflicts (or at least the worsening of relations between them). Compulsory compensation aimed at protecting one group of women's rights and interests most likely will result in infringement of another group of women's privacy and human rights.

Another debate aroused by the revision of the Marriage Law centres on the child-bearing right (*shengyu quan*). The Marriage Law revised in 1980 stipulated that 'both man and wife have the duty to carry out family planning', which, in fact, reflected China's basic state policy (i.e. on family planning), and the principle of the Constitution (i.e. the equality between men and women). This law, however, only addressed the issue of childbearing from the perspective of duty. It did not define clearly the rights of childbearing. The most important law in this respect, the Law on the Safeguarding of Women's Rights and Interests, based on the basic principle of the Constitution, stipulated that 'women should have the childbearing right in accordance with the state policy concerned, and have the freedom not to bear child', thus women, and only women, were entitled the childbearing right. Others could not infringe this right, not even the husband. But in the proposed draft of the revised Marriage Law, the article that 'man and wife are entitled equal child-bearing right' was added. Those who were against this article pointed out that childbearing was the basic right of a woman's control over her own body, the symbol of the liberation of women, and the enhancement of women's social and family status. They argued that pregnancy, giving birth and nurturing babies were the unique characteristics of women's bodies, and should be given special protection. However, those who were in favour of this article argued that childbearing was the duty and right of both man and woman, and man and wife should equally, correctly, legitimately exert this right. On 28 April 2001, the Twenty-First Meeting of the Ninth National People's Congress passed the revised Marriage Law, which was also put into effect on that day. In this newly revised law, the article that 'man and wife are entitled to equal childbearing right' was left out or deleted. Hence, the stipulation that 'women should have the child-bearing right in accordance with the state policy concerned, and have the freedom not to bear a child' remained unchanged in the Law on the Safeguarding of Women's Rights and Interests, thus avoiding a big conflict between the two laws. The differences and negotiations in the policy making during the process of the revision of the Marriage Law, on the one hand, revealed the complexity of the issue of women's rights and the protection of their rights. On the other hand, they also indicated that the making of policy or law lags behind the development of actual social life. The promulgation of the newly revised Marriage Law shows that when there are different views on the policy/law making concerning the protection of women's rights, the Chinese government now tends to choose the policy more favourable to women, and at the same time to take social stability as a priority.[6]

Unsolved Problems

However, in today's world, many problems concerning women's rights and the protection of these rights remain unsolved. The progress made in the field of women's rights in China is great only in historical terms. Many problems likewise remain in many aspects of Chinese social life. Great gaps exist between social reality and the requirements or stipulations of the Constitution, laws, policies, regulations related to gender equality and the protection of women's rights and interests.

There is almost no clear-cut feminist or gender theory in China on which relevant policies are to be based or implemented. Problems concerning women are, more often than not, simplified to be a matter of economic participation. Government policies concerning women often lack consistency, and sometimes are incompatible with other socioeconomic policies, which in turn greatly reduces the effectiveness of the government's efforts to support and protect women as well as to enhance women's social status. To make things worse, the traditional thought of gender inequality is still in existence (Tan and Peng 2000: 163). In rural areas, it is still very common to regard men as superior to women, to kill or abandon baby girls, and even to maltreat women giving birth to baby girls. There are about 200 million illiterate people in China, among whom women account for 40 per cent. In remote and poor areas, the enrolment of girls in school is usually quite low, which means that the proportion of girls unable to go to school is high. Such phenomena as abducting and selling/trafficking women and children, men visiting prostitutes and having mistresses, women becoming prostitutes are quite common. In some rural areas, mercenary marriages, arranged marriages, different kinds of illegal marriages, and the wrongdoings of interfering in the freedom of marriage can still be found. Women, unfortunately, are always the victims of such doings.

Women and men are entitled to equal educational rights by law. More and more women have received formal education. In the 1990s, women's illiteracy rate was significantly lowered, and the average level of women's education was raised. The differences in scores/attainment between women and men were gradually lessened, and so were the differences between urban and rural areas. Nevertheless, women's education levels are obviously affected by different regional conditions, especially with regard to the unevenness of economic development and to the strong influence of traditional ideas. There remains a big difference between women and men in terms of years of education. There are also large differences between male and female education in urban versus rural areas. Sex differences in education, however, are much bigger in rural than in urban areas. The number of years of education a person receives affects his/her ability to improve his/her socioeconomic status in society. 'Chinese women as a whole are in a disadvantaged position in education compared to men. Educational disadvantage then leads to poor employment opportunities and poor political participation by women' (Tan and Peng 2000: 155).

With the development of the Chinese economy, especially after the implementation of the open-up policy, the issue of women's rights has been granted greater importance and viewed with much more concern. However, Chinese practice shows clearly that women's status can neither be enhanced automatically along with economic development in general, nor be improved by women's increasing participation in forms of economic activity in particular. Indeed, the high rate of women's economic participation would not seem to have reduced the gender difference in many aspects of social life. In short, the traditional attitude towards women's participation in the labour force has not thoroughly changed yet. The talk of women's return to the family can often be heard from the mass media in recent years (Tan and Peng 2000: 164). Women's social status might therefore have deteriorated in some way instead of being enhanced. Certainly, women seem more likely to fall victim to economic changes/reform than do men.

The employment of women is increasing with the development of China's economy, but female college graduates, although equally qualified, usually have to go through much tougher job-hunting experiences than their male counterparts under the same conditions, and the chances of employment differ greatly between the sexes.

There are also problems concerning women's participation in politics, e.g. a lack of awareness of women's political participation among both women and men in Chinese society, in the context of sex discrimination in society as a whole. China has remained a patriarchal society for thousands of years, and women were never allowed to play an equal part in decision making at any level (Tan and Peng 2000: 153). It is not easy for all the Chinese people to completely cast away such old ideas within a short period.

The above-mentioned are only some of the problems relating to women's rights that China, a developing country constrained by inadequate social and economic development and outdated mentality, is now faced with.

Notes

1. Foot-binding (*chanzu* or *guojiao* in Chinese) was an ancient Chinese custom or practice aimed at women. Originally an upper-class practice, it soon started to spread throughout China during the Song Dynasty. People used a bandage, or a piece of cloth, to bind the feet of a little girl in order to prevent the growth of her feet, thus leading to the deformity of the feet. Consequently, the scope of women's activities and the area within women's walking distance were greatly limited. An abnormal aesthetic view on bound feet was even formed in feudal China, particularly the smaller the feet, the more beautiful they were considered to be.
2. Anonymous (1994), Extensive Participation in the Administration of the State and Social Affair, *The Conditions of Chinese Women*.
3. Ibid.
4. The third party refers to a person who keeps an intimate relation with one part of a married couple. The third party was generally regarded as a destroyer/intruder of the couple's marriage, and was morally criticized by the whole society in the late 1970s and 1980s. Since the 1990s, Chinese society has become gradually tolerant toward extra-marital affairs, and the 'third party' has thus become a comparatively neutral term.
5. The spouse's right refers to the right to be spouses between a married couple. It includes the right of fidelity, companionship, etc., and should not be infringed upon by anybody. This right was not mentioned in any Chinese law before. The appearance of this right is aimed at defining the third party as the intruder into a marriage, and thus to rule on the third party for his/her infringement of the spouse right, and consequently to punish the third party.
6. After the submission of this chapter, The Law of Population and Family Planning was issued in December 2001, stipulating that every citizen, regardless of his/her sex, should have the childbearing right. Men's childbearing right is thus clearly stipulated by law for the first time in Chinese history. Nevertheless, it does not mean that women's childbearing right is weakened by men's childbearing right. In other word, men's childbearing right should not be at the expense of women's childbearing right, especially women's right not to bear child. If a man would like to exert his childbearing right while his wife does not want to bear child, this stipulation cannot be used to force the woman to bear a child. The worst result of the disagreement upon childbearing is divorce. In terms of gender equality, the law can still be considered favourable to women. This note has been added before the publication of this chapter.

References

He, Naixiu (2001), On Women's Political Participation, http://www.women.org.cn.
Jiang Zemin (1995), Speech at welcoming ceremony for the Fourth World Conference on Women. Official web site of the FWCW.
Li, Huiying (2000), Comment on Chinese Women's Political Participation in the Recent Five Years, http://www.women.org.cn.

Peng, Peiyun (1995), Speech at the Fourth World Conference on Women. Official web site of the FWCW, http://www.undp.org/fwcw.

Tan, Lin and Xizhe Peng (2000), 'China's female population', in Peng Xizhe (ed.) *The Changing Population of China*, Blackwell, Oxford.

Xu, Anqi (2001), 'The barometer of the transformation of society – A look back on the revision of the Marriage Law', in *China Youth Newspaper*, 1 June.

Wei, Guoying (ed.) (2000), *A General Introduction to Women's Studies*. Beijing University Press.

Yang, Honglie (1990), *The Developing History of Chinese Law*, Vol. II. Shanghai Bookstore (based on the photocopy of the book published by the Commercial Printing House in 1930).

Zheng, Xinfong and Fangqin Du (eds) (2000), *Gender and Women Development*, Shanxi People's Education Press.

Chapter 17
Women's Rights and Gender Issues

Jane Lewis

Introduction

It is now rare to hear fighting talk in the UK about 'women's rights'. Rather, it is 'gender issues' which are very much alive here and in Europe generally, particularly in relation to the problem of combining work and family responsibilities. Ostensibly, the UK-in-Europe thus stands at a conspicuous remove from China, with regard to the formal recognition that government has given to the problems that women experience as mothers and workers, at least since 1997. However, there is a broader issue about how paid and unpaid care work might be shared between men and women, which is common to all countries. The UK has lagged behind other European countries in addressing this issue, which may provide a salutary point of departure for Chinese observers. In the context of both changing female labour market behaviour and changing family structures, the UK shares with China the tendency of policy makers to focus attention on 'the family', and on family law as well as family policies.

The first major post-war UK government document on family policy (the Home Office's *Supporting Families*, 1998) talked about 'parenting', even though the major responsibility for the unpaid work of care continues to fall on women. Indeed, it is fair to say that most so-called gender issues arise from the persistence of gender inequalities, for it remains the case that women in the UK experience lower pay, inferior occupational status, and lower levels of representation on public bodies of all kinds than do men. Yet, as in the Chinese case, legal steps have been taken to treat men and women equally in the workforce, via the Equal Opportunities legislation of the 1970s, and in the family via changes in family law (particularly in respect of divorce in the 1970s) and more recently in family policy (particularly in respect of the provision of child care).

Debate has raged over how far the persistence of inequalities is due to women's own preferences (Hakim 2001). For example, if good-quality, low-cost, widely available child care were to be introduced for all children over two in the UK tomorrow, how many women would use it and enter the labour market as full-time workers? It is difficult to answer such a question. Indeed, answers would in all likelihood differ between different Western European countries and between different regions and different cultures in the same nation state. There are undoubtedly many women who want to work part-time while their children are small. But this does not mean that they necessarily also feel that this work should attract little by way of recognition or value. Fundamentally, the issues of women's rights and gender inequality raise the age-old problem of equality and difference. It seems that what men do usually attracts the most rewards, thus the problem becomes how far to treat women the same as men and to expect them to do the same things, or how far it is possible and/or desirable to make provision for difference. When the problem is posed in this way, any solution seems to require collective action and to draw in government.

Western governments have been explicitly committed to gender equality for a generation. The only social policy included in the original Treaty of Rome, which set up the European Union, took the form of a commitment to equal pay for men and women (Meehan 1993). In the main, equality has been defined as 'sameness' and early equal pay legislation required women to find a male comparator. In what follows, I suggest that the recent trends in the UK have moved in the direction of assuming ever greater individualization on the part of men and women, whether in terms of family formation or economic autonomy, and that this has penetrated both family law and social policies. Such a set of assumptions treats men and women as if they are indeed similarly placed and means that legislation runs the risk of being out of step with the social reality and the differences (and inequalities) that characterize the position of men and women in practice.

Individualization and Behaviour

The dominant set of assumptions informing UK family law and policies for the first three-quarters of the twentieth century revolved around the idea of a 'male breadwinner family model', whereby men would be employed full-time and would take primary responsibility for earning, and women would take primary responsibility for the care of young and old dependants in stable families, and be to a large extent economically dependent on their husbands. During the years immediately following the Second World War, this set of assumptions as to how the family operated came closest to matching the social reality, even though a 'pure' male breadwinner model, in which women were not employed at all, never existed. However, from the 1980s, family and labour market change served profoundly to erode the firm assumptions about stable families and full employment for men. Family breakdown and lone-mother families became more common, male labour market participation fell slightly and female labour market participation increased considerably. As a result, it became more possible to assume that men and women were becoming 'individualized'.

Elizabeth Beck Gernsheim (1999: 54) has characterized the process of individualization in relation to the family in terms of 'a community of need' becoming 'an elective relationship'. In this interpretation, the family used to be an entity held together by the obligations of solidarity. But women's increased participation in the labour market, together with family change and instability have resulted in new divisions between biography and family; to use Burns and Scott's (1994) term, male and female roles have become 'decomplementary'. But the precise extent of the erosion of the male breadwinner family model is complicated. While almost a quarter of children are now living in a lone-parent household in the UK, the vast majority of families are couple rather than lone-parent families. Nor has there been any simple move from a male breadwinner to a dual career model family, for instance. Men and women have not become economically autonomous. It is now widely accepted that women will engage in paid work and attitudinal surveys have shown consistent increases in the acceptance by men and women of female employment at all stages of the lifecourse (Dex 1988), but to what extent – full-time or some form of part-time – varies considerably according to social class, ethnicity and sometimes region.

The male breadwinner model has eroded, but the social reality is still far from a family comprising self-sufficient, autonomous individuals. While women's behaviour has changed substantially in respect of paid work, they still perform the bulk of unpaid care work. Men have changed much less in respect of the amount of either paid or unpaid work they do (e.g. Gershuny et al. 1994). The pattern of paid work between men and women in households is now much more difficult to predict, but patterns of unpaid work have not changed so much.

The British General Household Survey shows that while in 1975, 81 per cent of men 16-64 were economically active and 62 per cent of women, by 1996, this figure was 70 per cent for both men and women (ONS 1998, Tables 5.8 and 5.9). Married women are as likely to be employed as non-married women and Table 17.1 shows the rapid increase in the proportion of women with small children in employment. But short part-time working is very common for women. Almost a quarter of British women with children under ten worked 15 or fewer hours per week in the late 1990s (Thair and Risdon 1999), and 24 per cent of all female employees worked under 20 hours a week (Rubery et al. 1998).

In respect of family structure, the pace of change in the recent past for the UK has been greater than in regard to the labour market. The divorce rate increased threefold – and the rate of unmarried motherhood fourfold – within one generation (see Tables 17.2 and 17.3). Cohabitation (see Table 17.4) has been the driver of much of the change. It is now sequel and alternative to marriage and has contributed to the increasing separation of marriage and parenthood, which constitutes a more profound shift than the 1960s separation of sex and marriage (Lewis and Kiernan 1996). British Household Panel data show that cohabiting relationships in the UK continue to be four times more unstable than marriage (Ermisch and Francesconi 1998). The net result of all these family changes has been an increase in lone motherhood (see Table 17.5).

The increase in women's labour market participation has effected a change in the male breadwinner model: the increase in female employment and in the incidence of the dual-earner family cannot be denied, even if women's participation is often part-time, making it less of a 'revolution' than is often supposed. This in turn has shaken the whole fabric of gender roles, which had been widely assumed – by government and by people – to flow from the model. At the same time, the increase in lone motherhood makes it appear as though women are increasingly able to 'go it alone'. At some point, the gap between changing behaviour and the normative expectations flowing from the male breadwinner model becomes too great, and the rupture gives rise to a new set of normative expectations. Female employment is expected, although to what degree is unclear. Indeed, expectations may actually run ahead of behavioural change, on the part of people and policy makers. This in turn has profound implications for the gendered division of carework and for the extent to which care is located in the public or private, formal or informal spheres.

Individualization and Policies

Policy makers have recognized the existence of greater individualization with regard to labour market and family behaviour, without taking on board the complexities of the way in which the male breadwinner model has been eroded. The reasons for the shift are complicated, but relate both to external and internal pressures on Western welfare states. Anxieties about securing greater and more flexible labour market participation in face of increasing competition, together with concerns about the 'welfare dependency' of the growing proportion of lone-mother families in particular, have served to promote the idea of a citizen-worker model.

A striking example of the pendulum shift in the assumptions underpinning policies took place in the UK and the Netherlands in the mid-1990s, in respect of lone mothers. This group of women has always been a particularly problematic group for a male breadwinner regime, because it must be decided whether and on what terms the state will step in to replace the father (Lewis 1998). Both national governments swung from treating lone mothers as mothers, with no requirement to register for employment until their youngest child was 16, to treating them as workers, regardless of the fact that a majority of married mothers were already actually working part-time (Lewis 1997). The rationale in both countries had much to do with reducing dependence on state benefits, but was supported by arguments regarding the greater labour market participation of married mothers, without it being acknowledged that the vast majority of these women worked short part-time hours.

The new set of assumptions behind social policies amounts to 'an adult worker' rather than a male breadwinner model family. It is noteworthy that, at the level of European Union policy making, the European Commission has focused in the main on the need for active labour market participation, stressing the importance of adult labour market participation in order to increase competitiveness. Both the EC (CEC 2000a) and the OECD (2000) have emphasized the importance of policies to 'make work pay' and, in the words of the EC, of strengthening 'the role of social policy as a productive factor' (CEC 2000b: 2). But this ignores the implications of the gendered division of work, unpaid as well as paid, that is experienced (or desired) by many women. In many respects, women's labour market participation has become the new norm and it is increasingly assumed that both men and women will be formally employed. However, there is evidence to suggest that the assumptions made by policy makers regarding women's status as 'workers' is rapidly outrunning the social reality, which, in many countries, takes the form of part-time and often 'short' part-time work (Lewis 2001). This becomes crucially important if it is also assumed, to any significant extent, that individuals will, in the future, be able to make greater provision for themselves, especially in respect of pension provision (Ginn et al. 2001).

It is also the case that the persistence of the gendered division of the unpaid work of care has not been anywhere near the forefront of the policy agenda. Thus the coherence of policies with regard to care is markedly less than that for policies delineating the new insistence on labour market participation for all; and the monies allocated to care are considerably less than those designed to get people into work and make work pay. Anything to do with care tends to be poorly valued. Wages in the formal care sector are low and benefits and allowances for carers in the informal sector are also low. This means that in a world in which individualization and the capacity for self-provisioning is increasingly being assumed by policy makers, carers are profoundly disadvantaged. It also means that care continues to be associated with women rather than with both the sexes.

The nature of family change also encourages policy makers to treat men and women as fully individualized for the purposes of family law. The law of divorce was substantially relaxed, as a result of which it was no longer necessary for the courts to decide which party was 'at fault'. Mary Glendon (1981) characterized this as the 'deregulation' of the law governing private relationships. However, as divorce rates increased, so policy makers became more determined to make men and women in their roles of fathers and mothers responsible for ordering their affairs in respect of their children, while recognizing their right to do as they wish in their capacity as husbands and wives. Thus, the 1996 Family Law Act assumed that men and women would be able and willing to engage in face-to-face communication and negotiation. This model of marriage assumes that husbands and wives are able to take responsibility for sorting out their own difficulties, and relies also on the assumption that they can be treated as fully (and equally) individualized. However, given that women continue to do a disproportionate amount of the unpaid work of care and are usually not fully economically independent, their negotiating power is likely to be less. Thus again there are dangers for women in the increasingly popular assumption that they can be treated as though they are similarly placed to men.

Conclusion

The male breadwinner model family institutionalized female dependence on men and to that extent may be termed patriarchal. An adult worker model family holds out more promise for women in many respects, but what is important is the terms on which such a model is introduced. Problems always arise when governments legislate on the basis of an 'ought' rather than an 'is'. Just as the male breadwinner model treated women as dependants of men and ignored their contributions, paid and unpaid, so the adult worker model ignores the fact that women are not 'the same' as men and are not completely individualized.

The problems of moving towards a full adult worker model in respect of the gender dimension alone are fourfold. First, unpaid care work is unequally shared between men and women, which has substantial implications for women's position in the labour market. Second, given the lack of good-quality affordable care in the formal sector, many women have little option but to continue to provide it informally (what Land and Rose 1985, referred to as 'compulsory altruism') and to depend to some extent on a male wage. Bradshaw et al.'s (1996) cross-national comparative study of lone mothers' employment rates showed access to affordable child care to be the key explanatory variable. Third, a significant number of female carers feel that it is 'right' to prioritize care. Fourth, women's low pay, especially in care-related jobs, means that full individualization is hard to achieve, on the basis of long part-time or even full-time work.

The tensions in respect of equality and difference that revolve around the place of care in an adult worker model are too grave to be ignored. It is useful to look at two other Western models – the Scandinavian and the American – in this regard as well.

Both have a fully individualized, adult worker model. However, in the USA case, the obligation to enter the labour market is embedded in a residual welfare system that often borders on the punitive, whereas in Sweden and Denmark it is supported by an extensive range of care entitlements in respect of children and older people. The position of lone mothers – always a borderline case for the study of social policy – is particularly instructive in this respect, because of the problem of combining unpaid care work and employment. The USA has gone much more wholeheartedly than Britain down the road of treating these women as paid workers, and imposing time-limited benefits. Employment rates of lone mothers are thus high in the USA; the push factor being strong. But employment rates are higher still in Sweden and Denmark, where lone mothers' poverty rates are much lower than in the UK or the USA. Indeed, Sweden comes closest to having achieved the adult worker model: in that all citizens, male and female, are obliged to engage in paid work in order to qualify for a wide range of benefits, which then permit them to leave the labour market. However, Swedish lone mothers get almost as much income from the state as they do from earnings (Lewis 1998). The system is based on a commitment to universal citizenship entitlements, rather than, as in the USA, grafting equal citizenship obligations on to a residual welfare model.

Put simply, the Scandinavian model recognizes care. All able-bodied adults are treated as citizen-workers but, after that, permission to exit the labour market in order to care with wage replacement is granted, and formal care services are provided. In effect, Sweden and Denmark operate a similar sex equality model to the USA, but their systems have the capacity to graft on respect for a difference that manifests itself in the form of an unequal division of care work (Lewis and Astrom 1992). Nevertheless, notwithstanding a low pay gap between men and women, Sweden does have one of the most sexually segregated labour markets in the Western world.

There is, unhappily, no perfect gender model available to us for export elsewhere; in any case, policy development in this area is profoundly culturally embedded. But in the struggle to achieve gender equality it is necessary to revisit the issue of women's agency and voice. It is significant that in the Scandinavian countries, where most effort has been made to recognize and value difference, women have also had the largest presence in formal political institutions. Whereas, in the UK, where women played virtually no part in the policy making that inscribed the male breadwinner model in post-war policies, their political representation remains relatively low.

Table 17.1 Economic activity of women aged 16–59 with dependent children, Great Britain 1973–1996 (%)

Age of youngest dependent child*	1973	1979	1981	1983	1985	1989	1991	1993	1994	1995	1996
Youngest child aged 0–4											
Women working full-time	7	6	6	5	8	12	13	14	16	16	16
Women working part-time	18	22	18	18	22	29	29	32	30	32	33
All with dependent children											
Women working full-time	17	16	15	14	17	20	22	21	23	22	22
Women working part-time	30	36	34	32	35	39	36	38	37	38	39
No dependent children											
Women working full-time	52	51	48	46	47	51	48	46	48	46	45
Women working part-time	17	18	18	18	21	22	23	23	22	25	24
Total											
Working full-time	34	34	33	31	33	37	37	35	36	36	35
Working part-time	23	26	25	25	27	29	29	30	29	31	30

*Persons aged under 16, or aged 16-18 and in full-time education, in the family unit and living in the household.
Source: ONS (1998).

Table 17.2 Divorce rate per 000 married population

1950	2.8
1960	2.0
1965	3.1
1970	4.7
1975	9.6
1980	12.0
1085	13.4
1990	13.0
1995	13.6
1999	13.0

Source: *Marriage and Divorce Statistics 1837–1983*, Historical Series, FM2, no. 16, table 5.2 (London: HMSO, 1995); OPCS, *Marriage and Divorce Statistics 1837–1983*, table 2.1, FM2, no. 21 (London: HMSO, 1995); ONS, *Marriage, Divorce and Adoption Statistics 1997*, table 2.2 FM2, no. 23 (London: Stationery Office, 1999).

Table 17.3 Marital and extramarital births per 000 women aged 15–44, 1940–1998

	Marital birth rate per 1,000 Married Women	Extramarital Birth Rate per 1,000 Single, Divorced and Widowed Women
1940	98.8	5.9
1945	103.9	16.1
1950	108.6	10.2
1955	103.7	10.3
1960	120.8	14.7
1965	126.9	21.2
1970	113.5	21.5
1975	85.5	17.4
1980	92.2	19.6
1985	87.8	26.7
1990	86.7	38.9
1995	82.7	39.6
1998	82.3	40.3

Sources: Office of Population Censuses and Surveys (OPCS), *Birth Statistics Historical Series 1837–1983*, Table 3.2b and c, Series FM1, no 13 (London: HMSO, 1987) OPCS, *Birth Statistics: Historical Series 1837–1983*, Table 3.1, Series FM1, no. 22 (London: HMSO, 1995); ONS, *Birth Statistics 1998*, Tables 3.1b, Series FM1, no. 27 (London: HMSO, 1999).

Table 17.4 Percentage of women aged 18–49 cohabiting by legal marital status (Great Britain)

Legal Marital status*	1979		1981		1985		1991		1998	
Percentages cohabiting										
Non-married										
Single	8		9		14		23		31	
Widowed	0	11	6	12	5	16	2	23	8	29
Divorced	20		20		21		30		31	
Separated	17		19		20		13		12	
% of all women who are cohabiting	3		3		5		9		13	

Bases = 100%.
*Women describing themselves as 'separated' were, strictly speaking, legally married, but because the separated can cohabit they have been included in the 'non-married' category.
Source: *Living in Britain, 1998*, General Household Survey, ONS (London: HMSO, 2000), Table 12.7.

Table 17.5 Distribution of the different types of lone-mother families with dependent children 1971–1999

	Percentage* of all families with dependent children			
	1971	1981	1991	1999
Single lone mothers	1.2	2.3	6.4	9.0
Separated lone mothers	2.5	2.3	3.6	5.0
Divorced lone mothers	1.9	4.4	6.3	8.0
Widowed lone mothers	1.9	1.7	1.2	1.0
All lone mothers	7.5	10.7	17.5	23.0

*Estimates are based on three-year averages, apart from 1991.
Sources: John Haskey, 'Trends in the Numbers of One-Parent Families in Great Britain', *Population Trends* no. 71 (Spring), 1993: 26-33; ONS, *Living in Britain 1998*, Table 3.4 (London: The Stationery Office, 2000).

References

Beck Gernsheim, E. (1999), 'On the way to a post-familial family: from a community of need to elective affinities', *Theory, Culture and Society*, 15, 3–4: 53–70.
Bradshaw, J., Corden, A., Eardley, T., Holmes, H., Sutton, S., Kilkey, M., and Neale, J. (1996), *The Employment of Lone Parents*, Family Policy Studies Centre, London.
Burns, A. and Scott, C. (1994), *Mother-headed Families and why They have Increased*. Lawrence Erlbaum, Hillsdale, NJ.
CEC (2000a) *Report on Social Protection in Europe 1999*, Com (2000) 163 final, CEC, Brussels.
CEC (2000b) *Communication from the Commission to the Council, the European Parliament, the Economic and Social Committee and the Committee of the Regions: Social Policy Agenda*, CEC, Brussels.
Dex, S. (1988), *Women's Attitudes towards Work*, Macmillan, London.
Ermisch, J. and Francesconi, M. (1998), *Cohabitation in Great Britain: Not for Long, but here to Stay*. Working Paper 98-1, ESRC Research Centre on Micro-Social Change, University of Essex.
Gershuny, J., Godwin, M. and Jones, S. (1994), 'The domestic labour revolution: a process of lagged adaptation?' In M. Anderson, F. Bechhofer, and J. Gershuny (eds), *The Social and Political Economy of the Household*, Oxford University Press, Oxford.
Ginn, J., Street, D. and Arber, S. (eds) (2001), *Women, Work and Pensions*, Open University Press, Buckingham.
Glendon, M.A. (1981), *The New Family and the New Property*, Butterworth, Toronto.
Hakim, C. (2001), *Work-Lifestyle Choices in the Twenty-first Century: Preference Theory*, Oxford University Press, Oxford.
Home Office (1998), *Supporting Families*, Stationery Office, London.
Land, H. and Rose, H. (1985), 'Compulsory altruism for some or an altruistic society for all?' in P. Bean, J. Ferris and D. Whynes (eds), *In Defence of Welfare*, Tavistock, London.
Lewis, J. (ed.) (1997), *Lone Mothers in European Welfare Regimes*, Jessica Kingsley, London.
Lewis, J. (2001), *The End of Marriage? Individualism and Commitment in Intimate Relations*, Edward Elgar, Cheltenham.
Lewis, J. (1998), 'The problem of lone-mother families in twentieth-century Britain'. *Journal of Social Welfare and Family Law*, 20, 3: 251–84.
Lewis, J. and Astrom, G. (1992), 'Equality, difference and state welfare: labour market and family policies in Sweden' in *Feminist Studies*, 18, 1: 59–87.
Lewis, J. and Kiernan, K. (1996), 'The boundaries between marriage, non-marriage and parenthood: changes in behaviour and policy in post-war Britain', *Journal of Family History*, 21, 3: 372–87.
Meehan, E. (1993), *Citizenship and the European Community*, Sage, London.
OECD (2000), *Economic Studies*, no. 31, 2000/2, Paris: OECD.
ONS (1998), *Living in Britain: Results from the 1996 General Household Survey*, Stationery Office, London.
Rubery, J., Smith, M. and Fagan, C. (1998), 'National working-time regimes and equal opportunities', *Feminist Economics*, 4, 1: 71–101.
Thair, T. and Risdon, A. (1999), 'Women in the labour market. Results from the Spring 1998 LFS', *Labour Market Trends*, March: 103–27.

Chapter 18

Social Care and Voluntary Action in China: The Policy of 'Societalizing Social Welfare' and its Effects

Tao Chen

Introduction

Many people did not recognize fully the significance of the policy 'societalizing social welfare'. They always criticize the poor quality of services provided by some private welfare agencies. But if we don't have many fish in the pool, how can we choose better ones from amongst them? And how are the vast amount of welfare needs to be met?

These words are from a speech made by an official to a seminar recently participated in by local civil administrators and scholars in social policy. This official is from the social welfare department of the Ministry of Civil Affairs, in charge of social welfare policy planning and administration. His sayings express the idea, familiar to us Chinese, which is that it is necessary 'to fill the pool with water to foster fish' *(fangshuiyangyu)*. The Chinese are also familiar with the reasoning of an old Chinese saying: 'if the water is too clean, there won't be any fish in it' *(shuizhiqingzewuyu)*.

However, the disputes around the current social welfare policy and its effects have not been ended by this official's speech. Indeed his speech has gone to show just how severe are the disputes between the officials on the one part – especially higher-level officials – and scholars on the other. Officials, on behalf of the government, insist on the necessity of societalizing social welfare in order to meet increased and still increasing demands for welfare services; while the scholars often worry about the decline in the quality of services and, following this, the decline in the conditions and status of service users. Furthermore, scholars are very cautious of the new policy's implications for the state's commitment to welfare care for the disadvantaged. Some of them think this policy of 'societalizing social welfare' means in fact that the state wants to transfer this responsibility to other actors; rather than merely to change the ways in which it takes responsibilities.

To make the task even more complicated, we may talk about the possible impacts of this policy on voluntary action, or in a broader sense, on the general development of the voluntary sector. How can we evaluate properly both the short-term and the far-reaching effects this policy might have in these respects?

China finds itself indeed in a very complex situation. We need lessons from abroad to help clarify both the present case and its future possibilities. When we have such, we may in turn be able to offer some lessons to worldwide undertakings for social welfare and human well-being.

This chapter offers a tentative outline analysis of the Chinese government's policy on social welfare reform – the so-called policy of 'societalizing social welfare'– and of some of its effects, as are already becoming evident. Naturally, it can only address a few main topics. But the author hopes it will assist readers to grasp the whole picture.

Societalizing Social Welfare

In practice, 'societalizing social welfare' has been a theme in the field of social welfare since the 1980s. However, it was at the end of the last century that the government clearly put it forward as a policy and offered a systematic depiction of its meaning. In the spring of 2000, the Ministry of Civil Affairs held a national conference in Guangzhou to publicize this policy and to push the administration system forward to implement its agenda. At that conference, an official document named 'Opinions on speeding up the materialization of societalizing social welfare' became well known. This document was drafted by the Ministry of Civil Affairs (plus another ten ministries and committees such as the State Planning Committee, the Ministry of Education, Ministry of Finance and Ministry of Labour and Social Security). It was permitted and issued by the State Council. So it represented the government's formal standpoint.

In the *Opinions*, the guiding ideal of social welfare reform was presented thus:

> The developing of the forms of providing and caring should continue in the direction of maintaining in-home care as its core foundation, community care as a support, and social welfare institutions as a complementary resource; and by this, to explore a new way of developing social welfare enterprises in which the state advocates and subsidizes, whereas various social actors actively set them up and manage (Ministry of Civil Affairs, etc. 2000).

The *Opinions* also pointed out the targets for societalizing social welfare:

> By 2005 in the country, there will be established fundamentally such a network of social welfare services that will be made up of four parts: state-run social welfare institutions as examples, other social welfare institutions in different forms of ownership as mainstream, supported by community welfare services, all based on home care and provision (Ministry of Civil Affairs, etc. 2000).

As for how to achieve these goals, the *Opinions* listed four operational directions as follows:

> The first is to make the investment (in social welfare enterprises) plurally sourced. This means the state, collectives and individuals can all invest in social welfare services through different channels, so as to form a structure of social welfare institutions with different types of ownership.
>
> The second is to extend the target group so as to cover the entire public. This means social welfare institutions should open to all the elderly, the disabled and other people in need, rather than being oriented exclusively toward certain particular categories of the

population, viz. the traditionally defined vulnerable groups, such as the people without labor force capacity, source of living and family (the so-called 'three nos').

The third is to make the forms of service diversified. In other words, a new delivery system of social welfare service should be one in which both centralized services and community-based services and even home care services are viewed as equally important components, all accessible to needy people.

The fourth is to make service personnel professionals. Personnel operating at different levels and in different agencies should gradually be trained and registered as professionals. To this purpose, social work education and other types of training should be strengthened. Meanwhile, voluntary service should be encouraged and institutionalized (Ministry of Civil Affairs, etc. 2000).

From the above, we can see clearly the shift in policy orientation. In short, it implies not only certain changes in the welfare delivery system, but also a transformation of the structure of responsibility. In respect of social care and voluntary action, we might surmise that the overall effects could be favourable to the development of voluntary service and professional social work. In the long run, it may also provide more room for the growth of the voluntary sector and for new professions in Chinese society. However, what might these effects be like in detail? Are there any new problems now occurring, worth discussing?

Voluntary Action: The Focus of Debates

In the period of the planned economy, there was no voluntary action in essence. In providing welfare care for people in need, the work units (*danwei*) in cities had played the chief role; the collectives (people's communes) had taken the same role in rural areas; while the department of public welfare had only a marginal role. Financed by the state, the work units had provided their workers with all kinds of welfare, from housing, pensions and health care to other things. But we cannot describe this as an occupational welfare model in Titmuss's meaning of the expression (Titmuss 1974). Rather, it is another form of state welfare. Since the majority of citizens in urban areas were employees of different work units, they were in fact covered by this caring system. The department of public welfare only had to take care of those people uncovered by the *danwei* system. Normally, in practice, these were non-employees without family. The civil administration often set up welfare institutions to provide a mixture of services for them.

In short, before the reform, the welfare needs of all citizens were met either by the *danwei* system or by state welfare institutions established and run by the civil administration. There was no role for voluntary action in this field. Indeed, there were no voluntary agencies or so-called NGOs at that time.

However, following the process of 'societalizing social welfare', more and more non-governmental welfare agencies have materialized. Indeed, according to the China Civil Affairs Statistical Yearbook, by the end of 2000, the number of beds provided by non-governmental welfare institutions had increased to 30,940, an 86.1 per cent increase on the previous year. Likewise, the number of personnel working in these non-governmental residential institutions had increased to 4,366 persons – an increase of more than 98.1 per cent over the previous year. Again, the number of residents cared for by them had increased to 19,451, an increase of more than 87.3 per cent over the previous year. Here, we see a significant expansion of non-governmental welfare agencies, which has definitely been in response to the policy of 'societalizing social welfare'.

Apart from this, there has also been a growth of non-governmental agencies in other fields of social care. For example, in some big cities like Beijing, Shanghai and Shenzhen, hotlines have been set up for such as adolescents, young people and women by various different individuals and organizations. They provide counselling services for people in trouble. Also at the level of community, various groups of volunteers participate in providing care for certain residents, or social services for the common good. In 1999, the All China Youth Federation set up a network for registering youth volunteers all over the country. These are all signs suggesting that the scale of voluntary action has increased outstandingly in China.

Yet the debates continue. How many of these services are to be regarded as truly voluntary? How are these different agencies, organizations and groups to be assessed as to whether or not they are really voluntary? Who should make the judgements? Moreover, even if all these non-governmental agencies were to be turned into voluntary actors, how then are they to be sustained?

The focus is on the nature of all kinds of non-governmental agencies, some of which are certainly not voluntary. They are private agencies, providing profit-making services. This has caused the quality of some services to decline. For instance, some private nursing homes for the elderly charge very little for providing care. But they may spend even less on housing, food or other things for their residents. So they can still make a profit. However, the government just thinks of them all as welfare agencies, not minding whether or not they are private or voluntary. In other service fields, the situation is similar. Some hotlines may operate according to the logic of a profit-winning actor. But the authorities don't care either way.

The government's attitude is clearly expressed in the speech quoted at the beginning of this chapter. It may be an understandable attitude, considering the scale of China's needs and the new ideology. Nevertheless, the problems uncovered should be addressed. In this period of transformation, perhaps the following points merit discussion in determining policy for the future. The need to:

- build up the assessment mechanism for NGO and voluntary services;
- reform the administration framework for voluntary services;
- set up financing arrangements to support voluntary action, including in respect of tax and donation systems.

The Development of Professional Social Work

When we turn to professional social work, we should appreciate that social work education had been developing in China before the communist revolution. Since the 1930s, a few universities and colleges had been providing social work programmes. Indeed there were about 20 programmes up until 1949. But after 1952 there were no more programmes like this; until in 1988, a social work programme was set up in the sociology department at Beijing University. This was the first, after the reform movement had begun. It should be pointed out that this programme was requested of the University by the Ministry of Civil Affairs, and that the first trainees were all from the civil administration system. Since this time, more and more social work programmes have been developed in different universities, colleges and schools. Among them, the China Youth College for Political Science established a department of social work and administration in 1993, which was the very first department of social work in post-reform China. By the end of 2000, according to an informal source, there were 70 to 80 social work programmes operating at various levels.

Besides this, overseas social work faculties have also taken an active part in training professional social workers or social work educators for mainland China. More and more people have gone abroad to take social work programmes, especially in Hong Kong. Some of these have come back to China, to teach in universities or to practise in different settings.

For many faculties of social work in China, the employment situation for their graduates is quite favourable. They don't need to worry much. In fact the choices are wide-ranging. Graduates can choose to be administrators in governmental organizations or to be managers in various institutions. Or they might work at community level, in street offices. It would seem that all the different levels and settings are in need of their services. Sometimes, indeed, such graduates wouldn't even choose to be frontline workers, owing to the other opportunities open to them. One could say that this last is correlated to the very process of 'societalizing social welfare'.

However, the link between social work education and the field of practical social care has so far mainly been built by individual faculties and agencies. It is only as the process of social welfare reform develops that the government becomes more conscious of its role in coordinating these two parts. At the end of 1999, a delegation from the Ministry of Civil Affairs, with the participation of several scholars, went to Hong Kong. Its mission was to investigate the registration system for social workers in Hong Kong and to draft suggestions for the Ministry of Personnel on setting up a similar system in China. This can be seen as a clear step towards the professionalization of social work.

In the viewpoint of officials from civil administration, it's both an urgent demand and a long-term strategy to turn its personnel into professionals. Since many critiques of recent policy have been for its effects on the declining quality of services, professionalization may be a solution. From a long-run perspective, it's also very important for professionals to contribute to welfare care so as to societalize social welfare. Although the advocacy of the Ministry of Civil Affairs for registering and ranking all social workers has not so far borne fruit, some programmes have materialized at municipal level. For example, the municipal civil administrations of Beijing and Shanghai have taken measures to register trained community workers. And in Shanghai, the authority is even exploring a ranking and rewards system for professional social workers and other social welfare personnel.

Perhaps the correct depiction of the current situation as regards the development of professional social work in China is as follows. The education has gone ahead of the practice, with the gap between the two yet to be closed.

Question to be Answered: What Prescriptions might there be for China's Situation?

The Chinese government's policy on 'societalizing social welfare', coupled with its orientation towards the development of non-governmental welfare agencies and professional social work, may be thought a reasonable response to the new situation. In the *Opinions* mentioned above, the necessity and urgency of pushing forward societalized social welfare was justified by current circumstances: the coming of an aged-population society, the changes in family structure, and the poor conditions of providing and caring for the elderly, the disabled and orphans. Surely these are true situations which together generate increasing demands for social welfare services which only a societalized social welfare system can meet (Ministry of Civil Affairs, etc. 2000). However, the policy choice to societalize social welfare is not to be justified by such objective facts. Rather, it is to be better understood in the context of the socialist market economy. The *Opinions* pointed out clearly the positive implications of societalizing social welfare for expanding domestic demand, sponsoring economic growth and increasing employment (Ministry of Civil Affairs, etc. 2000). In other words, this policy has a very important economic goal.

This can, in part, explain why the government is not too much bothered about the distinction between private and voluntary services. Or we can say that the government so far sees only the market as an alternative to the state in taking over roles and responsibilities for providing welfare care. It doesn't really recognize the role of the voluntary sector in this respect. But this is just reflecting the government's whole way of thinking after the reform. Isn't it?

Because of such a way of thinking, both government and society have taken a let-it-be attitude to non-governmental welfare services, without there being any clear definition of or encouragement for voluntary service. In the *Opinions*, we can see the role of voluntary actors only as complementing regular service personnel, which amounts to a marginal role in the whole welfare system. By contrast, the private sector has acquired an institutionalized and dominating role in reality. When people make more and more criticisms of the poor quality of services provided by private agencies, they just turn to professional social work for a solution.

Yet in this postmodern era, criticism of the professionals has been growing to the same extent as that of the private services, or even more. So how are we to rely on professionalism to safeguard the service users' rights and satisfaction?

The answer may be clear. The development of voluntary action is of key importance, not only for its own sake but for the sake of social care. Considering the political reality and social traditions of China, however, it may have a very long way to go. In this respect, questions of social policy have much to do with social politics.

References

Department of Social Welfare and Social Affairs, Ministry of Civil Affairs of China (2000), *Collection of Documents on Work for Societalizing Social Welfare* (internal).

Department of Finance and Administration, Ministry of Civil Affairs of China (2001), *China Civil Affairs' Statistical Yearbook 2001*, China Statistics Press, Beijing.

Ministry of Civil Affairs, etc. (2000), 'Opinions on speeding up the materialization of societalizing social welfare', in *Collection of Documents on Work for Societalizing Social Welfare*, (ed.) Department of Social Welfare and Social Affairs, Ministry of Civil Affairs (internal).

Titmuss, Richard (1974): *Social Policy: An Introduction*, George Allen and Unwin, London.

Chapter 19
Voluntary Action, Social Care and Social Work: A UK Response

Nicholas Deakin and Ann Davis

Introduction

The blanket expression 'societalizing social welfare' (Tao Chen, previous chapter) will not be familiar to political, academic and professional audiences in the UK. Yet the items embraced under this heading in China – the precise role and responsibilities of the state *vis à vis* other agencies in the field of social welfare; the boundaries between what should and should not properly be termed 'voluntary action'; shifting perceptions with regard to the nature and prospects of professional social work – should certainly strike a chord in Britain. All the same, there are glaring contrasts of context and 'path-contingencies' to be taken into account. The fact that Britain happens to have had a longer and more continuous history of development in the voluntary welfare sector, and thence also in notions of (e.g. voluntary versus statutory and professional versus 'amateur') social work, does not of course put this country automatically in a position to offer lessons to China, as if both were simply at different stages along the same path towards the same objectives.

What we can do, however, is to offer summary accounts of recent relevant developments in the UK, in the hope that these may serve as a useful, cautionary points of reference for professionals, researchers and policy-makers in China.

In the first section below, Nicholas Deakin reviews the characteristics and directions of the voluntary sector in the UK. In the second section, Ann Davis considers the ways in which the transforming terrain of social welfare in the UK has impacted on social work and social care.

The Voluntary Sector in the UK

Over the past decade, the question of the future pattern of relations between state and voluntary (or 'third') sector has become a major issue both in the UK and other developed Western democracies. The trajectory of the debate about these relations has been traced in detail in the major international comparative study being undertaken from the United States by a team from Johns Hopkins University (Salamon and Anheier 1997). This study, which extends beyond the United States and Western Europe to encompass the so-called 'transition' countries and other less developed states has produced a shelf full of country monographs based on a common system of classification (the ICNPO) developed by the coordinators of the study and has exposed a series of common themes.

From these studies and other recent investigations of these topics (e.g. Borzaga and Defourny 2001) the main driving forces behind the emergence of these issues can be summarized as being, first and primarily, the so-called 'retreat of the state', driven by a loss of confidence in the capacity of the public sector to deliver services in contested areas with the efficiency and of the quality (legitimately) expected by the recipients of those services.

Some of the factors precipitating this retreat have been the more assertive role played by the users of services and a general impatience with what has been perceived as the poor performance of large public bureaucracies and the risk they pose of producer capture – the tactics of 'bureau maximizing' anatomized by the public choice economists.

These perceptions led, in their most extreme form, to the move from the 1980s onwards towards the privatization of public services and, in less dramatic versions, to a drive to 'modernize' the state apparatus by withdrawing from carrying out functions that had previously been performed entirely by public agencies and recasting the form of those services retained within the state sector by the introduction of techniques and disciplines drawn from the private sector. (This is the 'managerialism and market orientation' referred to in the previous chapter, known generically in OECD countries as 'The New Public Management').

These developments are by no means confined to the areas of welfare and human services, but their impact is especially clear in these sectors. Change has acquired additional momentum by the introduction of the concept of citizens as consumers, seen as having needs which have to be satisfied on terms and conditions as close to those in the marketplace as possible. This thinking lies behind the approach adopted by the previous (Conservative) UK government and its 'Citizen's Charter'.

Alongside this withdrawal of the state – executed unevenly and at different rates in different countries, but a universal phenomenon across the OECD – there has emerged what Lester Salamon and Helmut Anheier have termed the 'global associational revolution', based on the rapid expansion of voluntary activity that their studies have documented. This widespread perception of the growth of the 'third sector' has led in turn to the view that the sector now has the competence to carry out functions surrendered to the welfare state during the period of its expansion. Furthermore, it is widely held that this is a healthy development, on wider policy grounds: the expansion of voluntary action, it is suggested, encourages self-help, enhances citizen responsibility and helps to build up and reinforce 'civic culture' (Brown 2001).

There is indeed substantial evidence that there has been a rapid expansion of the UK voluntary sector over the past ten years. Work undertaken for the (2001) current review of the voluntary sector's role being carried out in the Cabinet Office by Les Hems of University College London shows that this expansion has fallen into two phases: a period of rapid expansion in the first half of the decade, followed by a period of relative stagnation. By the turn of the century, there were 185,000 registered charities and between 300,000 and half a million voluntary and community organizations (complex questions of definition, as always in this field, make greater precision impossible). The total income of general charities was estimated at £14.2 billion, a third of which was concentrated in the 150 or so largest organizations. The total assets of general charities were estimated at £65 billion, and there were 514,000 paid workers in the sector, representing 2.2 per cent of the total UK workforce. These charities benefit from the contribution of over 3 million unpaid volunteers (Hems 2001).

The voluntary sector generally benefits from government financial support, now officially estimated as running at over £1 billion per year (Hems 2001) and from private donations – the total sums donated each year now amount to £7.750 billion, of which £6 billion are individual donations, £1.3 billion from foundations and trusts and £450 million from companies (Wright 2002). Rates of participation in giving are relatively high in Britain compared with other Western countries, although the average amounts donated are low and have only increased marginally, despite attempts by the government to promote a 'culture of giving' (Passey et al. 2002).

The notion that the UK voluntary and community sector has the potential in terms of scale and access to resources to undertake a more significant role therefore rests on more than simply rhetoric. However, such claims for enhanced roles and responsibilities for voluntary organizations raise a number of problematic issues, which have been widely debated in the UK in the recent past.

The first and obvious practical question is whether voluntary agencies do in practice have the capacity to deliver a much wider range of services to the standard now required. Comparative studies of small-scale providers of services in areas like care for the elderly suggest that the comparative advantage that the voluntary sector possesses in terms of efficiency and customer satisfaction is not great (Taylor and Hoggett 1994). Moreover, large bureaucratic organizations are not to be found only in the state sector: similar problems of scale and sensitivity to users' needs also occur in some larger voluntary sector organizations. And smaller organizations, which might be expected to be more flexible and adapt more readily to users' preferences often lack the capacity to deliver high-quality services and the necessary range of skills and expertise (Rochester 1998).

These difficulties are exacerbated when voluntary bodies have to function within the restrictions imposed by the New Public Management, which imposes the same regime of tests of quality to be delivered and targets to be attained that it requires of other contractors. By entering the universe of the 'mixed economy of welfare' and competing for contracts with agencies from the private (and public) sector, voluntary bodies are of necessity required to surrender some of their distinctive qualities, in order to be able to compete successfully. The introduction of business values and techniques, refracted through the systems imposed in the New Public management and the insistence on competition in that environment are examples that have often been given of this process of convergence in style of operation, management and organizational structure. These developments have attracted much commentary and criticism: in the more extreme form, voluntary bodies have been accused of selling their souls for financial security (Dahrendorf 2001).

One point that critics have strongly emphasized is that service delivery should not be seen as the only or even the main legitimate role of voluntary bodies. The tasks of representation and campaigning can be compromised by overemphasizing provision, just as the introduction of greater professionalism in delivery (as suggested in the Chinese paper) may tend to squeeze out distinctive third-sector values.

There is a further, and in some respects even more complex issue, and that is accountability: to whom and how should voluntary organizations performing tasks, funded in part or in whole out of public funds, be accountable? There are a number of possible answers, none of them wholly satisfactory. Clearly 'funders', particularly those who make public money available on contract terms, have a legitimate expectation that the providers will be accountable for the service they are contracted to provide. But the local community and their elected representative also have a legitimate interest: so do the users of the services (the 'consumers'), and the staff – and volunteers – engaged in providing the service. Not all these different forms of accountability can be satisfied in the same way: performance measures can be constructed that may be sufficient to satisfy funders but conceal the impact of internal changes that affect staff and fail to meet tests of closer community involvement.

In a number of Western countries, significant anniversaries have recently provided opportunities to reconsider these themes. In England, there has been the four-hundredth anniversary of the founding statute of English charity law (1601); in France, the hundredth of the Loi Waldeck-Rousseau (1901), legitimizing the role of associations previously held to be problematic by centralists of all political hues. There has further been some rethinking of the state's regulatory functions, including a Commission of Inquiry in Scotland (Scottish Executive 2001) which is likely to lead to legislation in the devolved Parliament in Edinburgh. Similar questions are being explored in England and Wales, first by an independent inquiry mounted by the NCVO (Tumim 2001) and latterly by the Cabinet Office's investigation (yet to report at the time of writing). Issues around the definition of charity and the benefits that should flow from it in he various common law jurisdictions have been the subject of a number of international conferences. The notion that in order to attract tax exemptions and other legal benefits', charitable activity must be demonstrably of public benefit has been gaining ground. There is an implied bargain here: the state as regulator exerting its jurisdiction over the different forms in which philanthropic action is taken in order to ensure that collective gains flow from individual activities.

Just as the issues around the state's relationship to voluntary action are common, so have been the attempts to resolve them. The means most favoured currently is 'partnership'. Key examples here are the introduction in 1998 of the government-voluntary sector compact in England (followed by similar action in Scotland) and in France, the charter signed in July 2001 (flattering the Anglo-Saxons by sincere imitation). The intention of all these initiatives (and other similar ones taken elsewhere in Europe and in Canada) is to codify rights and responsibilities and draw a clear demarcation line between the state and the third sector. In practice, distinctions blur – some third sector organizations have crossed the line and become state agencies in all but name; others operate on the state's turf, with its funding and on its terms, yet have succeeded in retaining their independence of action. One of the important features of the original English Compact is that it entrenches the right of voluntary bodies to criticize and dissent – statutory bodies have in the past often found it difficult to accept that they may on occasion find themselves funding their own critics.

As William Plowden's recent critique has demonstrated (Plowden et al. 2001), the role and status of smaller bodies and those seeking to represent unpopular groups or to advocate controversial ideas is at perpetual risk of being compromised. Yet it can be too easy to sentimentalize small bodies, to talk – as Conservative politicians, following Edmund Burke, so often did – of the 'little platoons' to which we owe our primary loyalties. The active citizens whom they sought to summon up in defence of traditional values (and property, in the case of their 'Neighbourhood Watch' schemes) can, given other circumstances, become vigilantes, not reinforcing but subverting the rule of law.

The essential point, and the one that makes all generalization about state-voluntary organization relations perilous, is that in reality there is no such thing as a 'voluntary sector', in the sense of a coherent entity with sharply demarcated boundaries. Rather, there is an infinite diversity of different kinds of organizations of different types and sizes, performing different functions in different styles. Such diversity is the hallmark of a healthy civil society: it is in many respects self-correcting: if the older organizations become compromised (and some have and more will), new ones will emerge to pursue independent objectives. The critics of current developments are right to warn of dangers that are real enough, but their pessimism can be overdone. Provided that the web of relations now being spun is sufficiently flexible to license dissent and admit the critics and advocates of unpopular causes and those that cater for the excluded, a closer working understanding between all parties can only be beneficial.

Social Work in the UK

Social work in the UK has had, over the past 150 years, a continuous but changing presence in the voluntary and state social care sectors. Its remit, and the space it occupies in the social welfare field, has been shaped and reshaped over time by governments responding to the troubling or troublesome situations of citizens. It has, throughout its history, mediated between such citizens and the state with a mandate to provide both care for, and the surveillance of, those with whom it comes into contact. Positioned as it is, it highlights the changes through time of the state's relationship to citizens and their families. This is a politically and socially contentious area of work and one which occupies what Parton has described as 'an essentially contested and ambiguous position'(Parton 1996).

The methods and skills used by social workers embrace interventions with communities, groups, families and individuals. In contrast to other European countries, social workers in the UK focus primarily on the social welfare sphere – rather than making a wider contribution to the spheres of employment, social security, education and community development (Munday and Ely 1996; Payne and Shardlow 2002). Within the state and voluntary social welfare sectors, social workers are employed in a range of services-known as the personal social services. These services constitute a very small part of government welfare expenditure and have contact with a tiny minority of citizens, most of them being from poor and socially excluded groups. (Glennerster and Hills 1998; Baldock 1997).

The personal social services comprise a diverse range of activities and provision, designed to care for and control individuals and families who find themselves unable to meet their own needs for welfare. They respond to individuals and families whose vulnerability or behaviour are assessed as warranting intervention. Such responses are provided from community and residential bases for older people, disabled people, young people, children and families.

It is estimated that one million workers are employed in the state, voluntary and commercial social care sectors in Britain. Only 14 per cent of these workers are actually social workers – 90 per cent of whom hold a professional qualification. Some 80 per cent of the remainder – i.e. social care staff – have no job related qualification (TOPPS 2001). The distinction made between social care and social work in the UK is one which defines social care as 'activities which provide ongoing supervision, support and care', as distinct from 'the focused, interventions, assessments and legal duties' undertaken by qualified social workers.

There is currently a lack of qualified social workers in the UK. Recent estimates are that 70 per cent of state sector social services cannot recruit enough qualified social workers to deliver their front line services. As a response to this growing crisis in social work recruitment and retention, the government launched a national campaign in 2001 to encourage more people to become social workers. At the same time the government is pursuing major changes in relation to the training, accreditation and regulation of the profession. These changes will be introduced in 2003. They will bring in a requirement for Universities to design and deliver three year programmes of social work education and training which meet national requirements with regard to the academic and practice learning curricula.

This new form of training will prepare social workers to enter employment for a probationary year, during which they will be asked to demonstrate their competence as practitioners, in order to be registered as qualified professionals by a new government appointed body: the General Social Care Council (GSCC). This body, chaired by a lay person – and with a membership in which service users and lay people will be in the majority – is being funded by government to protect the public, to accredit training and to regulate membership of the profession through registration. Its objectives, as outlined by the government's *Modernising Social Services* white paper, include ensuring that, together, social care and social work staff provide a service 'which allows and assists individuals live their own lives' (DoH 1988: 88). To achieve this, a range of initiatives is also being launched to address the basic training needs of existing and potential social care workers. These latter initiatives are typically offered in ways which accredit the practice of employees in social care agencies.

The current position of social work in relation to social welfare, social care and voluntary action in the UK has been shaped by the changing social and political terrain of welfare policy and provision, as outlined above in this chapter by Nicholas Deakin. At the same time there have been specific influences on the demands made on social work, as the result of demographic and wider social changes. Whilst it is true that social work makes only a small contribution, quantitatively speaking, to welfare in the statutory and voluntary sectors, its contribution is nevertheless symbolically significant. For this reason, tracking the relationship of social work and social care to voluntary action and state intervention in the UK, can offer key insights into the potential significance of such relationships for other societies in social and economic transition.

The Origins of Social Work

The origins of social work in the UK can be traced back to the ways in which nineteenth century Britain, struggling with the social and economic transformations consequent upon an emerging capitalist order, began to manage the welfare needs of its citizens. Early social workers – mainly unpaid and untrained women from the middle classes – worked in a growing range of voluntary sector welfare organizations. Their remit was to supplement basic and residual state welfare provision by assessing and meeting the needs of the rapidly growing numbers of poor people and their families, who were unable to maintain themselves in a rapidly changing, industrializing social order (Brook and Davis 1985; Rooff 1972; Walton 1975). From these beginnings, social work in Britain reflected a concern to both protect and strengthen society, and at the same time conditionally to support some of its most vulnerable members: those most suffering the socially undesirable consequences of nineteenth century economic enterprise and development (Jordan 2000, 2001).

Recognition of the distinct contribution of social work to social care in the largely voluntary sector-based welfare organizations of the twentieth century, was reflected in the gradual involvement of Universities, from the first decade of the twentieth century, in social work training. These early efforts at professional education, drawing on the social sciences, aimed to integrate values, knowledge and skills in the pursuit of better practice. The hallmark of the UK's approach to training for the profession was one of working to integrate academic and practice learning (Walton 1975).

The establishment of what became known as the 'Welfare State' in Britain, in the late 1940s, played a significant part in shifting the location, as well as the training and employment prospects, of social workers. Expanding state provision in health, welfare and education services opened up a wealth of new opportunities for social work and social care, and increasing numbers of men joined this burgeoning profession (Brook and Davis 1985; Orme 2001). Social workers were expected at this time to provide a final safety net for individuals whose needs had not been met by other services in the state sector. In responding to this mandate, more and more social workers found themselves moving, in effect, from being the employees of a diminishing number of voluntary sector welfare agencies, to becoming government employees in local authority, health and education services.

This shift of social work to the state sector during the 1950s and 1960s, meant that it established itself alongside other welfare state professionals such as doctors, teachers and nurses (Langan 1993). The contribution of social work to social welfare at this time was recognised, in the early 1970s, with the establishment of unitary local government social services and social work departments. This new 'fifth social service' was intended to replace the hitherto fragmented array of specialist personal social services. In short it was to be a universal state service – alongside health, education, social security and housing – responding to individual and family needs; with a mandate to build stronger communities, by enabling 'the greatest number of individuals to act reciprocally, giving and receiving services for the wellbeing of the community' (Seebohm 1968: 15).

To further the establishment of social work as a generic profession, rather than a federated grouping of specialisms, a generic professional qualification in social work, was introduced in 1971 by government – the Certificate of Qualification in Social Work. This offered a system of education and training, through Universities and Colleges, which was designed to combine assessment of practice with academic studies, in equal measure.

Marketization, Managerialism and Marginalization

The election of a government, headed by Margaret Thatcher, with her strongly declared opposition to public sector welfare in 1979, marked the beginning of a move away from the 'Welfare State' response to the provision of social welfare in the UK – and with it a new direction for social work and social care. Successive Conservative governments made it clear, thereafter, that it was the family that should be taking major responsibility for meeting the welfare needs of its members. Independence from state provision was the hallmark of the responsible citizen. This emphasis on increasing private and decreasing public responsibility for welfare provision in the 1980s and 1990s, brought with it two privatizing patterns of reform (Clarke et al. 2000), which were to reshape the relationship of social work to social welfare.

On the one hand, there was a drive to introduce marketization into the provision of welfare services. To realise this, state social welfare organizations in the 1980s were given a remit to assess the need for personal social services and then to purchase these from providers in the voluntary and commercial sectors. This promotion of a 'mixed economy' in social welfare transformed the practice of many social workers within the state sector. Social workers found themselves withdrawn from their previous role of working proactively and preventively with individuals, families and communities. They were required instead to undertake needs- and risk-assessments in order to determine which citizens were eligible to receive packages of services from a range of providing agencies (Holman 1998; Jordan 2000).

It was in the area of work with vulnerable adults that the most radical changes were made to the role of state welfare services and, thence, to the role of social workers within them. The Griffiths Report on Community Care (Griffiths 1988) recommended that local authority social service departments should cease to be major providers of welfare services. Instead, they were to become assessors of need and brokers to a range of suppliers of care services. The National Health Service and Community Care Act 1990 enacted these recommendations, bringing in the most far reaching changes in the financing, organization and delivery of social care services since the 1940s. As a result of this legislation, state sector social workers were assigned the role of care managers, assessing needs and organizing the delivery of packages of care by voluntary sector and commercial agencies.

At the same time, recourse to these services was increasingly being framed as a mark of individual and family failure. Dependency on state welfare provision, across the range, was seen as evidence of irresponsibility. In pursuing this theme, successive governments took steps to restrict the circumstances in which citizens could access publicly funded welfare services. These steps increased the stigmatization of state social welfare. As a result, both its recipients and those employed to make decisions about access to services, found themselves subject to criticism and hostile scrutiny by government and the media (Franklin and Parton 1991). As Clarke et al. comment 'these privatising shifts both diminished the scale and significance of public provision and celebrated the value of the private (in both senses) over the public' (Clarke et al. 2000: 3).

This transformation of the organizational, legal and political frameworks in which social workers practised, was delivered by new managerialist approaches to the organisation of the personal social services. Government increased its centralizing role in setting standards and indicators of delivery and performance; and social workers were increasingly subject to such forms of scrutiny and monitoring (Clarke and Newman 1997). In this climate, social workers found themselves in the 'firing line' symbolizing, as they did, a past, discredited approach to social welfare provision. The value-base of a profession which subscribed to the promotion of social justice and anti-discriminatory practice was vilified – and, with it, so was social work as a credible modern response to need. Social workers' practice became subject to increasingly negative scrutiny in the public arena, and members of the profession found their work devalued and critiqued (Langan 1998).

The changes in social work education and training introduced in the early 1990s represented an attempt, by government, to bring social work in line with the transformed social welfare order. A new professional qualification – the Diploma in Social Work – was introduced. It required Universities and colleges to enter into partnerships with employing agencies in order jointly to deliver training courses through two year programmes. These partnerships were subject to a set of national requirements detailing the value-, knowledge- and skills-base necessary for practice competence in social work.

Despite these major changes in the organizational and legal context of the occupation, the majority of social work practitioners remained directly employed by publicly funded welfare organizations (Balloch et al. 1999). In the voluntary sector the numbers of qualified social workers represented a tiny minority of its growing and largely unqualified social care workforce. Social work continued to be a predominantly female workforce at the front line, but with men occupying most of the top managerial positions (Davis 1996; Balloch et al. 1999). Women also constituted the majority of the users of social work services.

As Schorr observed, in his review of the major state social work agencies in the UK in the early 1990s, 'the most striking characteristic that clients of the personal social services have in common are poverty and deprivation' (1992: 8). Since Schorr's review of social work, its strong connection with poverty has intensified. Not least, the increase in the numbers of citizens living in poverty in the UK during the 1980s and 1990s has resulted in a growth in demand for state social welfare services (Becker 1997). Faced with this reality, state-funded social welfare agencies have became increasingly involved in rationing, through their assessments of need in the face of relatively diminishing resources (Glennerster and Hills 1998).

While the return of a New Labour government in the late 1990s implied there would be new approaches to the field of social welfare, particularly as regards recognition of the impact of poverty and social exclusion on family and community life, the New Labour establishment was also to keep faith with some of the ideas developed by previous governments. In describing its distinctive 'Third Way' for social welfare, the first New Labour administration referred to the need 'to move the focus away from who provides the care and place it firmly on the quality of services experienced by, and the outcomes achieved for individuals, their carers and families' [DoH 1988: 8).

The 'Modernising of Social Services: promoting independence, improving protection and raising standards' government white paper (DoH 1998) set in place centrally determined regulations, standards and qualifications for accrediting, targeting and measuring outcomes in social welfare, social care and social work.

These are now being used to monitor the performance of social services departments, in respect of a continuingly restrictive and conditional set of requirements that social workers are expected to deliver. The initiatives which New Labour governments have set in place to combat social exclusion and poverty in disadvantaged communities are being funded through new partnerships, between the voluntary and statutory sectors, that effectively exclude social workers and their employing agencies from playing a key role (Jordan 2001).

Prospects for Social Work?

Social work in the UK has been shaped and re-shaped in recent years by a variety of factors relating to changes in the social, political, legal and organizational structures delivering social welfare. Social workers in the statutory and voluntary welfare sectors in Britain remain critically positioned, at the point where social inequality shapes choice, direction and the possibilities of life, for some of the poorest citizens. The themes of family life, poverty and social exclusion still powerfully construct the encounters which daily take place between practitioners and service users (Davis 1991; Becker 1997). Faced with this reality, social work has continued to subscribe to a value-base which talks of the need to empower those who are disadvantaged and address issues of oppression and discrimination. Yet it has become increasingly confined in its scope and creativity, as it works through a fragmented patchwork of state, voluntary sector and commercial agencies that are required to meet tightly prescribed standards and outcomes, within restricted budgets.

Operating within what Jordan has described as 'a new regulatory landscape', social work is struggling to assert itself as a profession with a potential to work responsively and creatively, in partnership with those who are socially excluded. Its values, which emphasize the promotion of social justice and anti-discriminatory and empowering practice, cannot fully be articulated within the organisational frameworks in which it finds itself. The challenge currently facing social work is how *conceivable* it is to deliver – according to its own appreciation of, and concern for, issues of social justice – from the restricted position it now occupies in Britain's social welfare arena.

Conclusions for China?

It is not necessary to be passing through – or anticipating – precisely the same sets of predicaments in order to be able to learn lessons from the experience of others (see Chapters 2 and 3 in this volume). Britain and China are manifestly some distance apart with regard to the treatment, rights and life-chances of particular vulnerable groups; the scope for manoeuvre on the part of non-statutory, non-profit, social service providers; and the prospects for the emergence/consolidation of an independent, fully professionalized, popularly accredited, social work profession.

Yet one does not have to invoke elaborate theories of convergence in order to assume that, in the context of globalization and hence workshops such as ours, there will be increasing opportunity as well as intention to try to cherry-pick the fruits of others' experience. Let us hope that it will indeed be workshops – rather than mere international traffic on a one-off grant/self funding or profit-making basis – which informs what looks set to be a mounting traffic in 'international exchange'.

References

Baldock, J. (1997) 'The personal social services and community care' in P. Alcock et al, *The Student's Companion to Social Policy*, Blackwell, Oxford.
Balloch, S., Maclean, J. and Fisher, M. (eds) (1999) *Social Services working under Pressure*, Policy Press, Bristol.
Becker, S. (1997) *Responding to Poverty: the politics of cash and care*, Longman, Harlow.
Borzaga, C. and Defourny, J. (2001) *The Emergence of Social Enterprise:* Routledge, London.
Brook, E and Davis, A. (eds) (1985) *Women, The Family and Social Work*. Tavistock Publications, London.
Brown, G. (2001) *Civic Society in Modern Britain*, The 17th Arnold Goodman Lecture, The Smith Institute, London.
Clarke, J. and Newman J. (1997) *The Managerial State: Power, Politics and Ideology in the Remaking of Social Welfare*, Sage, London.
Clarke, J., Gerwitz, S., Hughes, G, and Humphreys, J. (eds) (2000) *New Managerialism, New Welfare?* Sage, London.
Dahrendorf, R. (2001), *Challenges to the Voluntary Sector*, 18th Arnold Goodman Lecture, Charities Aid Foundation, London.
Davis, A. (1991) 'Hazardous Lives: social work in the 1980s: a view from the Left', in M. Loney et al (eds) *The State or the Market: Politics and Welfare in Contemporary Britain*, Sage, London.
Davis, A. (1996) 'Women and the personal social services' in C. Hallett (ed) *Women and Social Policy: An Introduction*, Prentice Hall, London.
Department of Health (1998) *Modernising Social Services: Promoting Independence, Improving Protection, Raising Standards.* Cm. 4169. Stationery Office, London.
Franklin, M. and Parton, N. (eds) (1991) *Social Work, The Media and Public Relations*, Routledge, London.
Glennerster, H. and Hills, J. (eds) (1998) *The State of Welfare: The Economics of Social Spending*, Oxford University Press, Oxford.
Griffiths (1988) *Community Care: An Agenda for Action*, HMSO, London.
Hems, L. (2001), *The Organizational and Institutional Landscape of the Wider UK Non-profit Sector*, Performance and Innovation Unit, Cabinet Office, London.
Holman, R. (1998) Neighbourhoods and Exclusion in M. Barry and C. Hallett (eds) *Social Exclusion and Social Work: Issues of Theory, Policy and Practice*, Russell House, Dorset.
Jordan, B. (2000) *Social Work and the Third Way: Tough Love as Social Policy*, Sage, London.
Jordan, B. (2001) 'Tough Love: Social Work, Social Exclusion and the Third Way'. *British Journal of Social Work*, 31: pp 527–546.
Langan, M. (1993) 'The rise and fall of social work' in J. Clarke (ed) *A Crisis in Care? Challenges to Social Work*, Sage, London.
Langan. M. (1998) 'The personal social services' in N. Ellison and C. Pierson (eds) *Developments in British Social Policy*, Macmillan, London.
Munday, B. and Ely, P. (1996) (eds) *Social Care in Europe*, Prentice Hall, Harvester Wheatsheaf, Hemel Hempstead.
Orme, J. (2001) *Gender and Social Work: social work and social care perspectives*: Palgrave, Basingstoke.
Parton, N. (1996) 'Social theory, social change and social work: an introduction', in N. Parton (ed) *Social Theory, Social Change and Social Work*, Routledge, London.

Passey, A., Jass, P., Wilding, K., Wainwright, H. and Hems, L. *The UK Voluntary Sector Almanac 2002*: NCVO, London.
Payne, M. and Shardlow, S. (eds) (2002) *Social Work in the British Isles*, Jessica Kingsley, London.
Plowden, W. et al (2001) *Next Steps in Voluntary Action*: NCVO and Centre for Civil Society, London.
Rochester, C. (1998) *Juggling on a Unicycle*: Centre for Civil Society, London.
Rooff, M. (1972) *A Hundred Years of Family Welfare: a study of the Family Welfare Association*, Joseph, London.
Salamon, L.A. and Anheier, H. (1997) *Defining the Non-Profit Sector: a cross-national analysis*, Manchester University Press, Manchester.
Schorr, A (1992) *The Personal Social Services: an outsider view*, Joseph Rowntree Foundation, York.
Scottish Executive (2001) *Charity Scotland*; The report of the Scottish Charity Law Reform Commission, The Scottish Executive, Edinburgh.
Seebohm (1968) *Report of the Committee on Local Authority and Allied Personal Social Services*, HMSO, London.
Taylor, M. and Hoggett P. (1994) 'Quasi-Markets and the Independent Sector' in Bartlett, W. (ed) *Quasi-Markets in the Welfare State*, Bristol, Policy Press.
TOPPS (2001) *Annual Report on Social Care*, TOPPS, England.
Tumim, W. (2001) *For the Public Benefit?* A consultation document on charity law reform. NCVO, London.
Walton, R. (1975) *Women and Social Work*, Routledge and Kegan Paul, London.
Woodroofe, K. (1962) *From Charity to Social Work*, Routledge and Kegan Paul, London.
Wright, K. (2002) *Britain's Culture of Giving*, Centre for Civil Society, London.

Chapter 20

Afterword

Catherine Jones Finer

As explained at the outset (Chapter 1), this book is the product of a workshop, held at St Antony's College Oxford, October 19–20, 2001, on *Social Policy Reform in Socialist Market China: the Scope for Lessons For and From Abroad*. But, as was also implied, the project was intended to function as part of a broader and longer term comparative social policy endeavour, in respect of both China in particular and Asia Pacific in general. At this stage, therefore, it is worth reflecting on possible next steps.[1]

Certainly the workshop was well attended, not merely by interested academics and notably Chinese graduate students from within Oxford University, but by a range of other academics and researchers from 'near and far', at least within Europe. The quality of the audience, in conjunction with the quality of the speakers, made for vigorous and rigorous question-and-answer sessions punctuating proceedings, both formally and informally, throughout the period of the workshop. Predictably, the final rumbustious, evaluative session was primarily about 'what should come next?' (a positive variant on the *so what?* factor!) as a follow-up to what the workshop itself had managed to achieve and to stimulate. At this most basic level, therefore, the workshop exercise had at least passed 'GO'.

Suggestions for the Future fell into Three Broad Categories

First and most obvious, there were those emphasizing the need for much more detailed follow-up collaborative research and writing, in relation to each of the social policy sectors introduced in Part 2 of this volume. The enormity of the social policy challenges and dilemmas facing China, coupled with the evident willingness of its experts to consult abroad, ought – other things being equal! – to signify optimum prospects for future 'sectoral' comparative social policy (CSP) colla-boration; provided funds are made sufficiently available, from somewhere. How long before *Chinese* definitions of 'policy sectors' (e.g. with regard to different categories of workers, or families or residents) come to dictate a CSP agenda, remains an open question.

Second, were those emphasizing the need for varieties of basic research of the sort the present, 'practical', policy-useful, project could not hope to have encompassed. On the one hand, there was the need for enhanced theoretical, conceptual research into the nature of different systems of social welfare provision and how these were to be distinguished from one another (whether or not on an east-west basis). On the other, as was also emphasized, there was need for a sustained programme of 'consumerist research' in China, if only to map the evidently shifting states of popular opinion and confidence with regard to the future.

Third and finally, questions were raised as to the extent to which China should be regarded as part of the Asia Pacific region, for CSP purposes, as opposed to the one-off experiment in 'a socialist market with Chinese characteristics' which so many of its publicists have emphasized. Once again this takes us right to the heart of the comparative endeavour. To what extent is CSP supposed to be comparing 'like with like' (as arguably in the case of welfare state Europe or, alternatively, the Tigers – Japan included – of Asia Pacific), as against conspicuous 'unlikes' who may nevertheless have identifiable common problems and common points of response. Or, alternatively again, is China simply to be regarded as incomparable?

This last would surely be a staggering admission of self-denying defeat for CSP.

Notes

1   I am indebted to three key attendants at the workshop – who were not themselves paper-givers – for contributing to the following observations: Jane Duckett, Head of the Chinese Studies Programme at Glasgow University; Hatla Thelle, Senior Researcher at the Danish Centre for Human Rights; and Lin Ka, Researcher in the Department of Social Policy and Administration at the University of Tampere, Finland.

Index

academia, policy process 41–2
Academy of Social Sciences, Beijing 2
Age Barriers Project 150
age discrimination, and early retirement 150
All-China Federation of Trade Unions 108
Aristotle 11

Blair, Tony 89
blat 18
Britain
  charities 234–5
  council house sales 192–3
  divorce rate 221
  family policy 215–16
  JSA 121
  labour market
    deregulation 120
    gender differences 117–18
    standards 120
    unemployment 117
  Labour Party, Third Way 241
  New Deal programmes 122–4
  pension reforms 145–8
  poverty
    and employment 92
    programme 89–90
  PRC, comparison 89
  social inequality, measurement 91
  social work 238–42
  trade unions, role 120
  unemployed workers, training 121–2
  unemployment
    benefits 120–21
    policy 120
    regional variations 118
  voluntary sector 233–7
  welfare reform 122
  welfare state 10–11, 29
  women
    births, marital/extramarital 222
    cohabitation 222
    economic activity 221
    lone-mother families 223
  workless households 118–19
British Academy 2

British General Household Survey 217

care work, unpaid 218–19
CCP (Chinese Communist Party) 2, 25
  economic reforms 38–9
  organizational structure 26
  policy
    formulation 42–4
    implementation 44–6
  policy making, dominant role 37–8
  policy process 47–8
  political
    campaigns 45
    reforms 39–40
charities, Britain 234–5
China *see* PRC (People's Republic of China)
China/UK CSP workshop 2
civil affairs, expenditure 56, 57
civil society, PRC 26
cohabitation, women, Britain 222
contexts
  and historians 10–11
  national, and public policies 7, 9, 10, 11–12
  and universals, interaction 12
contextual knowledge, and economic models 9
contingencies, and lesson drawing 12–13
convergence theory, socialist states 30
council house sales, Britain 192–3
CSP (Comparative Social Policy) 1
Cultural Revolution, PRC 8, 25, 32

danwei 39, 227
Deng Xiaoping 39
Denmark, labour mobility 119
deregulation, Britain, labour market 120
developing countries, welfare provision, need for 83
divorce law, changes 219

early retirement
  and age discrimination 150
  and pension reforms 144
Eastern Europe, housing system 191–2
economic changes, and social benefits

entitlements 158–9
economic competitiveness
　and poverty 81
　and social inequality 81, 92
economic growth
　catching up 19–20
　PRC 52
　and unemployment 61, 63
economic models
　and contextual knowledge 9
　limitations 9–10
economic policy, PRC 25
economic reform
　CCP 38–9
　PRC 32
　and social inequality 92–4
economic state
　meaning 30–31
　PRC as 31–3
EEHM (Eastern European Housing Model) 191–2
　Ivan Szelenyi on 192
egalitarianism 75
EHCP (European Community Household Panel), poverty, and unemployment 121
elderly, health services 163
employment
　by types of enterprise 62, 98, 160–61
　change frequency 100
　and health problems 151
　informal contacts, use 98, 99
　state sector 98
　see also unemployment
employment policies
　John Major 122
　Margaret Thatcher 121
employment status, and labour mobility 100–101
entitlement groups, health services 161–2
Esping-Andersen, G., *The Three Worlds of Welfare Capitalism* 11
ESSRC (Economic and Social Science Research Council) 2
EU (European Union)
　pension reforms
　　details 144–5
　　and early retirement 144
　　and the labour market 148–50
　　and longevity 144
　　pension postponement 150
Europe, welfare state, development 17–18

expenditure
　civil affairs 56, 57
　welfare provision 60

family, and welfare provision 18
family policy, Britain 215
family structure, and individualization 216–17
friendly societies, development 18–19
Fukuyama, Francis 18
fungibility, policies 7

GDP (Gross Domestic Product), PRC 20, 51
gender differences
　British labour market 117–18
　laid-off workers 101
　migrants, labour mobility 104
　unemployment 102
gender issues, and gender inequalities 215
Gini coefficient, social inequality 72, 90–91
globalization, and social inequality 73–5
GPP (General Public Policy) 3, 28
　model 33–4
　PRC 33
　socialist states 29
　welfare state, as part 30
　see also social policy
grameen banks 18
guanxi 18

health care
　OECD countries 172
　PRC
　　flexibility 172–3
　　supply side 173–4
　WHO league table 170
health care finance
　'Singapore model' 155
　urban 155
health insurance, reforms 163–5
health problems
　and employment 151
　and retirement 150–51
health services
　elderly 163
　entitlement groups 161–2
　reforms 162–6
Heraclitus 11
historians, and contexts 10–11
history, and lessons from history 11
HIV/AIDS
　epidemic 158

prevention 163
household registration system 159
housing
 high prices 183–4
 high-rise estates, sustainability 184
 housing policies
  models 196–8
   efficiency 197–8
   equity 196–7
  typology 194, 200
 housing projects, World Bank 186
 housing provision chain 193–5, 199
  role of state 195–6
  and the wider system 198
 housing system
  Eastern Europe 191–2
  economic factors 182–3
  entitlements 180, 181
  poverty 180–82
  problems 180–85
   responses 185–6, 187
  social exclusion 182
  social inequality 180
  urban 177–80
   discrimination 178
   reforms 178–9
   rural, separation 184–5

income
 maintenance, and unemployment 119–20
 replacement, and unemployment 119
individualization
 and family structure 216–17
 and policies 218–19
inequality *see* social inequality
institutions
 labour market construction 106–9, 113
 policy process 41
  limits 47
Internet policy, PRC 14

Jiang Zemin 38, 41–2, 206
JSA (Job Seeker's Allowance), Britain 121

labour contracts 108, 113
labour market
 Britain
  deregulation 120
  unemployment 117
 EU, pension reforms 148–50
 women in 216–17, 221
labour market construction 97

development 98–9
institutional support 106–9, 113
and social inequality 111–13
and social security reform 106–7
and urban poverty 109–11
labour market standards, Britain 120
labour mobility
 Britain/PRC, compared 119
 Denmark 119
 dimensions 97
 and employment status 100–101
 and health problems 157–8
 increase 99–100
 migrants
  age variations 104
  future 105–6
  gender differences 104
  type of employment 104–5
  wages 105
 and pension reforms 130
Labour Party, Britain, Third Way 241
Labour and Social Security, Ministry of 57
labour unions
 membership 108
 services 108, 109
labourers, rights protection 107–9
laid-off workers
 gender differences 101
 poverty 109–10
 re-employment 101–2
 relief payments 106
lesson drawing
 and contingencies 12–13
 desirability 13, 14
 feasibility 13, 14
 sequencing 16–17
lessons
 from history 11
 meaning 12
 sources 14–15
Li Peng 44
lone mothers 218
lone-mother families, Britain 223
longevity, EU, and pension reforms 144

McDonald's, internationalization 12
Major, John, employment policies 122
Marriage Law, PRC 209–11
medical needs, changing patterns 156–8
Minimal Living Security, and urban poverty 80–81
models

GPP 33–4
  housing policies 196–8
  policy analysis 24–8
modernization, PRC 8

New Deal programmes, Britain 122–4
news media, PRC 38
NPC (National People's Congress) 208

OECD, health care 172

pension reforms
  aims 129–30
  benefits, and contributions 131
  Britain 145–6
    Pay as You Go 146–8
  EU 143–6
  implementation 130–36
  and labour mobility 130
  rural/urban divide 151–2
  Sweden 148
  viability 136–8
pensions, SOEs 129, 130, 133, 134
policies
  fungibility 7
  and rationality 24–5
policy
  analysis, models 24–8
  formulation, CCP 42–4
  implementation, CCP 44–6
  initiation, PRC 40–42
  making
    CCP, dominant role 37–8
    and society 27–8
policy process
  academia 41–2
  CCP 47–8
  evaluation 46–8
  institutions 41
    limits 47
  PRC 40–46
  professionalization 46
  and the rule of law 48
Policy Research Institute, PRC 41
political campaigns, CCP 45
political reform, CCP 39–40
politics, in the PRC 25–6
population
  PRC 13, 51, 65
    percentage changes 156
    rural/urban split 159
poverty

anti-poverty programmes 91–2
and economic competitiveness 81
and employment, Britain 92
housing system 180–82
laid-off workers 109–10
meaning 90
measurement 90
programme, Britain 89–90
rural 75–7
  anti-poverty programmes 76
unemployed workers 109–10
and unemployment 119
urban 77–81
  anti-poverty programmes 79–81
  features 78–9
  and labour market construction 109–1
  Minimal Living Security 80–81
  social factors 78
  unemployment 78
see also social inequality
PRC (People's Republic of China)
  Britain, comparison 89
  cities, economic growth 157
  civil society 26
  Cultural Revolution 8, 25, 32
  economic
    development 16, 52
    policy 25
    potential 14
    reform 32
  as economic state 31–3
  GDP 20, 51
  GPP 33
  health care
    flexibility 172–3
    international comparisons 169–74
    supply side 173–4
  Internet policy 14
  Marriage Law 209–11
  modernization 8
  news media 38
  policy
    initiation 40–42
    process 40–46
  Policy Research Institute 41
  politics, nature of 25–6
  population 13, 51, 65, 156
  public expenditure 59
  relationships 16
  resources 13–14
  retirement age 65
  social policy

emergence 2
internationalization 94–5
unemployment 61–3
welfare provision 17, 23
  women
    historical status 203–6
    outstanding problems 211–13
    rights promotion 206–7
  and the WTO 2, 8, 16, 66
  see also CCP (Chinese Communist Party)
public expenditure, PRC 59
public policies
  analysis 8
  comparisons
    problems 8
    purpose 8–9
  and national contexts 7, 9, 10, 11–12

rationality
  and human irrationality 26–7
  and policies 24–5
re-employment
  hidden 107
  laid-off workers 101–2
  policies 102, 103
  training 103
  and unemployment 103
re-training, and unemployment 61
retirement
  and health problems 150–51
  see also early retirement
retirement age, PRC 65
rights protection, labourers 107–9
rule of law, and policy process 48
Russians, mutual trust 19

Shanghai Municipal Government 41
'Singapore model', health care finance 155
social benefits, entitlements, and economic changes 158–9
social exclusion, housing system 182
social inequality
  Britain, measurement 91
  and economic competitiveness 81, 92
  and economic reform 92–4
  Gini coefficient 72, 90–91
  and globalization 73–5
  housing system 180
  increase 71, 72
  inter-regional 72
  and labour market construction 111–13

market transition 73
political factors 74–5
rural/urban 72
and the WTO 82
see also poverty
social insurance coverage 64
social policy
  extent 1–2
  PRC
    emergence 2
    internationalization 94–5
  and the welfare state 29–30
  and the WTO 82–3
social security system
  reforms
    issues 65–6
    labour market construction 106–7
social welfare proposals, World Bank 63
social welfare system
  level of provision 63–5
  reforms 53–8, 226–7
    Britain 122
    problems 58–65
  rural/urban entitlements 159–61
  societalizing 225–7, 230
  SOEs 52–3
social work
  Britain
    future 242
    managerialism 240–41
    marketization 240
    origins 238–9
    qualifications 241–2
    variety 237–8
  professionalization 229
socialist states
  convergence theory 30
  GPP 29
  and state socialism 28–9
society, and policy making 27–8
SOEs (State Owned Enterprises)
  deficits 59
  economy, share 59
  pensions 129, 130, 133, 134
  redundant workers 61–3
  reforms 58–61, 66
  social welfare system 52–3
  working hours 107
SOMM (Survey of Occupational Mobility & Migration) 97
Soviet Union, welfare provision 17
state, role, housing provision chain 195–6

state sector, employment 98
state socialism, and socialist states 28–9
STD (Sexually Transmitted Diseases) 158
Sweden, pension reforms 148
Szelenyi, Ivan, on EEHM 192

Thatcher, Margaret 89
   employment policies 121
   welfare services, marketization 240
Third Way, Britain, Labour Party 241
Thucydides 11
trade unions, Britain, role 120

UN World Conferences on Women 206, 207
unemployed workers
   Britain, training 121–2
   poverty 109–10
unemployment
   age variations 102
   benefits, Britain 120–21
   Britain, regional variations 118
   and economic growth 61, 63
   gender differences 102
   and income maintenance 119–20
   and income replacement 119
   policy, Britain 120
   and poverty 119
   PRC 61–3
   and re-employment 103
   and re-training 61
   reasons 102–3
   registration 103
   relief payments 106–7
   and urban poverty 78
   see also employment
universals, and contexts, interaction 12

voluntary action, increase 227–8
voluntary sector, Britain 233–7

welfare provision
   developing countries, need for 83
   expenditure 60
   comparisons 19
   and the family 18
   PRC 17, 23
   Soviet Union 17
   urban/rural differences 63
welfare state
   Britain 10–11, 29
   Europe, development 17–18
   as GPP pattern 30
   and social policy 29–30
   and social solidarity 18
WHO (World Health Organisation), health care, league table 170
women
   Britain
      cohabitation 222
      economic activity 221
      lone-mother families 223
      marital/extramarital births 222
      in the labour market 216–17, 221
   PRC
      historical status 203–6
      Marriage Law 209–11
      outstanding problems 211–13
      politics, participation 208–9
      rights promotion 206–7
   see also gender differences
working hours
   non-SOEs 108
   SOEs 107
workless households, Britain 118–19
World Bank
   housing projects 186
   social welfare proposals 63
WTO (World Trade Organization) 2, 8, 16, 66
   and social inequality 82
   and social policy 82–3

Xinhua News Agency 41

Zhu Rong Ji, Prime Minister 41